NORT

January 1, 2012

This book is a work of fiction. Names, characters, places, and incidents are the product of the author's imagination or are used fictitiously. Any resemblance to actual events, locales, or persons, living or dead, is coincidental.

Copyright © 2011 by Philip G. Peterson Sr.

All rights reserved. Except as permitted under the U.S. Copyright Act of 1976, no part of this publication may be reproduced, distributed, or transmitted in any form or by any means, or stored in a database or retrieval system, without the prior written permission of the author and publisher.

Dedication

To those farmers who lost equities and assets during times of Prohibition.

Introduction for Northern Moon

"Phil Peterson has created a work of fiction based on an industry that was an active part of the economy during the Prohibition era. At that time the manufacture, distribution and sale of alcoholic beverages was outlawed. Throughout the country people evaded "the dry laws" in many and various ways. Phil focuses on illegal activity in making liquor, better known as "moon" in an area along the St. Croix River north of St. Croix Falls, Wisconsin.

The characters while fictitious are real. I have met all of them again and again through my research on Prohibition in the St. Croix Valley. Many people made moon not because they themselves needed a drink, but because they needed to put food on the table for their families.

Several factors contributed to the success of making moon which Phil vividly and accurately describes. Much of the area is remote, but water for making mash and running the stills was plentiful. The product could be transported, "bootlegged", to the major markets in St. Paul and Minneapolis in a matter of hours.

This business was not without drama. Federal agents were always on the prowl looking for Prohibition law violators. Many were caught in raids. Also in the mix were Syndicates who bought liquor in large volume from local operations.

Yet, you will not find criminals in this book of the film noire variety; there are no shootouts between agents and moonshiners. Yes, these people broke the law, but after combing newspaper files and numerous interviews with participants I found ordinary and good people who were trying to make a living when they had no alternative. Phil has "distilled" my extensive research into a single story. I am pleased with the result. The story that Phil tells is one of survival in dire economic times that happened over and over again in this area."

Ward Moberg, *former editor of* The Dalles Visitor

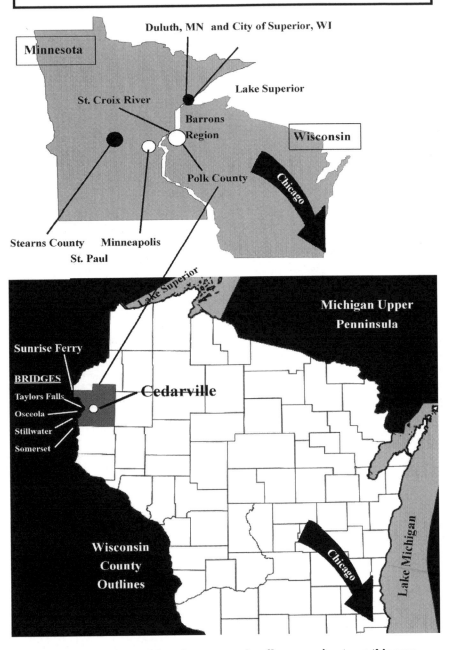

NORTHERN MOON

Preface

Between 1920 and 1933, America amended the Constitution by prohibiting the manufacture and sale of alcohol for consumption. Like today's two-party politics of elephants and donkeys, back then you were wet or dry. Those wet lamented, fought, ignored, and circumvented the law based on the degree of their thirst, need, or greed. Those dry, supported, evangelized, and demanded enforcement of the laws to a degree commensurate with their religiosity and particular vision of life without the abuse associated with consumption of alcohol.

Interestingly, America's legal efforts to stamp out the evils of alcohol, which excludes the *illegal and therefore unrecorded drinkers*, may have motivated more Americans to drink than had before passing of the 18th Amendment. It also spawned the illegal and immensely profitable, industry of illegal alcohol, which grew throughout Prohibition's thirteen-year period of discouragement. Many feel the 18th also spawned crime syndicate participation, Ala Scarface Capone himself. Prohibition also created the opportunity for hundreds of non-criminals to morph into those wanted by the law for producing and delivering moonshine. Many farmers turned moonshine into a harvestable crop to make mortgage payments on their farms and put food on their families' tables, which much of farming could no longer provide.

Advocates on both sides, wet or dry, made interesting history. The Women's Christian Temperance Union became one of the first organized groups offering protection to women from spousal abuse, drunken behavior and wasting of family funds, activities which soared in importance following the crash of '29. On the other hand, wets, not intimidated by what most felt to be foolish, inappropriate law, were thought to have saved the U. S. from dying of thirst, via hidden stills, stealthy deliveries, and cooperative wet efforts.

Today, it is still worthwhile to learn of each side's participation. Prohibition made some wealthy, some poor, gave some power, imprisoned others, and became one of the largest of political footballs during Prohibition years.

Taking advantage of documented research, Northern Moon is a glimpse of one small area of Middle America. The fiction element of the story is not difficult to imagine. Prohibition was a creative era of history.

Northern Moon is a story of some rural farmers of Wisconsin, their families, and how, together, they maneuvered their way through the beginning of the Depression that followed the crash of '29. Pushed to the edge and in desperation, some violated firmly established moral and ethical principles, by purposely breaking the law. These were honest, normally law-abiding people who practiced their religious faiths and worked hard to instill those same principals in their children. They were the last you would expect, to break the law, avoid discovery, and even enlist the aid of those children.

Why did they make this most difficult choice? The Depression destroyed most farm income. They stood to lose family farms to foreclosure, as some friends already had. The only thing keeping them functional was sustenance derived from the poultry, livestock, and few crops they could still raise. Depressed income from harvests no longer afforded even the costs of spring planting. Because of increased risk, banks began refusing spring-planting loans. The circumstances of those suffering were best described by a most often heard comment among them, "What the hell do we do now?"

Syndicates capitalized on Prohibition by providing as much illegal alcohol as possible but cooking smelly corn mash is difficult to hide. Just an hour or more from Minneapolis and St. Paul was an isolated region of north-west Wisconsin, known as the Barrons. Threading through its forested hills were unmarked and unmapped abandoned lumber roads, small family- farms, former logging camps as well as lakes and streams that fed into the St. Croix and, eventually, the Mississippi River. The magic ingredient of *available water* draining the rolling landscape of the Barons made the region well-suited to become a Midwest Appalachia. As federal pressure increased on shiners of Minnesota, *the Barons* became an attractive syndicate option with a work force of farmers desperate to keep food on the table and save their family farms from the banks.

Thus, one day, a man some farmers hardly knew, who had purchased eggs and chickens from them just weeks before, said, "How would you like a job?"

That was their introduction, as it is now yours,

to

Northern Moon

Part I

"What the hell do we do now?"

Chapter 1

"No."

"What do you mean, no, Mr. Anderson?" a stunned Andre responded.

"It's not that I don't want to, Andre. The bank has too many mortgagees failing to keep their payments on schedule. We're having too many foreclosures. Now, with crop prices so low and still falling, spring planting loans have become too risky. The bank's board won't let me approve your loan this year."

"I've repaid that loan, on time and with interest, for the last seven years! How am I supposed to keep up with my mortgage payments if I can't plant?" Andre was angry now, and his anger was fueled by fear. His mortgage payments were bigger this year than last, because just last year, this same bank had approved a loan to expand his acreage and the equipment needed to farm it. Neither he nor Clair had expected any change in the annual planting loan they used to cash flow the farm.

"We've had to turn down a long list of old customers, Andre, not just you. Banks have to stay solvent, too," Anderson finished.

Andre and Anderson talked for ten more minutes. Their discussion became emotional and heated, especially on Andre's side, but the last word from the Bank's Anderson was still "No."

After storming out of the bank, Andre drove home with anger and frustration pushing on the gas pedal. Seeing him drive up the long driveway from the main road, Clair sensed something was wrong. She met him as he slammed the truck's door.

"What's the matter?" Clair asked seriously with eyes wide.

"Anderson just turned down our spring planting loan, the same one we've gotten from him for the last seven years and always paid on time. He says we are too big a risk, that we won't make enough from harvest to make the mortgage payments and that there's nothing he can do about it!" Andre spit.

"How can that be, Andre, we always repaid that loan. What has changed?" Clair questioned.

"It's called the depression. I don't know what we're supposed to do Clair. I'm a farmer! He says even if he could give us the loan, nobody has money to buy what we grow. This is nuts! Here we sit, with this acreage of prime farmland, tractor, trucks, and the gear we need for a bumper crop . . . and no seed to plant!" Andre Cartier shook his head as he mirrored the discouraged expression on his wife's face.

"We've always been able to borrow seed dollars, sell crops or livestock to repay the planting loan, and when nothing else worked, we could work harder, put in more hours and even work another job to make up the difference. Now, no one is hiring. I can't get another job anywhere and our friends are facing the same problem! What the hell are we supposed to do? What is anyone to do? I used to know what to do next and the bank really liked the way I organized and farmed. They used to have confidence in me. That gave me confidence. Now . . . for the first time . . . I don't know what to do."

"Something will work, Andre," Clair responded. "This is not the end. We can't let it be. We can live on what we raise ourselves, and many others will continue to need what we raise."

Andre nodded, "Yes, some will, but already some like Mrs. Johnson yesterday are asking for credit. When they ask if they can pay for the eggs next week, it's not easy to say no . . . at least I couldn't yesterday." Seeing her expression change he quickly added, "I wrote it down on the pad by the chicken coop door, three-dozen eggs for Johnson's. And as bad as it looks for us, we are better off than all those who don't have a farm. We have food, they don't, and they are going to come to us to get it, Clair."

Worst of all, so bad in fact that he didn't want to bring it up to Clair, they had only a small savings they could tap for mortgage payments until that ran dry. A year before the crash, they agreed to follow Andre's wishes and borrowed from their bank to buy an additional fifty acres and necessary equipment to farm it, along with their existing acreage. When the loan closed they bought a used, stake-bed truck for hauling bigger loads. New trucks were prettier, but Andre's conservative nature and depression-times dictated, *used*. The two trucks would complement the sedan and pickup they'd driven for the last few years. He already had a tractor, and was trying to do less with the work-horses and more with gasoline. It had seemed the smart thing to do back then. Extra acreage would result in a larger harvest, and more profit to pay back loans sooner. Andre wasn't afraid of the work. In fact, he wanted to work harder. Now, though, another mistake was surfacing, which he had refused to acknowledge until hindsight forced him. That problem was the way he had negotiated the loan. He actually hadn't negotiated at all. He let the bank arrange it. He remembered now how he'd rationalized it at the time. *I'm a farmer, not a banker. The bank knows what it is doing. Anderson has always treated me fairly. I'll listen to his advice.*

Anderson, had advised wrapping the smaller, existing mortgage they'd inherited from his father and paid on for ten years, with the new mortgage. "Everything bundled into one package," was how Anderson put it. "That way, Andre, you will only have one mortgage, and one mortgage payment. It will be easier to keep up with." It sounded good at the time, but he wished he had taken a second mortgage instead of combining the two. That way, in a pinch like now, should he lose the additional land he had purchased to foreclosure, he would still retain his original property. Now, because of combined mortgages, if he missed payments everything was at risk. All he and Clair owned was now vulnerable to foreclosure and he was scared. Andre was a hard worker, young and aggressive, and back then had been anxious to grow his holdings with that new equipment and acreage. He knew then that he and Clair and the kids were going to make that farm pay off. He envisioned bigger profits to result from his investment of money and labor. Now, everything looked different. The mistakes just beneath their dwindling cash were becoming more visible. Andre and Clair were learning what a Depression was. Now, he couldn't even get a planting loan.

"Without income Clair, we have three to four month's cash at best. After that, we can't make mortgage payments. We've got to figure something out . . . now," he finished.

"What?" she asked. "Figure out what? Sievertson's lost their place last month. It was much smaller than ours. When I saw her at church Sunday, I said I was going to try to help Mildred with some of our kids' old clothes. How can we not help them, Andre? This isn't your fault. I don't know what to do either, but we've got Carolyn and Henri to protect, too."

Andre and Clair had known this conversation was coming for months. Both had avoided it as long as possible. The Depression and its cascading psychological depression, had been settling over their region for the last year. It didn't matter where you were, or who you spoke to, people's smiles were slighter; they worried more and talked less, unless unloading anxiety in an ineffective torrent of invectives aimed at the government, the banks, and those moneyed, who seemed to have no worries. Though it did no good, it was at least, a cathartic action, which seemed better than no action at all.

"We've got to do more than talk about it," Andre said, as he headed for the barn at chore time.

Clair did not know what to do with that last statement from Andre. She watched him walking toward the barn, his head bent down, with a slower stride that made him look older.

The Cartiers' led a simple, small farmer's, family life. Andre and his fourteen-year old son, Henri, took care of the four milk cows, the horses, and a dozen head of beef. They took turns slopping the pigs, which Henri considered his least favorite chore. Andre, on the other hand, knew taking turns with his son would pass on the knowledge and discipline demanded by animals via chores. Carolyn, at sixteen, took care of the chickens, eggs, ducks, and sometimes the half-dozen pigs, when Henri either forgot or rebelled. Carolyn didn't mind her brother's stubbornness, and didn't want her dad getting angry at him Each time she replaced Henri's pig- efforts, however, she told him she had done it, but hadn't told their dad, which was a reminder that Henri owed her.

Cartier's had several customers who called on them weekly to pick up vegetables in season, eggs, and chickens, beef, or pork when they were butchering. With his pickup, Andre delivered eggs to two stores in Cedarville, eight miles east of their farm on highway 17. Carolyn cleaned the eggs, packaged them into cartons of twelve, then put the cartons into large cardboard egg crates. Her dad delivered the crates to the stores. She and her dad brought in steady money with the chickens and eggs. Often, she would let Henri know she brought in more dollars than he did, which irked him considerably. She and Henri weren't really aware of the Depression, though. Their parents tried not to share it with them.

There was little stress or dissension within the family, other than sibling bickering, but the year was 1930, which followed the Crash of '29. It was going to be a year to reckon with.

Chapter 2

"What are you going to do, Ralph?" Andre's eyes bored his question into Ralph Johnson as they stood talking at the gas station in Cedarville. Boyhood friends since the seventh grade, they had attended a one-room school house on the west side of Cedarville before high school. Andre and Ralph arranged to have desks beside each other for several years, losing them only when separated by their teacher, usually due to horseplay. Both farmed with their fathers as they grew from boys to manhood, and both inherited their father's farms. Uniquely, each lost his father as well. Ralph's died of pneumonia at age sixty, when Ralph was twenty-five, causing him to take over the farming duties with his mother and sister. Andre lost his dad in a freak car accident on highway 8 as his dad was driving to Minneapolis. Twenty-four at the time, Andre, too, had to quickly assume the role of farming his parent's acreage. The commonality of losing fathers forced both to mature quickly. That shared burden made them even closer as friends. Though a year younger, Andre was more mature which made the transition to adulthood easier for him. When Ralph hesitated with decisions, Andre would often quietly nudge him in the right direction. Now, as an adult, Ralph still usually followed Andre's leanings as he had in their school years. It was easier.

"I don't know, Andre. Each time I figure something I think might work, I hear someone's already tried it and failed, or someone with money tells me it won't work. No matter what I think of to raise, build, or sell, someone says don't bother because no one has any money to pay me for it anyway. I'm getting to where I'm scared to do anything but work for someone else. If I didn't have this gas station job right now, Andre, I'd miss my mortgage payments!" Ralph almost choked on that one. He cleared his throat and said, "I can't hang on much longer. Bill has been good to me here at the station, giving me all the hours he can, but he told me Monday that by next month I will be down to half-time. I've got three kids to feed, and Maureen can't find any work. I took that second mortgage on the farm when we added on to the house to make room for our three kids. I inherited it free and clear, but now I've got the house monthly. It's never been this bad before, Andre. I've always been able to figure something out, put in more hours, even work nights when no one else wanted those shifts. But, now there just isn't anything I can find to do. It scares hell out of me!"

"That's about the way I see it too, Ralph. Clair and I were talking about it last night. I have even bigger problems, because I took that loan to expand last year.

It's crazy! Now I have 125 acres, two used trucks, a tractor, just two-years old, and nothing to do with them because the bank declined the annual spring-planting loan. They've approved that loan for the last seven-years and were always paid on time, Ralph. Now they say no!" Andre took a deep breath, let it out slowly, as he and Ralph locked eyeballs in understanding.

With a wave of his hand, Ralph excused himself from their talk, and walked quickly out to the gas pump. An expensive looking, four-door Oldsmobile sedan was pulling up to the pump. A well-dressed, no suit, but no farmer either, man got out of the car. "Fill it up will you?" he asked, "and check the oil too, please. I bought the car used last week at an auction, and I don't know if it uses oil or not. There are so many cars available at auctions now," he added, "all those repos. This one's got sixty-two big horses under that hood, and it goes like hell," he laughed.

Ralph grimaced at the thought of auctions, thinking of his ongoing conversation with Andre. He filled the gas tank and checked the radiator by removing the twist-off cap at its top. It had a fancy ornament mounted to the cap. As he was twisting the ornament, left, to unscrew it, the cap exploded straight up in a cloud of steam! As he watched it fall to the ground beside the front wheel, Ralph rubbed his hand against his belly, removing the heat of steam from his fingers. The ornament had not broken off the cap. It lay on the ground, undamaged.

"Oh hell, I thought you were just going to check the oil," the man said, as he watched steam pouring skyward from the radiator. "She runs hot, and I've been pushing her hard all the way from Minneapolis. I hope you didn't burn your hand! Thanks for checking it."

Ralph reached for the long-spouted can of water the station used to top off radiators, and began to fill it.

"Not too fast with the water," the car's owner said, "I don't want to crack the block."

When Ralph finished filling the radiator, which took a half gallon, he set the can down and tried to lift the side panel of the Olds hood. Most car's oil dipsticks were on the driver side of the engine, but he couldn't find the door-latch.

The man grinned, "I couldn't find it either," and then showed him the spring-loaded catch at each end of the panel.

Ralph folded the door on top of the hood, then pulled the dip-stick, wiped it with his pocket rag, dipped and read it again. After re-inserting it, he said, "The oil's fine."

The man paid for the gas and asked, "Is the owner of the station around?"

Ralph glanced at the side of the building where Bill parked. "He's not in until noon today. Can I help you with something?"

The guy was friendly. He smiled again, "No, but can you give me his name and phone number? I'd like to contact him about some possible business."

"Sure, it's on this card here," Ralph said as he handed him one of the business cards Bill kept beside the cash register. "If you want to leave your name and number I can have Bill give you a call."

"No, that's ok; I'll get in touch. Thanks for the help." With that, he entered the Olds and drove off to the east, obviously not heading back to the Twin Cities.

"Who was that?" Andre asked.

"I don't know," Ralph answered, "This is the third time this week I've seen him in here, but the first time with that car. He drove a Hudson the first two times I filled him up. Nice wheels today, huh? Big, shiny, Oldsmobile! He must have money, he looks like money. I wonder what he wants to talk to Bill about."

They talked for another ten minutes, while Ralph had no customers. The topic never changed. *What the hell are we both going to do? What's anybody going to do?*

Andre drove off in his Ford pickup to fetch a short list of things Clair asked him to get at the grocery store. He dropped off the two cases of eggs Carolyn had packaged in the last two days.

"Thanks for delivering eggs, Andre," the store manager grinned. "You know, every week or two old man Brown tries to get us to buy eggs from him, but he refuses to package them in cartons like your daughter does. We tried one delivery from him, but then we had to take them from the case and package them into dozen packs ourselves. Nobody liked that. And when we saw how dirty his eggs were, we realized Carolyn was also cleaning the eggs better before putting them in dozens. Tell her she's doing a great job, and she doesn't have to worry about Brown."

"That's great, Jerry. She does wipe them down and I've never seen her break a single egg. I guess I'm a proud papa. By the way, can we just work out a trade of groceries for eggs, rather than me paying cash? That would help me with cash flow and wouldn't hurt you any." Andre saw Jerry's face go more serious.

"I'm not sure, Andre. Let me talk to my Dad. He gets touchier by the day about cash. Lots of folks asking for credit, and some aren't paying for what we've already given. I think I can talk him into it, but give me a couple of days till your next delivery."

Andre drove home, thinking of how everyone was suffering *depression*.

Chapter 3

12-11-18

Carolyn was coming out the chicken coop door when her dad drove up. "Hello, young lady. I've brought you some empty twelve-packs and egg cartons from Nelson's grocery. You should hear the manager go on about the quality of the eggs you package for him. He said old-man, Brown, tries to sell them eggs all the time, but he likes your service and you've got his egg business! I'm proud of you!"

She beamed with pride, and helped her dad unload the cartons from the pick-up. She was sixteen going on twenty, dramatically cute, physically and mentally sharp and her mother laughingly told her she was going to have to be careful about having those new curves, with a smile. Carolyn smiled back and asked, "Why?"

"Because it attracts attention, as you will soon find out," Clair added.

Carolyn was always fun to be around. It seemed none of the family could get enough of her, including Henri. She noticed some boys at school had begun to look at her differently. She wasn't quite sure how it was different, just knew it was. Right now, her favorite man on earth was her dad, and she hadn't thought much beyond that, but she was beginning to. She asked Henri why some of the boys looked at her as they did. All he would say was all the boys looked at girls like that. He didn't want to say, "I'm beginning to look at them differently, too, though." She really liked her brother. He was two years younger, but big enough to look a couple years older. One day at school, she discovered no boys were going to mess with her when Henri was around. He didn't have to say anything. Just the look on his face was enough when the other boys saw it. She found that a comfort.

Henri came out of the barn just as Andre and Carolyn finished unloading the egg boxes. "Hey, dad," he asked, "What's the matter with Betsy? She just keeps cribbing in her stall. Pretty soon we'll have to build a new one. I didn't know horses ate wood."

"Something's bothering her throat," Andre said. "Keep giving her a little of that pine tar every day, I think she's getting better. Are all the animals fed?"

"All but the pigs. I thought Carolyn could feed them," Henri grinned, "while I move the beef over to that other pasture. They need more grass if they are going to fatten up," he finished.

"That's your chore and you know it, Henri, and I'm getting tired of having to remind you. Get at it," Andre demanded. "You're not a little kid anymore."

Carolyn smirked.

Henri hated it when his dad sided with Carolyn, which seemed to him to happen too often.

Andre smiled, thinking, *they're still kids, but not for long. It's a good thing these two don't know how close we really are to financial trouble.* He loved hearing them banter, argue and laugh. Remembering his own childhood, that's how he wanted them to be, and the next thought that hit him was, *how the hell am I going to hold everything together for them?*

Chapter 4

"Why me?" Sampson spit as he glared at his supervisor.

"Because you are the most experienced man I've got for the problems they're having up there," O'Hara answered. He'd been Sampson's boss in the Chicago office for the last three years. He didn't like much about Sampson, in fact disliked many things, but he couldn't deny that Robert Sampson was effective.

"But you still need me here," Sampson said. "Shit, who's going to make things happen around Chicago as I've done? Without me your arrest budget will disappear!"

"I'm concerned about that, Sampson, but people give me orders, too. I have to follow them, and so do you. It's not like this will change your life forever; it's a one-year training run. Chief says Minneapolis needs our help and I have to give it to them. His last words to me were, 'and make damn sure you send someone that knows how to train men and ferret out the runners, or I'll have your ass before the board!' You are not the only one with his butt on the line, Sampson. You are one of only three unmarried men I've got. You don't own a home; you live in an apartment. You don't even have a car for God's sake; you drive the state's. Add that to the facts that you have the highest arrest rate in Illinois and are one of our top trainers, and you've selected yourself," O'Hara finished.

"If I'm that damn good, why don't they pay me more? I should retire from the force and become a bootlegger myself. This is a bullshit assignment," he retorted.

Sampson wanted it to seem he really did not want any part of this new assignment. He intended to resist it mightily, make them beg to get him to go. He wanted all his field agents, most of whom also disliked him, to be joking about how pissed Sampson was about being sent to Minneapolis. He wanted them laughing behind his back about how he got screwed into this job against his will. He wanted things that way because he had worn out his welcome in Chicago. He'd heard some crime bosses of Chicago were beginning ask about a certain Federal Agent and was well aware those bosses had ways of dealing with those they asked about. Sampson was what other Federal agents called "a real bastard." When your own men think of you that way, it just might be true. When crime bosses started thinking specifically of you, it might be time to switch pastures.

Sampson was acting this façade of disappointment and anger because he knew the more he bucked the assignment, the more determined his boss would be to see he got it. He'd known O'Hara didn't like him for a couple of years.

O'Hara doesn't like to see me going up the ladder, because all he gets to look at is my ass, he thought. Sampson also knew he needed some new ground to dig in, a place where no one knew him, a place a long way from the Chicago syndicates where he would be less of a target. He wanted this assignment. He just didn't want anyone to know he wanted it. He had a plan for working out of Minneapolis.

He was thirty-one years old, had been an agent in the Chicago office for five years and a beat cop in Chicago three-years before. He had a high school education, and a real education from the Chicago streets. He considered himself smarter than most Federal agents, smarter than most people. He was tough, loved to fight, and needed, almost had, to win. Sampson couldn't stand losing at anything, which is why his marriage had lasted only two years. He'd married someone smarter than himself, couldn't admit it, and on top of that, his wife would not be pushed around. Their marriage really lasted only one year, because that second year couldn't be called a marriage. With hindsight, the only good thing about their marriage was they split before having kids. Since the divorce, Sampson's psyche had been on a downward slide. He was always getting even with the world or someone on it. He was mean; somewhat a bully, a dedicated womanizer, and loved to demonstrate power to those he worked with, especially those he arrested. Sampson was a real bastard. The Chicago syndicate was starting to feel the same way about him. To them, his arrest record of bootleggers glowed in the dark.

"You're going up there and get this done for us, Sampson. Chief Lundquist, your new boss up there, says booze is pouring across the Canadian Border like a second Mississippi. Not only haven't they been able to stop it, they haven't even slowed it down. My boss was up there for a one-week look-see last month. He thinks Chief Lundquist in the Minneapolis office doesn't know if he's afoot or horseback and his agents are worse. I don't know if he's right or wrong about that. I talked to him again this morning and I want you to know exactly what I told him."

"So what did you say?" Sampson grimaced, shaking his head as if in disgust.

"I said I was sending my best man up there under one condition. You were to be the head honcho, the number one trainer, and the trainer of any other trainers, in your territory. You were to call the shots, design the actions, and see them through. I said, Sampson answers to me, he's on loan to you, and I want him in charge of the Revenue agents he has to work with. You can assign him to wherever you want him to be. But, if he bears the responsibility for results, he has to have commensurate authority. That's how it's got to be, or I'm not sending him," O'Hara smiled. "Lundquist agreed, just for one year, but he agreed. I also told him you still answer to me, Sampson. If he has any problems with what you are doing, he's to notify me. If that occurs, you and I will work out the problem. Don't screw this up, Bob. Lundquist is your superior officer. You have some free license to call the shots, but don't abuse it. He must have your respect."

Sampson was getting a warm feeling in his stomach, the kind he had after a special drink, or after punching someone out during a fight, or getting laid, all of which sometimes triggered an orgasm. He felt good. His hidden plan to make money up north was inadvertently being set up for him by O'Hara and by Chief Lundquist up in the Twin Cities. They had no idea.

"It's still a bullshit assignment, O'Hara. If I go, I want a step up in grade and a different car. Not just a car either, I want one of the hot ones the patrol uses."

O'Hara knew he was winning the argument now that Sampson was maneuvering for perks. He so wanted to be rid of him!. He was next to impossible to manage, and kept O'Hara on his toes by constantly rallying other agents against their supervisor. Sampson did have a high arrest record, but hated to share credit with the rest of the department. Lately, when he made arrests he'd been tipping off a newspaper friend, which resulted in the arrests being credited to him instead of the entire Revenue Department. When O'Hara challenged Sampson on this latest practice, Sampson all but told him to shove it, unapologetically saying, "Who made the arrests?" O'Hara knew it would only become more difficult to have him remain under his direction. This was his opportunity. He did, in fact, have at least two other agents he thought would be better to send north, but given the opportunity to send anyone, he wasn't going to miss the chance to get rid of him.

"I can't do that Sampson. A step up in grade is possible, after the first sixty days on the job up there. If things are moving along with the help you give them, I can justify that." *Fat chance*, he thought to himself. *Once I get you out of here you will not get another dime out of me.* "But I can't get one of those cars. Hell, every man on the patrol wants one and they only bought a dozen. I can only buy eighteen cars this year for our whole department, and they sure aren't the high-priced patrol cars. I'll assign you one of those next month. I can cover that so nobody here knows you have it. That's a favor I'll do for you, but that's it! That's all I can do. You've got to do the rest. We'll announce this assignment to your squad next week. You'll be in Minneapolis the following week. Let me know who's ready in your squad to take your place. It's your call. I want it by Friday."

Sampson knew his act had accomplished a lot. O'Hara thought he hated the assignment, and was even more convinced by how Sampson demanded the pay grade and car. He'd pulled it off, and he knew rumors of Sampson getting screwed out of his job, would be flying off the rumor-mill by morning. In his mind he was, by God, *one of the best damn manipulators he knew, and was proud of it.*

That night, after a pint of moonshine that didn't cost him a penny and some rough sex that left a reddening bruise on the cheekbone of the woman lying beside him on the bed, he said, "Yeh, after all these years of service, these bastards are sending me to Minneapolis to knock some sense into those Revenue agents. Who's going to take care of you the way I just did? You're gonna miss ol, Sampson, but I'm sure I can find someone friendly up there when those Scandinavian women hear about me."

She half-smiled an affirmative nod, which hurt in her swollen cheek, thinking, *miss you?*

Chapter 5

"Morning Sheriff," the druggist said, as Maun walked past him.

"Morning, John." *Everyone always greets the Sheriff*, Maun thought. *I guess that's one of the bonuses of wearing this badge.* He'd just dropped his kids off at school and was walking from Bill's gas station where he'd left the town's only police car to be greased. His office was one room in City Hall, with a sign that said, "SHERIFF" over the door.

The Cedarville law force was not complicated. Cedarville's population was about 700. The police force consisted of one police officer, who shared the one-room office with Sheriff Maun. There was a gentlemen's agreement between the County and Cedarville, which found itself within that County. The County paid Sheriff Maun and his one and one-half deputies. Cedarville paid their only town policeman. The agreement was, Cedarville would furnish the office space free of charge to the Sheriff if the Sheriff would help their only police officer enforce the city's law. Basically, it was the cheapest way to have law in both the County and Cedarville. It worked because there was so little crime in this small farming community. Their biggest problem was finding ways to keep three and one-half men busy enforcing the small amount of law needed. There were endless monthly discussions, at both County and city levels, as to why these enforcement tasks could not be accomplished with just three instead of three and one-half men.

Jason Maun liked his job, and felt he did it well. He was one of few not worrying heavily about the Depression. He got paid monthly, had no job-related expenses that weren't paid by the County or city funds, didn't have to pay for his car and the crime rate in the County was so low he didn't really feel any personal risk. Nearly everything he handled as Sheriff, or second town cop, related to too much alcohol, repossession of cars, trucks or tractors; and lately, the surprise the Council tasked him with, of evictions, due to unpaid mortgages. A mortgage foreclosure was the one assignment he hated. He'd done two. Drunks were common - there were more of them since the depression, people trying to drink away their troubles - but he was big enough to handle the worst of drunks. Losing a vehicle because they could no longer afford it was common and he'd handled many. But, mortgages involved families, wives, kids and relatives. Kicking someone out on the street was brutal; especially someone he knew, which had been the case in one of the last two cases he had to serve papers on. He was awake all night before going out with the banker the following morning to serve the Browns and their two kids. He did it apologetically in front of Anderson's bank partner, and it seemed to piss off the suit-and-tie-wrapped Mr. Corbit. All Maun said to Brown was, "I'm sorry, Jeff," expressing his remorse as he handed the papers to him. "I have to enforce the law; I have no choice." Jeff's wife, Sarah, had tears streaming down her face. Jeff said, "I know Jason, I know."

Sheriff Maun couldn't sleep that night. Being Sheriff, he had to walk a line that would keep him in harmony with the law and the Council. Consequently, he thought he had no choice in working with the banks and mortgage companies as the Council assigned him. He despised the manner in which they had foreclosed on Jeff. *I don't know how I'm going to do it, but I better get used to it,* he thought. *This depression is going to be here for awhile.* He promised himself to look into the law in this regard.

Chapter 6

"I've made three trips to Cedarville this week. It's about fifty-five miles northeast, just across the St. Croix River. It's a small farming community mostly, seven or eight-hundred people in the town. Most farms are around 100 to 200 acres and from the scuttlebutt some of them are really hurting," Jim Hutton explained to Manny Goldfin. "From conversations I've had with different people there, the local bank, run by the Andersons, has cut way back on their spring planting loans because they're afraid they won't get paid. Prices on crops those farmers normally raise are the lowest they've been since the war, and the bank and the guys at the local grain elevator think they're going to go even lower. That's ideal for us. There's going to be real estate bargains we can pick up if we find them before the banks foreclose."

Hutton had a real estate license and normally worked around the Twin Cities and also over in Stearns County west of the Twin Cities as well. He had landed an assignment from one of his best customers in St. Paul, Manny Goldfin. He'd been buying and selling properties for Goldfins for three years and always made money doing it. Three weeks earlier, Goldfin called Hutton to his office to discuss a new assignment. Manny thought it was a good time for some bargain hunting up in the Barrens region of Wisconsin. He thought a lot of small farms would be taken via foreclosure, and he thought there might be opportunities to buy some on contracts-for-deed from the owners, assuming their mortgages before the banks got hold of them. He told Hutton he would pay all his expenses and wanted him to go up there and find some interesting prospects. "Find out who's hurting. Start there. See what kind of opportunities there are. We can likely invent a way out for some, before they lose everything and still get it cheaper than we ever will from a bank. If we decide to buy any, I'll pay your normal commission as I always have. If we find some good deals, I'll even sweeten it a bit. I'll provide you wheels free of charge. My brother has an Oldsmobile dealership here in the Cities. I'll have him give you a different car every week, so people don't get too used to you being around. As usual, don't mention our names, or that you are working for us. Just say you're shopping for clients, the way we did that deal last year in St. Paul. I don't want anyone knowing about our new ventures until they are completed. Oh, one more thing to remember, Jim. We are especially interested in properties that have water on them, lake front, or flowing water, is always more valuable. Here's five hundred to cover your initial expenses," Manny said, handing Hutton a roll of cash, "Turn in the rest of your expenses weekly and give me a weekly update on what you find. And, Jim, if we can turn one or two of them into operations as we have in Stearns, you'll get your normal cut."

That was all the encouragement Hutton needed. The Goldfins always did business quietly, never wanting others to know what they and their partners were doing. Hutton understood what some of their business was, because he'd been steadily working with them for the last two years. He knew they were connected in the Twin Cities, likely part of the syndicates, and that they were involved in liquor importing, likely bootlegging as well, from Canada. He'd involved himself in their Stearns County operations three years before. The Goldfins of this world appreciated quiet people, especially quiet people who could get things done. He was happy to accommodate them as long as they kept the cash flowing. They did.

He saw Manny becoming impatient, waiting to hear what he had found. "Manny, you were right about there being opportunities up there. A lot of those small farmers are scared to death of losing their farms and homes. Not only is the bank unsympathetic with their plight, I get the idea the banks see opportunities too. The banks already collected their down payments and monthlies from those people on their mortgages. If they repossess those properties, they can get market price, which is lower, but another down payment which makes up for the low market price, and a whole new set of monthly payments on the same properties they've sold once already."

Jim Hutton could almost feel Manny grinning at what he was hearing, behind his poker face. He was hearing just what he expected to hear. That's why he'd asked Hutton to go up to the Barrens of Wisconsin in the first place.

Hutton went on, "I've looked at papers on properties in the County office, so I'm getting a handle on who owns what, and I've pretty thoroughly driven the west side of Cedarville. This week I'll do the south side. I'm staying within about a twenty-mile radius of the town. So far, there haven't been many properties with lakes, or on a river, available. The east and north sides of town is where the water is and I'll get to see much of that by the end of the month. I told you it would take me a month to scope it all out and I'm on schedule. Do you want me to do anything different than I'm doing, Manny? I've got a few people spotted who I think will provide me more info. I'll buy them lunch or a couple of drinks pretty soon, and I think they'll help me find what we are looking for. I definitely see opportunities to set up some Stearns operations over there."

"No. You're doing fine, Jim. Just remember to keep quiet about who you are doing the looking for," Manny finished. Jim felt dismissed. He was.

Chapter 7

Carolyn and Henri were typical farm kids. Born on the farm, that life was all they'd known. They loved animals, accepted them and their uses as part of life. They'd been given a firm set of principles to rebel against by their parents, raised Catholic, never missing church, unless weather or illness prevented attendance. They went to confession when their parents arranged it. It was easy for Carolyn, but Henri did not look forward to it. He always seemed to have more to feel guilty about than Carolyn did. At least that's the way Carolyn made it sound when they talked of confession. It was when facing confession that Henri usually thought perhaps he should take more care of the pigs instead of shirking that chore, or leaving it to his sister. He was also a boy. Boys seemed to like to fess up less than girls. He often resented his chores. Now that he was a freshman, chores often conflicted with school sports he'd like to participate in. He loved to run, but often wondered if those he had to run against who didn't have chores, had an unfair advantage.

They were sharp students, and good-looking teens, as well. Henri was strong, big for his age, and would be handsome like Andre. Carolyn was, as her mother described her, maturing and would be an attractive woman like her mother. Henri and Carolyn were close, allies in life, and though they would occasionally take each other on, or call each other out, woe be it to anyone else who attempted to push them around, or say something bad about either in front of the other. Nothing united them more quickly. Most of all, they had played together while growing up on the farm. The size of farms in the region discouraged youngsters playing together when small because of the distance between them. Consequently, kids of a family played more with siblings until they got into school. It wasn't until then that they regularly saw other kids anywhere else but church, and occasionally at one of the stores in town.

They enjoyed a spirited relationship. They grew up playing hide' n seek around the home and especially in their biggest barn. It was a typical barn of the day, two stories and long, with haymow on the upper deck, and stalls for horses and pigs, below in one end, and stanchions for milking cows in the other. It was a typically active barn below, with smells, noises, and animal messes running in the troughs, messes which had to be shoveled with regularity, another chore. It was shoveled and disposed of outside, via horse team and manure spreader to fertilize the farm fields. Carolyn avoided the heavy lifting in that department. She did rake out the chicken coop, though, and spread wood shavings and straw on the floor weekly, which she felt was equal to what Henri did in the barn. Henri felt his duties more manly than hers, and often with a grin said to Carolyn, "At least I don't have to put up with chicken shit." Either one of them could feed all the barn residents. They watched and helped their father so often the amounts of specific feeds for each animal were second nature to them. It was not unusual for either Carolyn or Henri to help the other finish feeding or distribute fresh water when one finished his or her chores before the other. Unless, of course, they were mad at each other, which seemed to happen more often now that they were in their teens. When mad, each loved to get out of the barn first, leaving the other with what they deserved.

It was the upper hay loft of the barn, the haymow, which was thought of as the play ground by Carolyn and Henri, even their parents at times. Anyone climbing the ladders to the upper realm carefully scraped their boot-soles first. That practice kept the wooden ladder rungs, which had to be grasped with bare hands, cleaner. The hay mow was always clean, dry, inviting, and a little secretive. Because of the elevated deck, everything stayed dry up there. Hay couldn't be put up wet without the real possibility of becoming a spontaneous combustion fire hazard. As you climbed the ladder from the darker, smellier, noisier, region below, the clean, dry, smell of hay welcomed you. Those large hay doors on each end, breathed old air out, and allowed fresh air in. "It's like going to heaven," Carolyn once said to her mother, when she asked Carolyn why she liked the hay mow so much. "Everything gets better as you go up. Isn't that like going to heaven?" Carolyn would often lie in the hay reading her school books and doing homework. It was her place.

Playing in the hay mow made it a sweet, lifetime memory. It was the place to be when you wanted life to be better, and, while playing there, its secretiveness became significant. It was a great place to hide. The lower barn was ok for hide-n-seek, because it had so many walls, cribs, and things to hide behind. Even animals would cooperate by shielding you from view, as long as you didn't sneak up on them too quickly. There was a silo as high as the barn roof on one end of the barn, but it was off limits to them, per Andre's instructions. "It is dangerous," he said. Henri had added, "You could get buried in a silage slide in there, and there's deadly gasses, or something like that." Henri liked to hide downstairs because Carolyn would tip toe around trying not to step in crap. He would hide in places surrounded by it, knowing she'd avoid it and not find him. Carolyn wouldn't walk in cow-wastes just to win at hide-n-seek. She developed her own strategy. When they were younger, she learned as soon as she stopped looking for Henri, he would come out. Carolyn loved to hide upstairs. She'd climb a few wooden rungs of the ladder and say out loud, "I can't find him down here, he must be upstairs," and then hurry the rest of the way up the ladder, knowing she would be hidden in the hay mow before Henri could get up there. As they got older, Henri wised up to that ploy, and the games became even more challenging.

The hay mow was almost as long as the barn itself, about 100 feet. Thirty-feet in from the north end there was a wall, with a door in it, behind which Andre stored animal feed in bags and containers. Outside that wall, the rest of the space on the upper floor was used for hay storage. They loaded hay into the hay mow through the big doors on the south end. A wheeled track on a metal beam ran north and south along the peak of the roof, from which hung a block and tackle with a hook on it. The hook could be raised and lowered between the peak and the floor of the haymow. With the block and tackle on rollers, you could hoist a canvas full of loose hay from a hay wagon below, high enough to pull it into the loft along the peak's track to the place on the floor you wanted to dump it. That apparatus allowed distribution of hay throughout the loft to maximize storage. At the end of haying season, the haymow would be full from floor to below the small open window at the peak. The space near the barn roof drew the remaining moisture out of the hay, and there was enough room that you could still crawl around up there. Then, as the season progressed, hay was forked down through holes in the floor, almost daily. When a hot spot was found, it was dispersed with pitchforks to eliminate fire danger. Surrounded by railings so you didn't accidentally nose dive into the darker regions, the hay piles would slowly shrink throughout the winter and spring. Because of that shrinkage, the hay mow was forever changing. One day it was this way, the next day that, as hay was moved, eaten, and used in different ways. That's what made it so much fun to hide up there. You could hide in the same place for a few days, then, all of a sudden that place was gone. But, there was always a new one.

As the hay mow emptied, the games changed. As piles lowered, the hook on the block and tackle kept getting closer to the floor, and farther from the ceiling. That made it a tempting swing, and Carolyn and Henri, sometimes Andre as well, would take turns flying all the way across the barn before jumping from the hook onto a soft pile of hay. Carolyn and Henri would take turns, riding and pushing each other, always trying to outdo the other in some spectacular way. Henri's size and strength usually enabled him to jump further, louder, and with more robust delivery, but both had fun. Carolyn's delivery was more theatrical. Sometimes she leaped with the form and precision of a trapeze artist, sometimes she crashed like a damsel in distress. Once, Henri mis-timed his release of the hook, dropping sooner than planned, which caused him to land on just enough hay on the floor to slide under the rail of one of the hay chutes, in slow motion, falling all the way to the floor of the lower barn. He was covered in crap, but unhurt, and neither he nor Carolyn could stop laughing. When his mother asked about his clothes he said he'd tripped while shoveling.. He wondered how he'd handle that little white lie at his next confession with Father Baptiste.

In the last weeks, they' invented and practiced a new skill, swinging on the block and tackle. They would each stand on a brace-wall platform which extended out about ten feet from each side of the barn to support the roof. Standing a few feet above the current hay level, they would swing the heavy hook and block back and forth across the hay to each other on each end of the barn. Each would catch it, stopping its swing, then, when ready, thrust it back across the barn to measure the accuracy of their of their aim. When that got boring, Henri hung onto the block and swung himself all the way across to Carolyn. Pretty soon, they were each taking turns swinging back and forth, changing places on each end of the barn. It was great fun, and they soon became expert at this new game. They did not, however, tell their parents of their latest accomplishments. Better that they thought their children's activities were limited to hide-n-seek.

When they tired of the barn and hay mow, they'd often go down to where the creek that crossed their lower farm fields ran through a culvert under the road. In the spring, they'd chase tadpoles, in the summer brook trout, in the fall, frogs. In the winter they'd often skate on the frozen water. The farm was a great place for kids to grow up. The culvert was two blocks down the road from the end of their driveway. They'd put skates on at the house and skate, walk, and fall all the way to the culvert before finding flat ice. It was tough on their blades, but kept their feet warm.

There was another thing that irked Henri. He always felt Carolyn got more time and attention from Andre than he did. It wasn't a big deal; he never made an issue of it, but the feeling seemed always to be there as his Dad and Carolyn worked the coop together, or delivered eggs together. He knew he did some chores with his Dad, but it always seemed like work rather than sharing time with him as Carolyn did.

Chapter 8

"His name is Jim Hutton," Ralph said. "He says he's a real estate agent in the Twin Cities, and he's here looking around for one of his clients. He says they think there will be some opportunities of picking up some farms inexpensively before banks foreclose on them," Ralph finished. The expression on his face telegraphed his current thought, *that his own farm could be one of those opportunities pretty soon.*

Thinking the same thing, Andre responded, "Well, he's right about that. If we don't get something going to raise money, and soon, we'll be at the top of his list."

"Yeh, but here's what's interesting, Andre. He said he is looking for some help, and he's willing to pay for it! He asked me who you were, too. He saw you in the station in your pickup one day when I filled up his Oldsmobile. Then he said he'd like to have lunch with us this week to talk about some possible work. He was in a hurry, so he just asked me to see if I could set something up for Thursday, and that he would see me that morning when he fueled up. This may be something we need, Andre. Can you be here at noon on Thursday? I think we should talk to him."

"I'm willing to listen to anybody with an idea right now Ralph. I'll be here." Andre went on, "I hope whatever he's after is legal. I don't want any problems with the law. I've got enough of my own problems already."

He filled the three five-gallon gas cans in the back of his pickup, loaded a wire basket of long-snout quart-bottles of 30- weight oil in beside the gas cans, told Ralph he's see him Thursday and headed home. He thought of Hutton all the way home. *They didn't know him from Adam, had only seen him gassing up his Olds, and didn't have any idea why he was willing to pay them, or what he might ask them to do.* Then, Andre remembered Clair's comment, "Something will work, Andre. It must."

Clair was an equal partner to Andre, both in their marriage, and in their business of farming. They were both in agreement that her priority was the kids, but when there was work to be done, even without Andre asking, she was there beside him as much as she could be.

Chapter 9

Sure enough, at 11:45 a.m., that shiny Oldsmobile pulled up to the gas pump. Andre and Ralph were standing just inside by the cash register. Hutton said, "Hi, Ralph . . . fill her up will you? I'll get the radiator. The oil's ok. She's not using a drop." With a practiced hand, he took a heavy bath towel from the rear seat, wrapped it around the ornament on the radiator cap and began twisting left. Steam began to shoot out, but with his hand wrapped in the towel, he held the cap tightly to the radiator receptor for the two seconds it took the steam's pressure to escape. Then he added, "I'll wait till you fill her, then start her up before adding water. Pouring cold water into a hot block without the water pump working can raise hell. I cracked the block on a Chevrolet doing that once."

As Hutton paid Ralph for the gas, he looked at Andre. "You must be Andre Cartier," he said behind his outstretched hand. "Ralph told me you are a good friend of his, and that you might be looking for some work. I'm Jim Hutton."

"I'm Andre, and yes, I could use some more income. With crops at their current prices I can't afford to plant this spring. That means no harvest. That means no money."

"I don't know what the government expects small farmers to do," said Hutton. "When shopping for a deal in real estate out here, I feel like I'm out here picking bones like a vulture, but real estate is what I do. And, believe me; I'm not getting rich either," he smiled. "Well, listen, I brought a great box of fried chicken and some more lunch with me from the cities . . . picked it up at one of my favorite restaurants. Why don't you boys ride with me? I'd like to see a place out by Lake Schellor. We can talk and eat lunch out there. For reasons I'll explain over lunch, I'll leave here, alone, and you two can meet me behind the Catholic Church. I'll be parked out in back."

Andre nodded agreement. Hutton got in his car and drove off. Ralph looked at Andre and asked, "Is it lunchtime?" Andre nodded again. "Bill, Andre and I are going for lunch. Do you want me back at 1:00?"

"Nope. Better get used to it, Ralph. I'm sorry, but you're going to half-time starting tomorrow," he added, shaking his head disgustedly. "We haven't sold enough gas today to even pay my wages. Could be worse I guess . . . at least I'm not a farmer."

As the two of them drove towards the church, Andre asked, "Why didn't Hutton want us to ride with him, Ralph?"

"I don't know. Last week he told me not to tell anyone but you that we were talking about work. It made me curious, too."

Chapter 10

The Catholic Church Andre and his family attended was a half-mile east of Cedarville. It was on the north side of the highway, just beyond an acre or two of pines, which made it invisible from the highway until you almost reached its driveway. Built at the turn of the century, it was about thirty years old, of red brick that sat beside a big but well groomed, graveyard. The Priest's home was also of red brick and modest in size.

As he and Ralph drove around between the church and graveyard, Andre remembered his father always laughing his way past this part of the driveway saying, "Kids, people are dying to get in here." But then Andre thought he should be thinking more seriously right now. *What am I doing here,* he wondered?

Hutton had parked in the far corner of the lot behind the church. They pulled in beside him, and got into the Oldsmobile, Ralph in front, Andre in back. "Welcome aboard, boys. Have you ever ridden in an Olds before? I hadn't until last week. She's a real honey on the road." With that, he started the engine and began pulling onto the highway heading east. "One of the places my client bought last month is that old farm behind Lake Schellor. It used to belong to Brad Robinson. Do you know him? Brad lost the farm to the bank . . . same problem . . . same deal as most others. No crops, no harvest, no money, no mortgage payments. My client bought the place from Anderson at the local bank.

"Why would someone buy that place now?" Andre asked. "It makes no sense. How does your client come out? Why does he want the farm?"

They were ten miles further east now, approaching the junction of County 29, which ran north and south across the highway. Hutton turned left on 29, winding his way around the northwest quarter of the lake. Lake Schellor was about six miles long, two to four miles wide throughout most of its length, with the widest spot being halfway down the lake. It was a fairly shallow lake, thirty to forty-feet deep off shore and wooded right down to its shoreline, everywhere except where the pastures of three different farms reached the shore. Robinson's farm was the least developed of the three, but had the most acreage on the lake, and also had a reputation of being somewhat unproductive according to what Andre had heard rumored around the grain elevator. Robinson, his wife and four kids, occasionally attended the same church Cartiers did, but they had never become more than casually acquainted. Andre sensed among the congregation that few members seemed to even notice the Robinson family.

Hutton answered Andre's question, "How he comes out is a secret many would like to know. Like anyone with substantial money, he is often envied, copied when secrets can be learned, and he's never anxious to make those secrets obvious. I admire the man . . . he's a smart cookie . . . and he's always made me money. I don't really know you boys, but from what I've heard around the community you're both honest, hard-working fellows who can be counted on. That's why I suggested we have lunch. Let's go down by the shore of the lake and eat. We can talk more there."

They chitchatted around the lake to the Robinson driveway. "My client allowed the Robinsons to live in the house for another month. Then they are moving down by Somerset, where Mr. Robinson has found work with a relative." As they drove past the farm house and barn, Andre's ner-do-well feelings about Robinson were validated by what he saw. The house was peeling paint; a few shutters hung cockeyed. The barn was a faded red that hadn't been touched up or painted in years. None of this was unusual. It was the Depression's time, and none but the biggest and best financed were paying much attention at all to maintenance, or even paint. There was something about this place that made Andre think it was likely substandard before the crash of '29.

They pulled up by the lakeshore where Hutton killed the engine. He got out, opened the trunk of the Olds, and as Andre and Ralph watched, lifted a basket and a folded canvas. Setting the basket on the ground, he shook out the folds and spread the canvas on the dry shoreline, next to the water. "Schellor's water is so clean I want to swim every time I get near it," he grinned. "Open that basket there and help me spread out this lunch. You're going to like it."

I can see why he's in real estate, Andre thought. *He's a natural salesman.* There was enough fried chicken in the box to feed three more besides Andre and Ralph. A whole apple pie, some fresh fruit, and a quart-Mason jar full of what looked like lemonade. Andre and Ralph were glad they had come, no matter the conversation, and were soon too busy chewing to talk.

Hutton distributed drinking glasses from the basket, filling them with lemonade, from the jar. He went back to the Old's trunk, rummaged around a bit, then pulled out another Mason jar, smaller than the lemonade-jar, and brought it over to the canvas picnic spread. "I have the perfect touch here to stir into that lemonade. This is Minnesota 13, from Stearns County over in Minnesota, some of the best moonshine known to man. At least, that's what my client tells me. Can I sweeten your drinks?"

Chapter 11

Andre didn't drink. He had nothing against it, couldn't be called wet or dry in the vernacular of the times, he just didn't drink alcohol. Neither did Clair. They had friends who drank ; which was fine, but they didn't. Ralph, on the other hand, had liked the grape, regardless of its form or packaging, since his first experience with some moonshine back when he was seventeen. He'd been at a threshing party where following the final thrashing of grain, beer and home brew of some nature had been readily available. A couple of his uncles had decided to initiate him, which didn't take much doing. That resulted in them unceremoniously pouring their nephew off a hay wagon in their brother's yard in front of the house. They fired off a twelve-gauge shotgun and disappeared from sight behind galloping horses, before the wrath of their brother could descend on them. Ralph's father had never quite forgiven them for how they had treated his son. He'd expected more, then, *remembered they were his brothers*. The damage had been done, though. Ralph had met the grape. From then on it had been a contest for Ralph. Sometimes he won, sometimes the grape won, especially during his early twenties. His on- button worked better than his off- button, right up till he was twenty-five. Then he met Maureen. Within six-months they married. In the next five-years, along came Robert, William, Roger and Lillian. From then on it always seemed there had been five fingers on Ralph's off-button. But those five weren't here today.

"No thanks, Jim. I don't drink, never have, but I appreciate the lunch and all," said Andre.

Jim smiled, "To each their own," then held the 13 jar towards Ralph, who readily held out his glass. Jim poured a healthy dollop, first into Ralph's glass, then his own, and recapped the jar. "Over in Stearns County in Minnesota, they say Minnesota 13 is one of the most sought-after moonshines in the country. It's hard to believe that Midwest booze could be popular in places like Chicago, New York, and California, but that's their claim. Some over there say they've even dealt with the likes of Al Capone with this stuff," he said while admiring the 13 jar in his hand. Ralph took a long cool drink from his glass, then another, and said. "It's good."

Andre wasn't paying much attention to their glasses. He was looking back up towards the buildings they'd driven by on the way in. "This place doesn't look like much . . . kind of a shambles. I mean, my place doesn't look like much now either, but that's because I can't afford maintenance right now, but it looks a lot better than this place."

"You're right about that," said Hutton. "Robinson was never much on maintenance, or even farming if you ask me, but my client's got big plans for the place. He's going to put some money in here, fix it up a little. He wants to turn it back into a productive farm again, thinks with almost half the property on the lake, this will be valuable in the future. He's going to hire others to do what Robinson didn't."

"I still don't get it," said Andre. "Your client is going to do all this just betting on the future? Explain that to me"

"Well, like I said, my client is never anxious to share his secrets. He knows what he's doing, though. And, he does make money for those who work with him. That's why I wanted to talk to you two right now," Hutton finished. He hesitated for a minute, looking down at the 13. "Want another, Ralph?"

"Yeh, I do. I haven't had a drink for months . . . I'm overdue . . . just one more though," he finished as he bit into his third piece of chicken. Andre hadn't seen Ralph looking this happy for months.

Hutton poured, first the moon, then the lemonade into Ralph's glass, adding, "I have to honor my client's wishes of keeping all this close to the vest. That's why I suggested you meet me behind the church. If no one sees you with me, no one will know we are even talking. If I divulge, I guess share is a better word, some of my client's plans with you two, I need to count on both of you to keep it confidential." He eyeballed them astutely following his question, measuring their reaction to what he'd asked. "Can I count on that?"

Andre thought, *Where is this going?* Ralph thought, *Hell yes! Pass the 13.*

While Andre thought, Ralph said, "Well sure. I can keep my mouth shut, and I want to hear how I can make some money. I'm damn near in the same shape Robinson was before they foreclosed on him."

Andre added, "I can understand the need to keep some things quiet. We aren't talking murder or bank robbery, here are we?"

Hutton laughed, "No, but I must know that I can count on you not to pass on anything I tell you, whether we end up doing some work together, or not. Can I count on that?" he finished, as he reached out his right hand, first to Andre, to shake in agreement. They locked eyeballs and Andre nodded affirmatively. Andre was not sure about this man, but what he was sure of was, he, himself, was a short distance away from becoming a different kind of man. The kind that fails his wife, his family, loses his farm to foreclosure and is left with nothing. He was not going to allow that to happen. He stretched out his weathered and calloused hand to shake agreement with Jim Hutton.

Hutton had known from the first time he saw Andre and Ralph in the gas station, that Andre was the savvy leader of this duet. Hutton then reached out to Ralph, who had already extended his hand, "I'm quiet as a mouse," Ralph smirked, with a hint of 13 glossing his upper lip. Then, he equaled the pressure on his hand from Hutton's.

Chapter 12

Sampson was half-way to the Twin Cities from Chicago. He had finished up his last two weeks, transferring all his work-in-progress to Ben Ambrotz. Ben had been in Sampson's squad for three years and was the one Sampson picked to replace himself as squad leader. He would run things in Chicago while Sampson was on temporary assignment up in the Twin Cities.

Ambrotz owed him a lot. Sampson hired him, trained him, made him extra money, and kept him out of jail once during the last year. He'd been assistant squad leader under Sampson for the past year as well, so was expected by the rest of the squad to replace him. Sampson pushed him hard for the first two years. He kept him overworked for nearly a year, just to see if he could take it. He loaded some bad assignments onto him for the same reasons. Ambrotz hung in there, and when he began complaining about not making enough money as an agent, Sampson arranged to bring him quietly into his own private enterprise of sideline-moon sales. Sampson had made a lot of extra money by quietly selling off contraband moonshine his squad captured in raids on stills and bootleggers. He had his sideline well-organized, well- hidden, and only one other agent in his department was aware of what he was doing. That was Ambrotz, which was exactly how Sampson wanted it. Sampson knew of another squad leader padding his income with the same sideline. It wasn't at all uncommon since Prohibition passed.

Though the timing was an accident, it was by design that Sampson clandestinely brought Ambrotz into secret moon sales. Now, he would continue Sampson's sideline operation, taking his cut plus another 10% Sampson promised him for running the show in his absence.

Not only did Ambrotz owe Sampson, he was scared of him as well. Sampson had arranged that, too. During his first year with Sampson's squad, Ben had seen Sampson strategically shoot a bootlegger while in a fit of rage, and he had done it right in front of him! Ben couldn't believe what he'd seen. Before this event, Sampson had slipped him cash a couple of times, telling him it was money from his sideline. Ben had readily accepted it, so was already compromised as an agent. Having arranged that, Sampson also wanted to be feared by him. The bootlegger was lying, face down unconscious on the road where Sampson had clubbed him with his pistol. Ben didn't know Sampson was acting when he shouted, "Did you hear what that son-of-a-bitch said to me?" The man on the ground would never walk normally again, because Sampson shot him directly in the back of the knee!

Before he could impulsively ask, "Why the hell did you shoot him?" Sampson sneered, "You've got to let em know who is boss, Ben! He'll never try me again." Sampson could see his trainee was horrified at what he had seen, which was just what he wanted. "This episode stays between us, Ben. That man was shot trying to escape. I only fired after he fired, got it?" With that, he reached down, took the pistol from the man's belt and fired it into the air. Then he placed it in the unconscious man's hand. "If I ever hear of this incident any other way, I will know it came from you, Ben. You don't want that to happen. I've had agents killed by the likes of this bastard," he finished, still acting enraged. Sampson then coached Ben with the story he expected him to use when explaining how the shooting occurred. Sampson was a good actor. Ben Ambrotz feared him.

Now, months later, Sampson had not only that incident, which by now would be considered aiding and abetting, but also had an exact record of the dates and amounts of money Ben had taken from the illegal sale of confiscated moonshine, which was supposed to be destroyed or disposed of before a raid was considered finished by revenue agents. To Sampson, Ambrotz was the ideal man to run things for him in his absence. Someone in his debt, someone he could destroy with evidence, and someone who was scared stiff of him. *Nice work, Sampson,* he thought as he drove north.

Sampson had talked with Chief Lundquist from his office in Chicago the day before. "I'm looking forward to these months of helping you, Chief," he'd said. We've been playing hardball with the big guys down here around Chicago, and learned how to do it. I know you don't have Capone and some of his henchmen up there, but I can pass on some of the methods we've learned about revenue enforcement and help you train your new agents to be more effective," he'd finished.

"Well, don't be too sure about that. I just got a report that Capone was right here in Stearns County just last week. He and some of his friends had a meeting, supposedly, about how they could better compete with all that Canadian booze coming down above the Dakotas. We're investigating it now," he'd responded. "Well, check in when you get here tomorrow. Goodbye, Sampson," and Sampson had heard the phone click. He'd left his Chicago office thinking, *nice start Sampson. No one here knows how happy you really are to be going to Minneapolis where you'll be out of sight of the syndicate for a year.*

Sampson was going to be Chief Lundquist's ally. He wanted him to be glad he was there and needed Lundquist to grant him some freedom in his training, operations, and raids, so he could set up another private enterprise on the side. It would not be in Lundquist's area of command, but over in the quieter regions of the Barrens in Wisconsin. There he could be a big cog in a smaller wheel, without attracting the attention of the big guys as he had in the Chicago region.

Sampson was smart. He learned from mistakes. He had gotten too aggressive in Chicago. He wouldn't make that error again. He didn't want to stay in the revenue business any longer than he had to, and had learned it's not healthy to have syndicate people looking for you. Things could happen to Revenue agents, especially those who became known to the big guys. He was going to make raids on the little guys, and was going to remain unknown to most for a while. He was relieved to be out of Chicago, especially as things were heating up. *Let someone else get shot at by Capone,* he thought, as he drove north towards Minneapolis.

Chapter 13

"My client's going to make moon here," said Hutton, watching the expressions change on the faces of Andre and Ralph. "Now, don't panic, just hear me out. You are going to like what you hear." They were sitting in Robinson's building.

Shit, Andre thought, *I knew it would be something illegal*, as he looked at Ralph, with a kind of "I told you so, look." Ralph didn't really care if what they were doing was legal or not. What he wanted to know was how he got money out of it. Hutton had asked, "How'd you like to make some money?" Ralph wanted to know. He needed to make some money.

Hutton went on, "My client's been making, selling, and bootlegging moon over in Stearns County for the last five years and has made a fortune. He knows what he's doing and has made a lot of money for a lot of farmers who were going broke before they hooked up with him."

Andre butted in, "Why's he coming over here if there's a fortune over there?"

"Because, Andre, things are getting too hot in Stearns County. For the last three-months they've been sending more and more Revenue agents in on raids. They've arrested more in the last few months than in the last few years. Three weeks ago they filled every jail in the County. Everything about the moon business and Revenue agents seems centered in Stearns County right now . . . three out of five people over there have something to do with moon, either cooking, hauling, hiding, selling, or bootlegging," Hutton continued. "My client says, though Stearns has made him rich, he wants to relocate some of his operation to a calmer region to create some new sources and avoid those agents. Now, don't let that scare you. These people aren't going to prison. I'll explain that in a minute."

"So, why come over here?" said Andre.

Ralph listened intently, watching Andre, as though he listened through Andre's ears.

"It's the same distance from the Twin Cities as Stearns County. It's wilder country, fewer people, more woods, lots of water, only an agent or two occasionally, and lots of farmers that are going broke. I'm sorry to make it sound that way to a couple of farmers, but you both know that's the case. Is there anything I've said that isn't true?" Hutton came across as honest, sincere, and like someone you would trust if you were doing real estate business with him. Everything he said was true, and Andre and Ralph knew it.

"So why are Ralph and I sitting here eating fried chicken and moonshine?" Andre asked with an edgy voice. Andre looked mad, and Hutton could tell.

"Once again, let me just say . . . relax . . . hear me out. You will like what you hear."

Andre responded loudly, "You keep saying that, but so far, I don't like what I'm hearing, Mr. Hutton."

Hutton went on, "Since the war ended, farming has been a downhill slide for years. Prices are so depressed banks won't even lend you money to plant. You can't live on ten-cent a bushel corn, and you and I both know your friends, maybe even you, are faced with defaulting on mortgages and losing farms that have been in your family for generations. Ralph said he took over his father's farm. It's the depression causing all this. It's not fair, it's bull shit, it's wrong, but there's not a damn thing any of us can do about it. I talk to farmers every day who say they can't hang on more than another six months, if that . . . none of them know what to do. Ralph told me last week, that that was exactly his situation, and he hinted yours may not be any better, Andre. What else are you going to do?" he finished.

Andre said, "Well, I'm not going to break the law, and go to jail, that's what. Playing around with moon breaks the law."

Hutton answered back, "Ok, I agree . . . it breaks the law. But, it's a stupid law, a law that never should have been passed. It keeps some churches and dry-people happy, but it's a law that will never last. It's just not right Andre." He waved his hand for effect, "Look at Stearns County. There's a ton of honest farmers over there just like you. They have the same farming problems you do, but they decided they had the right to save their farms due to a depression they didn't cause. Now, three out of five people over there are making money from moon. And those are the three out of five that are paying their mortgages and not losing their homesteads. Think about that, Andre, you too, Ralph. How are you going to pay your mortgages?" He looked at them seriously with another, "How? The Volstead Act, Prohibition, and the Depression on top of that are nothing any small farmer had anything to do with, or can do anything about. You guys can save your farms the same way the Stearns boys have."

"I truly don't know what I'm going to do, Jim, but at least I still know that, honestly," Andre said.

"This isn't just about honesty, Andre. I have a cousin over in Stearns. He used to talk just as you are talking. He did not want to break the law, ever. He was dragged kicking and screaming into the moon business. Everything he did, he did reluctantly. Then, after being in the business for six months, he said everything changed. He found he wasn't working with criminals or gangsters. He was working with neighbors, friends that all had kids to feed and clothe, mortgages to pay, and none of them felt like they were breaking a just law." Hutton went on, "On top of that, they passed the law while our country was still reeling from World War I, and then the Depression hit! Now, half the people who were pressured to vote the law in want to vote it out. It's 1930 now, and well over half the nation's politicians are saying Prohibition won't last much longer. Repeal is coming, and when it does all this Prohibition bull shit will not have changed a thing. In the mean time, the important thing for you is to not be one of those who loses their farms."

Each time Ralph heard Jim talk, the serious but curious expression on Ralph's face began to almost smile. He liked what he was hearing from Hutton.

Andre squared his jaw, then said, "That's a good speech . . . but it's still illegal. It is still breaking the law. There are still Federal Revenue agents. You can still go to jail," he finished. "What in hell would my wife and kids do with me in jail? My wife's my partner, Mr. Hutton. I'm not doing anything she doesn't agree with. Maybe you should have invited her for chicken and moon, too."

Each time Andre talked, Ralph's face drifted back downward. Ralph knew he wasn't sure about deflection of the argument in either direction, but he liked the sound of money. He cringed at the sound of jail. Illegal had a nasty ring to it. It was times like these when he liked Andre around. And, when Andre was around, Ralph listened more than he talked. Andre had just reminded Ralph he had a partner too.

Hutton smiled, then returned to a serious face and a serious tone, "Here's what's interesting about the illegal part, Andre. Stearns County has more arrests than any other County in the state, but there is little jail time, and when it occurs it is short. My cousin knows one of the judges over there. He says even the judges think it's a stupid law. The judge says the agents are pouring on the arrests to scare people away from moon, but they can't enforce the law, because there just isn't enough jail room. Federal agents can't get the judges to send mooners to prison. Only the worst of repeat offenders get that. Local law enforcement won't help the agents. Hell, even the Sheriff over in Stearns won't help them. He used to occasionally tip us off when raids were coming."

Hutton went on for another hour, explaining to Andre and Ralph why his client's approach of making moon a harvest crop in this area was going to work. His explanations and anecdotes from the Stearns County region were convincing, and they also relieved a lot of Andre and Ralph's building anxiety. Andre had most of it; Ralph didn't usually think things through far enough to create the same depth of concern. As they were cleaning up lunch leftovers, Jim said, "Look, just think this over for a few days, then let's talk again . . . say next Thursday. I can have the two of you working in a week, making good money, in a way you'll be pretty safe from the law. And we're just getting started. There's money to be made here, and there's no other way you are going to earn it. Remember our agreement, though; no matter what you decide, not a word to anybody. I know you'll have to discuss it with your wives, but just call it a job. You'll be working for a wealthy land owner who's restoring a farm. You'll be working some days, some nights, so you are free to continue working your own places to whatever degree you choose. To your family, you've taken on some extra work to gain some income. This will work, and from what I've seen of most of the Stearns County men, you won't regret it. Hold your hand out, Ralph," he finished.

Ralph did. Jim placed a twenty and a five-dollar bill on his palm. "How does that look?" Jim asked, and then added. "That can start happening two or three nights a week before the end of the month," he smiled.

Ralph was smiling now, looking at his palm. Then his smile faded as Jim picked up the twenty-five dollars again. He didn't offer to hand it to Andre. He'd made his point and knew Andre had heard it. "Ok, let's head back to town. We'll meet Thursday and I'll have a lot more information for you then."

They didn't talk much more as they drove back. Andre and Ralph wanted to talk alone, to evaluate everything they'd heard without, Jim, as the audience. After Jim dropped them behind the Catholic Church, the two of them sat in Andre's pickup and talked for an hour. By the time they stopped talking, they had almost reached agreement that it was a worthwhile risk. That's when Andre added, "We'll see, Ralph. Clair has an equal vote on what I do."

Chapter 14

"I know it's shady, Clair," Andre said. "But like you said the last time we talked, something will work out. Hutton's offer is the only something we are going to see. I was dead set against it at first, but the more I think about it, the more I think we should do it. Not only that, but the sooner the better."

"It just scares me, Andre. I don't know how the kids would handle it if their father was arrested for something illegal. I don't know how I would handle it. But, we are not losing this farm either. I think Hutton is likely right about Prohibition having added unnecessary laws, and it's not just prohibition either. How can farming get any worse than it is? Even if we could plant, we'd barely break even with a good harvest," she finished.

"Yeh, and that is if it's a good growing season, with no weather or drought. So far, we aren't planting this year, Clair. There may be no harvest. We need money again, and we need it soon. That's something else I learned talking to Hutton. He says the banks really get mad when his client comes in and buys up a place before they can foreclose on the mortgage, because they lose their opportunity to profit. If we are late on a mortgage payment, they aren't going to give us any more time." Andre was using his perception of facts to talk himself past the risks he was sure must be attached to this challenging new money opportunity. It was working. "Ralph wants to do it. I know he's not as careful as I am, but he's also more willing to admit just how desperate our situations have become. His father left him their place too, and they've got more kids than we do," Andre ended.

Clair added, "Andre, you know I'll back whatever decision you make. I know we have little choice. We must do something. You decide. You always hand me a 50-50 vote on big decisions, as I do you, so here it is. If you're in, I'm in."

Andre nodded, "I never thought we'd ever be in a situation worrying about mortgage payments, or even considering this kind of work, Clair. I am truly sorry it has to be this way. My father didn't leave this farm to the banks, or the government. He left it to us, with the mortgage that existed, and we've always kept up." He was mad now. "I'll be damned if they're going to take it away, no matter what I have to do. What *we* have to do," he added, penetrating her eyes with his. "It's as you said, Clair. Something will work out. I think it has," he finished.

"Just promise me one thing, Andre. Don't go to jail."

Chapter 15

Sheriff Maun and Andre had been friends for years. They'd finished their last years of school together. Maun was two years younger than Andre, but they'd spent time together in different ways; school activities, hunting as they grew older, threshing times on their father's farms, activities at their Catholic family's church, and while they'd not call each other *best* friends, they had a certain respect for each other. Andre had voted for Maun several times, and felt he was doing a good job as Sheriff. Actually, he wasn't sure of that, because there didn't seem to be much for the Sheriff to do here. But no one ever seemed to complain about him, so he must be doing something right.

Coming out of the grocery store with empty egg carton boxes, he saw Maun walking by. "Jason, how you doing?" Andre smiled.

"Great, Andre, how about you?"

"Well, I'm a far cry from rich, but I've still got eggs," Andre laughed. "What we raise is still keeping us out of jail, which is why I haven't seen you in a while."

"I hear that," Jason responded. "I don't know of any farmers making money! That situation is threatening to make my job a little tougher."

"How's that?" Andre asked.

"I've had to serve papers on three properties in the county this month, Andre. That is not a fun thing to do. I'd done it before on car loans and farm equipment, but I'd never seen anyone kicked out of their homes and lose everything that way." He shook his head slowly between sentences. "The first two weren't friends, or people I really knew, but I felt like a damn pirate, or a crook, or something like that, handing them those papers. It's part of my job, I know, but I think the banks should serve their own damn papers! Then Jase, the last one was Jeff Waters!"

"I've been hearing how bad it's getting for some. Hell, I don't know how much longer Clair and I can hang on. You are in a tough spot serving eviction papers, though. If I didn't have the animals and eggs we're raising right now, I'd be expecting you to show up on my steps with papers in your hand. What about Jeff?"

The Sheriff said hello to another man passing by, waited for him to get out of hearing, then said, "One of Anderson's men from the bank, Corbit is his name, was there at that serving. When I handed Jeff the papers, I told Jeff I was sorry. He said, 'I know Jason, I know.' His wife was on the step beside him trying to stop crying, and their three kids were hiding in the kitchen looking out the window. They looked whipped, just done in, and when Jeff called the kids outside, I think because he wanted the banker to see them. They were skinny as a rail. Honest, Andre, one of them looked like he was starving! I had no idea Jeff was in that kind of trouble!"

Andre lowered his head in empathy saying, "That shouldn't be, Jason. It just shouldn't be."

"I know it. I asked the bank's man if he couldn't give them another month or two, I mean, hell, they had no place to go! Where will they live? He just said, "No, because in two more months, they'll just be two more months worse off than they are today." He just looked Jeff in the face and told him he had to be off the property by the fifteenth. Then he turned around - got into his fancy car, well not so fancy, it was a Chevrolet, and drove off leaving me there with the saddest family I've ever seen. I didn't even know what to do, and couldn't think of anything worthwhile to say. I couldn't help them and I felt like it was my fault because I handed them the papers."

Dismayed, Andre just kept shaking his head, listening to Jason's cathartic purge. He knew he had to get this out to someone, and when he first saw the Sheriff walking by, Andre had impulsively decided to ask him some questions himself. He didn't know Jason was going to unload on him this way, so hadn't gotten to his own questions yet.

"Just between you and me, Andre, I had to do something for Jeff and his family. I came back to town, bought a bunch of groceries, and delivered them back out there that evening. I meant well, but hell, his wife started crying again, and Jeff shook my hand until I thought I might lose it. I didn't want their thanks for a few lousy groceries . . . I served their papers!"

Andre said, "Jason, you can't blame yourself for the problem caused by the government, the foreign war we've been suffering from these last years, the depression, prohibition. Hell, none of us caused all these problems. We're just the ones who have to live through them. Only those with money are trouble-free these days. But it's sure not your fault."

"I know that, Andre, but if I have to serve any more papers, I'll find another line of work somehow. That situation made me understand why so many people over in Minnesota started making moonshine. Hell, without the little money they get from that, somebody with a badge would likely be serving them."

That comment surprised Andre. He hadn't mentioned moonshine to Jason. He hadn't mentioned a word, even a thought, to make that subject come up. In fact, he'd been consciously avoiding it. On the other hand, Jason's comment created an opportunity Andre couldn't let pass.

"I keep hearing a lot of people are doing that. Well, they've got to do something. How do they keep from going to jail?" Andre thought that comment would now surprise Jason, but it didn't.

"Hell, that dumb Volstead Act, and all that legal crap. Nobody enforces it, Andre. It's a bunch of bullshit! When's the last time you saw a Federal Revenue Agent in Cedarville? They've got a whole herd of them over in Minnesota, west of the cities, but that's because that's the hub of booze action there, I guess. I hear in law enforcement info that comes to us each month that Canadian booze pours over the border in the Dakotas, then goes down to Chicago and gets bootlegged all over the country. They make moonshine like crazy there in Stearns County. That's where all those Federal Revenue agents are. I hear they make a lot of arrests, but as quick as people are arrested, they're out of jail and making moon again. Nobody wants to enforce those laws but the feds. I don't know why they even have them. I've never made a single Prohibition arrest. The most I've ever done is take away a few jars at town hall dances." Sheriff Maun was unaware that what he was saying was music to Andre Cartier's ears.

"Andre, I didn't mean to give a speech here. I kind of unloaded on you. Sorry about that. Listen, I see you've been delivering eggs. Do you have any left you haven't sold?"

"Yeh, I do. Just about four dozen, though," said Andre.

"Can I buy them?" Maun asked. "I've got another family that is so hurting for food. I try and help them out about once a week. Their farm has no mortgage, so they don't have to worry about that, but the man has been sick for weeks, and they are barely hanging on, with three kids."

"No, you can't buy them," Andre said, which shocked and showed up on Jason's face.

"Just take them off the front seat, no charge. What in the hell are people going to do if this mess gets any worse, Jason?"

Chapter 16

"Did you hear Mom and Dad talking last night, Henri?" Carolyn asked. "It sounds like we really have money problems."

"How could I not hear them?" Henri answered. "I've never heard either one of them talk that loud. I've heard them argue before, but never like that. I've seen Mom mad at Dad, but last night they were really upset."

"I know. When I heard Dad shout, I really started to listen carefully. I don't think they were mad and shouting at each other. It's more like . . . well . . . they were shouting at the bank. I think it sounds like they are running out of money," she added. "That's what they're mad about. Dad said the bank wouldn't loan them money this year. I didn't even know they borrowed from the bank every spring to plant, did you?"

"Well, Dad used to call Mr. Anderson his friend, but I've never seen either Mom or Dad do anything with the Andersons. It must have something to do with the bank."

Carolyn and Henri were typical teen-agers. Their parents did not share the family's relationship with the banks, or even many business details about their farming. As responsible and loving parents, they spent more time making the kids aware of their respective roles in operation of the family farm. They knew how to be responsible about their chores, and because of how their parents had taught them, were proud of their roles as productive members of the farm. They knew their parents sold livestock and crops and helped them deliver eggs to a couple of stores, and milk as well occasionally. They knew the land their farm's borders claimed and that it belonged to their family. They had heard their Dad frequently say something like, "Dad left this farm to us, and we will run it in a way that were he here, he would be proud of our work," to which their mother would quickly add, "He is here in spirit, Andre, and I know he is proud." So, both Carolyn and Henri always thought things were fine with the farm. They were both unaware of the additional mortgage their parents had added last year, or how it might affect them.

In the last year, however, both brother and sister had heard more and more discussions about problems with the economy, which didn't really mean much to them. The way they would hear about it was when someone didn't pay their monthly bill for eggs, or when another crop price in a long line of reductions, would cause one of their parents to say, "We can hardly afford to raise it if we can't break even in a good season," or "what do we do when these people we've always dealt with can't pay their bills?" The kids knew problems were growing, and they heard even worse stories at school. Two of their school friends had to move off their farm and were now living with one of their uncle and aunts. Carolyn had tried to comfort her friend, Molly, the day after they moved. Molly cried all day in school, and Carolyn had taken her off behind the school and shared lunch with her. Molly couldn't stop crying enough to eat. "We lost our home and farm, Carolyn, and if you think I'm crying you should hear my mom and dad!"

"I don't want us to end up like Molly Raft's folks," Carolyn said to Henri. "Maybe we should talk to Mom and Dad. I'm not sure, though. Maybe they don't want to talk to us about it."

"Molly's brother, Dan, said after the bankers and Sheriff left that day, her father drank so much moonshine he passed out on the kitchen floor!" said Henri. "Maybe it's something bad enough that they don't want to talk about it. I think that's how it is. Last night, they kept saying things about not knowing what to do about whatever the problem is. So, if they don't know, how can we ask them? I think we should just help as much as we can, you know, with the chores, the eggs, and that kind of stuff."

"That sounds good, Henri. I don't want to ask Mom either. I heard Dad say the Robinsons couldn't pay for the eggs they got in the last three-weeks. Maybe I'll start to ask people if they can pay when they pick up the eggs. That might help, but then I'd have to say they can't have more eggs. How do I do that?" Carolyn questioned.

"I don't know, Carolyn, but let's see if we can figure out what's happening," said Henri, "and we'll find a way to help."

"Ok," added Carolyn, but I did the pigs for you twice this week, Henri. That's your job. I didn't tell Dad, but I'm going to if you skip out again."

Henri nodded.

Chapter 17

Chief Lundquist spoke from behind his desk in St. Paul. "Glad to have you with us, Agent Sampson. We need some experienced help up here. O'Hara said he was sending me one of his best men. I hope you live up to his appraisal."

"I intend to, Chief. Tell me how you think you need my help." Contrary to his behavior in Chicago with O'Hara., Sampson was going to be *Mr. Cooperative* to Chief Lundquist.

Lundquist went on, "We've got a lot of Federal Revenue agents working Stearns County right now. That's where most of the action is. My guys here in the St. Paul office, say three or four out of every five people in the County are involved with moonshine. We've made so many arrests we sometimes run out of jail room. We've shut down and destroyed hundreds of stills, but they get back into business almost as fast as we shut them down. We get almost no cooperation from local law, and they don't like Federal Revenue agents."

"Same thing around Chicago," Sampson nodded, "I'm used to not being liked."

"The biggest problem we have is judges who won't commit the first time offenders to jail-time or prison. The majority of the population up here did not vote for prohibition and don't honor the law, or the 18th Amendment. We don't get any help. But, I've got more than enough agents over in Stearns. I don't need you there."

Surprised by Lundquist's statement, Sampson asked, "Where do you need me?"

"We've put so much pressure on the shiners around Stearns that they are beginning to spread out, outside of Stearns, into neighboring counties. There's kind of a 100 mile radius around Minneapolis and St. Paul that is beginning to hide a lot of the action. I think the best thing we can do right now is keep the pressure on in Stearns, and begin to set up small squads of near-invisible agents in that radius outside the Twin Cities. What I don't want to happen, is have all those surrounding counties gear up as they have in Stearns. I want to nip that action in the bud," Lundquist finished.

Sampson always felt good when he sensed opportunity. He felt good now. "So, where can I help?" he asked.

"I've got fairly experienced teams on the west side, south side too, and there isn't that much moonshine north of the cities. Its east, on the Wisconsin side, across the St. Croix River, out by Somerset, Hudson, St. Croix Falls, and Cedarville where I don't have any experienced Agents who know the region. When I mentioned that to O'Hara, he suggested I find some new agents and then train them under an experienced squad leader. That's when we started talking of you, Sampson."

"That's my kind of assignment, Chief," Sampson grinned. "I know how to find the right kind of agents, how to train them, and get results. If that's what you want I can handle it."

"Find yourself an apartment or something here in the Twin Cities. I don't want you living anywhere near Stephens County where you might be noticed. It's only Tuesday. Spend the rest of the week getting settled in. We'll go to work on setting you and this new team up to work Somerset and the Barrens next week." Lundquist seemed happy with their discussion, which was exactly what Sampson wanted.

Chapter 18

The following Thursday, Andre and Ralph signed on with Hutton. Andre was still innately reluctant; Ralph was anxious. Hutton had expedited their decisions by putting them into training the first week as cookers and laborers, working at the Robinson place, which he hoped at least Andre would be able to handle himself, eventually. He could have found many people with more experience with moonshine, but what he wanted was someone known in Stephens County, with a legitimate excuse for driving around, such as delivering eggs and produce. His hopes were on Andre, but he thought Ralph might have promise as well. Hutton explained to the two of them that in the capacity of cooker or laborer, no one ever went to jail even if arrested, which wasn't going to happen in this operation because they were careful. The more Hutton talked, the more Andre realized Jim had much more to do with moon than real estate. The closer they got to the innards of what Hutton was setting up for his client, the more he realized that Hutton knew all the secrets behind the scene of moon shining. When Andre asked, "What do cookers do?" Jim gave him a step-by-step rundown as though he was teaching a class.

"There's a lot more to cooking, in a good operation, than just cooking, Andre. My client's small operation out here is pretty much set up to train in new people. I'll start you there. The Robinson place is within ten miles of your place and you have a pickup, so transportation isn't a problem. I may arrange a different ride for the two of you too, so we don't arouse suspicion with you guys driving around. We'll see."

Hutton talked for another twenty minutes, telling them of materials handling, of sugar, the types of sugar used by different shiners - cane, beet, or corn - yeast, water, corn for flavoring, and adequate and mandatory cleanliness. He talked of plain wood fifty-five gallon barrels used for mash, mixing and fermenting. He talked of charred oak barrels used for storage and aging. He explained the rationale behind different recipes and when and why they were used. They would mix the mash in those uncharred barrels, according to the selected recipe, and then practice daily stirring of each drum as fermentation progressed. These were some of the things cookers did when they weren't cooking. When the active bubbling dropped off, a sign that the mash was almost through fermenting, the barrels were drained and strained into the cooking drum of the still. Hutton was talking high quality product, which was why cleanliness was crucial, as well as accuracy, in following the recipes. Once the mash was drained and strained, the strained mash was put back into the same barrel that had just been drained. Then new water was added along with some fresh corn and yeast, and stirred into active mash just as the preceding barrel's content had. The same mash dregs could be used multiple times, but never more than four or five, as long as the recipe amounts of each ingredient changed slightly to accommodate the used mash. Then, that barrel of new ingredients would go through the typical four to five-day fermentation before the cooking rituals were repeated. In an efficient operation, Hutton said cookers were used for all of the preparations before they cook. Most of those preparations were labor. Jim gave them just enough information to make them curious and get them fired up about working with him.

The day Andre and Ralph started working, Hutton met them behind the Catholic Church. They rode with him past the Robinson farm where they had eaten lunch by the lake, almost another quarter-mile north. He drove right past the run-down farm house and barn, and followed a rough field road, just a couple of tire tracks really, back into the more heavily-forested portion of the property. They drove into that wooded patch through big pines and underbrush, then, stopped at a long and narrow building that looked like some sort of chicken coop, but there were no chickens.

"We're going to keep you busy here for a few days and nights," Hutton explained. "When you're done here, you'll know how to make moonshine."

Inside, Jim introduced them to Gene Finley. Hutton explained that Gene had been working with him since Hutton's client had bought Robinson's farm about a month before. Gene had worked with Hutton over in Stearns County for several years and he was going to be their trainer in the making of moon. Hutton left shortly after the introductions, claiming he had some real estate business to attend to, and that Finley would begin training them this afternoon. Finley seemed like a nice guy. He didn't have much to say in the way of conversation, but they'd just met. As soon as Hutton drove off, Finley said, "Well, let's get at it. Hutton wants me to show you how we make moon. Let's take a hike down the building here and I'll show you what's going on."

The floor was on two different levels. For the length of the building, the floor of the right half was about three feet higher than the floor on the left. On the higher floor there was a row of ten barrels, with about a foot of space between them, running lengthwise down the edge of the elevated floor. The building was just over fifty-feet long, so the row of barrels stretched almost end to end of the floor. Each of the barrels had a loose wooden cover resting on top. Behind each of the ten barrels, were four more stretching straight back towards the outside wall of the upper floor. Behind the row of four barrels, there was about four feet of remaining space to the wall. In this area sugar sacks were stacked floor to ceiling against the wall the full length of the building leaving just enough space to walk the length of the floor between sugar and barrels. There were literally tons of sugar sitting on the wooden floor. The building smelled like the inside of a silo. Ripe corn and cornstalks, ground into silage, smelled this way on Andre's farm too, but here it seemed to have an even riper smell. A couple of water hoses came through the wall of the elevated floor, then stretched out along the floor behind what Andre and Ralph had determined were mash barrels, as Finley explained the operation.

Finley talked as they walked. "We fill the mash barrels with about forty gallons of water first. Then we lower one of these trays that hang above each of the barrels closest to the edge of the floor." The trays were two-by-three-foot rectangles, with sides about six inches high above the bottoms. Each hung from a rope from the ceiling, with a small block and tackle that allowed you to raise or lower the tray. "You two will get used to filling the trays with water and corn seed, which causes the seeds to sprout in about five days. "After forty-gallons of water are put into a barrel, sprouted seed is added, then replanted. Then, we add forty-pounds of cane sugar per barrel of mash. Hutton uses only cane sugar. Corn sugar requires about sixty-pounds per barrel, and beet-sugar about 100 pounds. Since we are making good quality moon here, like we did in Stearns, only cane sugar is used. No beet or corn sugar, just cane. This exact recipe is used for each barrel you set up to ferment. Right now, we're trying to keep five barrels in active fermentation at each station. Each is started one day later than the one ahead of it. It takes about five days to ferment it to cooking readiness. Four active barrels in each line enables us to cook one barrel a day for four days. We've just started producing here, so our system still needs some tuning up. It now gives us four active days of cooking, then one day to clean up. Cleanliness is essential to making good moonshine. Then, we start over with the same routine for the next week. When we empty a barrel to be cooked, we transfer only about two-thirds of the mash into the cooker. The one-third of raw mash left in the barrel kicks the new ingredients we add more quickly into fermentation, kind of like baking sour dough bread. It acts like a starter."

Andre was soaking it all up as Finley talked, but Ralph was beginning to scratch his head between comments. It was getting complicated in his mind, but he knew he could ask Andre questions later. It had been that way when they were in school, too.

On the lower floor to the left, a copper tub with coiled copper tubing coming out from the domed top sat opposite the wooden barrels on the upper floor. There was one cooking still below each line of barrels on the upper floor with four wooden barrels behind each of them. The burners below the kettles of the stills were all cold today because they weren't cooking.

"These stills can each produce about 250 gallons of moon a day if they are fed enough fermented mash," said Finley.

The stills sat three feet below the higher floor above where the barrels rested.

Space on the lower floor, other than that occupied by the stills, was open. Against the lower wall, outside the stills, there were at least a hundred five-gallon crocs with screw tops, stacked tightly against the wall to minimize space they occupied. There was a large, flat-bed wheeled cart, empty today, which appeared to be what they used to transport filled cans to the bigger doors on each end of the building for distribution.

Some chicken coop, Andre thought. He was impressed with how much Finley seemed to know about moon. Andre and Ralph worked three days the first week, primarily being educated by Finley, on what their jobs were. Hutton agreed to pay them ten-dollars per day for labor which had nothing to do with cooking and said he would raise them to fifteen-dollars per day or night, when they started cooking.

Andre and Ralph each brought home thirty-dollars cash that week. Clair had been right. Something had worked, "as it must." During that week, Andre and Ralph learned that Finley's home was over in Stearns. He had a wife and two kids, and had given up a trucking life to work for Hutton with moon. He was happy, making more money than he ever had, and was here just temporarily until Hutton found someone to replace him. He left no doubt in either Andre's or Ralph's minds that they had a good opportunity in front of them if they worked it right.

Chapter 19

Sampson did exactly what Chief Lundquist suggested. He found a small apartment just off Lake Street in Minneapolis. Everything was in the full bloom of spring. The apartment building's parking lot was surrounded with flowering lilacs, making it look like a pretty quiet neighborhood, which is what he wanted. He wanted to minimize his visibility, come and go as he chose whenever he wanted to, without too many people noticing it. His agent's rent allocation was more than adequate and he was only ten-minutes from the Revenue Agent headquarters in downtown Minneapolis.

His first weekend in town, he scoped out both Minneapolis and St. Paul's downtown areas. He found hot spot bars on Washington and Hennepin Avenues in Minneapolis and even a speakeasy in the bottom of a warehouse on Washington Avenue. Two days after arriving in the Twin Cities he had hired a girlfriend and found moonshine flowing like a fresh stream on some Twin Cities streets.

Newspapers generally showed Revenue Agents in dark suits, long coats and fedora hats, trying to look official, important, and to be feared. Consequently, Sampson dressed like a typical bar patron, on a hunt for a single can, bottle of moonshine, or a friendly woman. He drank a little more than normal his first night, at the Roaring Forties speakeasy, on Washington Avenue. Because his plans were working he felt like celebrating. He was having fun, and was three sheets to the wind, when a woman calling herself, Lucille, suggested she might help him with his next drink and even more fun after. They drank for the next hour, while Sampson plied her with casual questions aimed at tuning him in on Twin Cities booze and speakeasies. He was surprised at some of the dumb statements people in the bar made using names like, "Scar-face Capone," "Baby Face Nelson," and others that he felt quite familiar with. These name- droppers had not a clue about the reality of those Chicago gangsters; it was just edgy speakeasy talk. Sampson more than once wished he could unload a few facts on them, but knew he could not. The girls and some of the male patrons would talk about such things with him, but the bartenders would not. He quickly detected a hearty fear, almost dislike, of anyone unknown, who just might possibly be a Revenue Agent or one of their tipsters. Asking the simplest question without flashing the recompense of money before the bartender, quickly clammed him up.

Sampson awoke Saturday morning, with a fat head and a woman in his bed, who had never been there before. Per one of his favorite routines, she had a red welt on her cheek.

Part II

Hope

Chapter 20

The three of them were just sitting down to supper, when Carolyn asked, "Where's Dad?"

"He's working," was the explanation Clair returned.

As Henri scooped potatoes onto his plate, he asked, "Where? I can never figure out what he's doing. It seems like I do more and more of the chores and he does less," he complained.

Chores were an issue with Andre. The animals had to be fed and watered twice a day, the cows milked, and it took a minimum of two hours a day to accomplish chores when things were running smoothly. Any problems that arose took extra time. Andre didn't spend much time listening to Henri's complaints. He remembered well his own father's statements, *"Children are to be seen and not heard. Get on with it."*

"We are going to have to make some changes in our daily routines now," said Clair to Henri and Carolyn. "Your dad has found some part-time work that will require him to work off the farm some days and some nights. He is working for a real estate man who needs help shaping up some of the farm properties his clients are buying. He never really knows when he will need to work until they call him, so we can't count on him to be regular for chores, like tonight for instance, Henri. When you asked me why he hadn't fed the beef cattle or set up for milking, I realized I hadn't yet told you yet of his other work."

Carolyn added, "Henri and I were talking about this last week. We heard you and Dad talking about needing money. It seemed like you were almost fighting and it was scary. What is it all about?"

Henri nodded his support to her question.

"We didn't want to worry you kids about it. But," Clair added, "Times have changed. The years after the war have all but killed our farm's crop prices. This spring Anderson turned us down on our annual loan. He said that even if we planted, with prices as low as they are, we wouldn't earn enough to repay the loan. That's a big change for us, kids. We hope the work your dad's found will keep us going until crop and livestock prices improve. We are luckier than many of our friends, yours too, because we have our own supply of chickens and the other foods we harvest. The eggs and chickens we sell help us, but without money from crops we can't keep up the mortgage payment on the new land and the truck we bought last year. This work your Dad has found will help us through these tough times, but the three of us will have to pick up Dad's chores when he is working off the farm."

"That sounds like more work for me," Henri lamented, to which Carolyn responded with a distinct frown.

"We knew something was going on," said Carolyn, glaring at Henri. "I can drive now, both the tractor and trucks, so I know I can help,"

Henri quickly envisioned himself behind the wheel of one of those trucks. "I can drive too, Mom, and I don't want to get stuck with all the chores while Carolyn is out driving around."

"I'm older than you, Henri. Don't forget, I was first born," she grinned at him, enjoying his irritation.

Foreseeing a possible conflict, Clair butted in, "Stop arguing now. We need your help. Your, Dad, and I, talked it over. Tomorrow, we'll all sit down to discuss sharing and transferring some chores. I can do more, as we all can, but one thing Henri, I am not taking over the pigs!" she added with a smile. Carolyn grinned. Henri wasn't sure how to react. Then, Clair gave him a hug and they all laughed.

Though they had just been told they would be doing more work, Carolyn and Henri felt relieved having been brought into the conversational loop about the problems. They no longer had to worry about their parents fighting, nor of losing the farm, as the Raft kids had.

"Don't worry, Mom," said Henri. "We'll pick up the slack, and the extra work. I'll even do the damn pigs, but Carolyn isn't the only one that gets to drive!"

Carolyn nodded agreement, and then smiled, "Don't swear, Henri."

Chapter 21

It was mid-June and the days and nights were warming. Ralph and Andre had spent the first week mixing mash. Each day they mixed the contents of ten barrels along with other tasks. The following day, another ten, and so on, until all forty barrels on the elevated floor were filled with mash and fermenting, each row a day older than the one in line ahead of it.

Hutton and Finley had planned the schedule, so the day the first row of barrels was five-days old, they could begin cooking the fermented mash in those barrels. One obvious signal that fermentation was nearly complete was when normally floating mash sank to the bottom of the barrel. Only two-thirds of the liquid of each fermented barrel was put into the cooker. The sunken mash made it easier to siphon the liquid from the barrel to the stills on the lower floor, without having to strain all the mash. What mash was strained during siphoning was later returned to the same barrel it came out of. That third was used again, with added ingredients, as starter mash. Finley explained the leftover mash from each barrel could be used repeatedly, up to five times, before being discarded. Using it more than five times as starter caused a bad flavor in the moon.

Cooking was fairly basic, and dangerous as well. Many a still and its building had burned to the ground when its gasoline burners ignited the flammable mash within its kettle. Working with high temperatures, combustible gasses, and gasoline burners was a precarious environment.

There were literally hundreds of recipes for moon, each supposedly fixed with quantities of ingredients, used to create precisely the end product expected from that recipe. Smaller stills were less precise and more experimental with their ingredients, but not the large producers. The planning required to produce substantial quantities of moon did not allow recipes to vary much. Production requiring 10,000 pounds of cane sugar per week demanded they finish the week's production with no shortage of sugar, and no sugar left. Precise management of ingredients was essential to a good operation and good moon.

The recipe Hutton was using required that two-thirds of the liquid of each barrel of ripe mash be siphoned through a filter into the adjacent still's copper kettle on the lower floor. The filters were crude, almost burlap, and filtered out only the mash solids. The gasoline burners, eight on each of these stills, were ignited and burned at their high setting as the liquid slowly heated in the still's kettle, called a "copper cow" by cookers, until it reached about 170 degrees. Then the heat was reduced some to maintain the steaming liquid within constant parameters between 174 and 200 degrees. In that range, alcohol flowed as steam through the copper coils which exited the domed tops of the copper cows. The copper coils, called worms, were immersed in a water-tight jacket of cooler water, sometimes called "flake stands," that required a large volume of constantly flowing cool water to cause the alcohol to condense from steam within the worm and drip alcohol from its open end into the receiving container beneath it.

To maintain the cool temperature of the worm's cooling water, it was pumped through pipes by a gasoline-powered pump from the large pond outside the building. The cooling water flowed through the water-tight jacket surrounding the worm, then back out the discharge pipe into the pond to cool again. Fortunately, the pond was large enough to cool water for an entire day's cooking. Then, the pond would again cool to its normal ambient temperature overnight. Hutton estimated that, should they ever go to cooking round-the-clock, the pond would be too small. They would have to add a cooling water radiator between the pond and the stills to maintain a cooler water temperature.

Mash allowed to cook to any temperature above 212 degrees caused the alcohol to come out of the worm as steam. It then disappeared into the air as an ill-destined aroma that could attract attention instead of condensing into moonshine for the keg, or container, at the end of the coil. Cookers had responsibilities. Overheated cooking could quickly waste hundreds of dollars of quality moon into smelly air. Another reason to keep temperatures below 212 degrees was above that temperature you were also distilling water with the alcohol, which degraded the taste of the final moonshine product. Final taste, or the buyer's perception of taste, was one of the things that drastically affected the price moon could be sold for.

Hutton had been coaching them through the process with Finley for a couple of hours this morning and was just finishing with, "Each fifty-gallon barrel of mash produces roughly twenty-five gallons of moon. Each 250 gal still burns about eighteen gallons of gasoline per cook, and each cook of 250 gallons takes about six hours. Five-gallon crocks, wrapped in burlap to cushion breakage like those you see against that wall, are more popular when shipping smaller amounts than the ten-gallon kegs we use for bigger shipments. They weigh less, which makes them easier to store, smuggle and deliver," he finished.

After the first barrel's two-thirds of mash was into the still for cooking, its remaining third of mash dregs, was moved back to the far end of the line of one-day-older fermenting barrels, making it the barrel to be cooked five or six days later. The barrels were easier to move back to that spot while only one-third full. Next, the additionally required recipe contents, more sugar, yeast, corn and water were stirred into the dregs in that barrel, which, after stirring, triggered it all back into active fermentation.

After Hutton and Robinson showed them how to restore the contents of each barrel, they were assigned the task of stirring each of the day-older-barrels with a canoe paddle. They stirred each fermenting barrel daily, sometimes twice. The better-mixed contents expedited fermentation, keeping it between four and five days. It took considerable time to mix and stir all those barrels. The canoe paddles had flat bottom edges, so you could stir all things loose from the barrel's bottom, as well as stir the contents into a swirling, smelly, mix. When they began cooking, as well as mixing, the cookers became even busier, but got paid more, too.

Hutton's quality recipe demanded not just one cooking, but two. A second cooking of the first-cooked moonshine, enhanced the alcohol percentage and taste of the final product. In addition to a variety of moon recipes, there were different levels of quality as well. That quality often determined the price that could be asked. Smaller operations were known for single-cooks, which gave the resulting drink a well established reputation. It was referred to as *white lightning*, or *white mule*, and was infamous for sometimes causing illness, alcohol poisoning, blindness, and occasionally, even death from impurities, lead, heavy metals and/or chemicals it sometimes contained. Single-cooks usually tested at 80 to 120-proof alcohol content. Putting first-cook through a second-cook, increased the proof from that range to as high as 180-proof and removed most impurities through additional filtering, cooking, and condensing. It also provided an additional opportunity for flavoring. These improvements caused second-cooked moon to be looked upon and tasted as *quality moonshine*. Hutton knew the moonshine most in demand all over the country was Minnesota 13, named after a seed corn of the same name and produced in large quantity in Stearns County, Minnesota. He had a cousin there who could prove it, and Hutton had plans for 13. Hutton finished this training session with, "We'll get into flavoring and aging later on."

Finley showed Ralph and Andre the second cooking process, which was less complicated. The condensed moon of the first cooking was held in barrels until the first cook of the stills was complete. Whenever the timing fit into the production schedule, the first-cook from all three stills, was combined. About half the volume of the original mash-cook, it fit into just one still, which cut the cost of gasoline for heating dramatically.

During the second cook, moon dripped from the worm more rapidly, which kept the cookers busier. Consequently, during the second cook, they did little but cook, bottle, and stir mash barrels.

By the third week, they had accrued over 300 hundred gallons of second-cook moon. During an official tasting of cooled, but un-aged product, Finley said their first moon was great, and tasted so. Hutton said it was good, but not great. He advised them all they had a ways to go, *to great*, but fully intended them to get there. Ralph agreed with Finley. Andre didn't know what it should taste like, and thought it resembled the ethylene glycol mixture he put in the truck and tractor radiators in winter. Hutton had made Andre curious during training, when he said moon could be flavored and aged with oak chips and heat. He said five-year old moon could be made in just two months if one properly used the oak chips, heat, and a barrel-movement mixing process. Andre wanted to know about that process. Farmers always wanted to know how to grow something faster, better, or with a larger harvest.

They were in production, and Ralph and Andre had each brought home over 120 dollars cash in three weeks. Ralph kept asking Andre why they hadn't done this sooner. "Because no one invited us," Andre responded, thinking to himself, *When does the trouble start?*

Chapter 22

"Two months," Hutton answered to Manny's question of how soon he thought he'd be able to produce the amount of moon Manny wanted. "We've got two operations under way; one of them is producing well, and I think I can close on two more farms this month. Each one has water, buildings, and good night time distribution roads," he finished.

Manny smiled and said, "You've done a good job, Jim; every one's happy with what you've accomplished, but demand for moon is high and we need our share to keep financing the real estate side of all this."

"Frankly, Manny, if you'd told me what we were going to do with these properties sooner, I probably could have made things happen sooner, Jim added. "

"You have to move carefully in this business, Jim, and the money always makes the big decisions. We worked with you three years before deciding you might be our man. Quick decisions can make quick trouble we want no part of. We did what we had to do. Now it's starting to work. Now, the money wants their share of the moon, Jim. Just make it happen as fast as you can, without undue risk. No move is better than any move, when risk is high. There's been almost no revenue action over in that region, just a few agents around Somerset occasionally. They are pretty well focused on Stearns County, which is where we want to keep them. Keep doing what you're doing, and above all, keep it quiet. Be careful who you hire. We've been lucky so far, but there are rats in every barn Jim. It just takes one."

"I understand, Manny. The ones I've chosen have every reason to keep quiet. We're saving them from foreclosure, they're making some cash, and all have families that don't want them to go to jail. I've learned what I need to know about making moon. Those guys you hooked me up with over in Stearns a couple years ago really do know their stuff. Every time I think I've got production figured out, they tell me how to do it quicker, cheaper, and make better moon drip. They are some sharp cookies," Jim grinned.

"They also know how to handle rats." Manny said, quietly.

Chapter 23

"Just two of us are going to snoop around in Stephens County," Sampson said. "We don't want anyone to know any Federal Revenue Agents are around. First we will find out what is happening up there, then, we'll decide what to do about it." He was talking to three new agents he had hired the prior week. He was now beginning to train them as agents for his squad. Lundquist had come through as promised. He let Sampson select three agents from his roster of newly-recruited trainees already on the fed's payroll.

"Take your pick, Sampson," was how Lundquist put it. "You can have three men. You select them, you train them, and you supervise them, just as I told O'Hara."

With Lundquist's go ahead, Sampson picked three, all rookies, new at the game, with little experience. He didn't want anyone too savvy in police work. He preferred, inexperienced men whose behavior he could mold to his liking.

Sampson went on, "Brown, you will work directly with me next week. I want to cruise around that Somerset area where Lundquist says most of the action is. I will fill you in this afternoon on my plans. Eggert, you and Eastman will continue to work as trainees with the Stearns County force for the next two weeks. Learn all you can from the active Revenue Agents you are assigned with. I've arranged that each of you will work two or three days with a single agent then transfer to another for the next three. You'll keep doing this until I call you back. This will give you the opportunity to learn procedures, the law, and gain ideas from experienced agents. Learn as much as you can, as fast as you can, I'm going to expect results when our squad goes active," he finished with a stern look. "Remember, I'm from Chicago. Don't forget to learn how to be tough!" which left Eggert and Eastman thinking, *what the hell does that mean?*

Sampson was told by Chief Lundquist that Somerset was the center of moonshine activities east of the Twin Cities. He said it was small potatoes compared to what went on over in Stearns County and the surrounding area, but didn't want the area east of the Twin Cities to grow into more of a problem. Sampson wanted to see for himself. He had spent a week with some of the agents in Stearns County, one day each with seven different agents who worked for Lundquist. It gave him the opportunity to see how Lundquist's men performed, how well Lundquist directed his men, and to get a feel of how much activity there really was over there. He was impressed, in fact, more than impressed. There was far more moonshine being cooked, bottled, and shipped out of Stearns County than there was down around Chicago. Even a bigger surprise was that much of it was being shipped towards Chicago. One more big surprise, was that Capone had spent weekends in Stearns County, and Lundquist's agents swore that Capone and a number of other Chicago gangsters had held meetings in Stearns to work out problems between them over things like who bought from which source, distribution, shipping, and other common issues, as though they were Ford Motor Company execs.

He found Lundquist's men less aggressive than those he had supervised around Chicago. He didn't think they were as tough or determined as his squad in Chicago, and they didn't seem to have much of a plan. On the other hand, he was surprised to learn they were shutting down fifteen to twenty-five stills a month. He had no idea there was that much moonshine action up there. Mostly, they coaxed neighbors into ratting one another out. When they'd raid a still and arrest the cooker, they'd give him a chance to avoid jail time by tipping them off about another still or two. Neighbors would stay absolutely quiet until faced with the unique sentences dreamed up by some of the local judges, of shorter time in the Stearns County jail, for first offenders. Second-time, serious offenders, were sometimes even sent to Leavenworth prison in Kansas, many of them sentenced for *a year and a day*. That sentence allowed the opportunity of parole after six months. Anyone sentenced to more than a year and a day, was not eligible for parole at all during their first year of imprisonment. Judges who sentenced for a year and a day were actually doing those sentenced a favor. Faced with such consequences as threatened time in Leavenworth, those arrested became better able to remember neighbors who still might be involved with moonshine. It was mostly Federal Revenue Agents who made all the still arrests.

County law enforcement officers made few arrests in Stearns. They tended to be more involved with speakeasies and dances. In fact, one of the Revenue Agents Sampson spent the day with, claimed the local sheriff had more than once tipped off some stills of a potential federal raid. Consequently, when the agents raided they found the platform a still had been sitting on, empty, with no one around and not a hint of evidence on the site. Sampson was also surprised to find out how many *sitters* there were in Stearns' County. A *sitter* was one who had already done time for prohibition violations, either in Stearns County jail or in one of the larger prisons. Another agent told him that often, after a still raid and an arrest, the offender was out of jail in less than a week and right back in the moonshine business. He thought Lundquist had been joking the day he said, "Hell, we can't make any more arrests in Stearns this week . . . the jail is full!" It was no joke. It had happened and more than once. Learning all this had humbled Sampson, not enough that anyone else would notice, but he had come up here planning to show these yokels how to operate, and now discovered their action was bigger than his turf in Chicago. True, except for one aspect. Scar-face Capone headquartered in Chicago, as well as other big name criminals. Chicago accrued more booze and got more big headlines because of their *Who's Who* crime syndicates, which made that region appear to be the center of moonshine action. The Chicago area was bigger in volume of all kinds of alcohol, but Sampson was now impressed with the *moonshine activities* of Stearns County, Minnesota.

Chapter 24

Andre was having another conversation he wanted to have even less than the "what are we going to do" conversation he had with Clair a while back. He had exited ahead of his family and was standing just outside the front door of the Catholic Church at the bottom of the steps, waiting for Clair and the kids, when Jason Maun walked down the church steps with a friendly, "Morning, Andre,"

Andre couldn't avoid talking with him and hadn't imagined how nervous being involved with moonshine would make him when talking to an officer of the law, especially to his boyhood friend, Jason Maun.

"Morning, Jase. What are you up to that you shouldn't be?" he said, hiding his anxiety behind a smile.

"Oh you know me, Andre. Not a thing. My wife says I never do anything I shouldn't. She says it makes me boring. How about you?"

Andre knew a strong offense was his best defense. "I found some extra work to tide me over, so I don't have to worry quite as much about losing my farm as others around here. Clair and I are pretty happy about that."

Jason looked surprised. "I didn't know there was any work, how'd you manage to find it?"

Andre enthusiastically said, "Just got lucky. I was at the station talking with Ralph. A guy in the real estate business pulled in to gas up. We started talking and a week later he offered both Ralph and me some part-time work helping him fix up a farm he had bought. We're building a good-sized chicken coop right now. He works for some clients in the cities who want him to pick up some farms before the banks foreclose on them. He says they can get them cheap now and they expect them to be more valuable in a couple of years. Man, I hope that is true."

"So, why a chicken coop? I thought you had the chicken and egg business cornered in Stephens County," the Sheriff quipped.

"No, not me, Jason, that's Carolyn," Andre grinned. "The real estate guy says his clients are wealthy and can play some tax games with these properties if they make them productive. Chickens and eggs are more profitable right now than crops or beef, and cost less to set up than anything else."

"But, won't that be more competition?"

Andre had rehearsed this conversation over and over while driving to and from work with Ralph. He remembered Hutton saying repeatedly, *There are things you can, and can't, say about this operation. What we do with moonshine will always be behind a façade of something legitimate, and we will set everything up so the legitimate things are obvious and legitimate to anyone taking a look at us.*

"Well, I hope not, Jase. In fact, I have already pitched them to let me do their distribution of eggs and chickens, just like I do with Carolyn. They are considering it now. I've even volunteered to run their whole chicken and egg stable, for a percentage, of course. If I can make that happen, this could be the best thing that's happened to me in years."

"That's great news, Andre. The very last one I ever want to serve foreclosure papers on is you. What's this guy's n. . . ," just then Clair threw her arms around the Sheriff's neck, warmly, as Carolyn waited, as though in line for her turn, to do the same.

As Carolyn hugged Jason, knocking his hat off in the process, Andre said, "Clair, I thought you were never coming out of Church! We've got to get going! Out best cow may have dropped that calf already. She looked to me as though she was having trouble with it this morning. We've got to get back there!" he finished, waving goodbye to Jason as he began walking quickly to the car. "See you, Jase. Gotta run and take care of that cow." *I hope that went as well as I think it did,* Andre thought, all the way to the car, hoping Jason wouldn't finish his question with, "n . . . ame?"

Chapter 25

"We need an inconspicuous storehouse to keep this stuff, Andre," said Hutton. "I want to be able to get this moon off the premises as soon as it's finished with the second cook and into those charred barrels. That's how they do it up in Stearns County. It's all hidden in a number of different places, which no one but the head man knows about. By doing it that way, if they do get raided, there's nothing but inactive stills and no evidence of moonshine. The feds can't even prove they were once active. They can make an arrest, but can't make it stick, so there's no jail time or arrest record," he finished.

It wasn't really quite that simple, but he wanted Andre and Ralph to focus on work and to not worry about arrest. Plenty of arrests were made in Stearns County just for having hints of moonshine around. Copper kettles, tubing, bags of sugar, barrels, cans, jars, all had caused arrests and jail time, and for some, more than once. Jim had seen friends arrested over in Stearns and fully intended to protect Andre and Ralph and anyone else who worked with them. He had learned much about how to do that from his Stearns experience and would use that knowledge to protect this operation.

"We need a building that's accessible by car and truck, but hidden from Revenue Agents driving by on the main roads, Hutton stated. "A building that we can fill with something else as a diversion, that will hide the moon, and that will not attract agents, or anyone else. I've been looking all over Stephens County for a month. I've found a couple, but they're too far away. What can you think of, Andre, that's within ten miles of here? We've got 300 gallons in those barrels that need a place to hide and age. We've got to get them out of here."

Andre thought to himself, *just how involved do I want to get in all this?* He did have an idea, *but wondered if he should even bring it up.* "I'm not sure, Jim. Now that I know what you are thinking about, let me consider it tonight and see what I can dream up."

"Come up with something, Andre and I'll make it worth your while. I think you are cut out for this sort of thing. I know you don't like the idea of breaking the law, but you are careful, you think, and you don't talk much. I like the way you operate. Ralph, I'm not sure of, he's a little loose I think, but we'll see."

Andre said, "I wanted to tell you, I had to come up with a story for the Sheriff last Sunday."

Hutton's face froze, and his eyes grew. "How's that? What kind of a story?"

Andre filled him in on the encounter he had with Maun after church. "There was nothing else I could do, Jim, and the chicken and eggs angle was the perfect cover story for me, because of my own farm."

Hutton nodded, "That was good thinking, Andre. You denied nothing, and didn't hide anything. Which came first, the chicken, or the egg?" he laughed. You just gave me a great idea! How'd you like to expand your egg and chicken business? That may be the perfect cover for the next year or so."

They talked then, about possibilities, and one of the things Andre liked best about it was that Hutton kept pointing out how Andre could earn even more money, and it would be, almost honest. Almost honest, sounded much better than the things he had heard Hutton say about his cousin's dealings with agents over in Stearns County.

That evening, he and Clair talked about it. Ending his third week of working with Hutton now, he and Clair hadn't spent a lot of time together lately. She talked of how Henri and Carolyn were picking up slack on the chores. "You'll be proud of how Henri is taking on more of your chores, Andre. He looks older, acts older, especially when he tells Carolyn he doesn't deal with chicken shit," she laughed. "And of course, Carolyn comes right back at him with something about the pigs. They're actually out-doing each other, and all the work is getting done," she finished proudly. "Carolyn still spends a half-hour with me on the piano each night. She'll soon play better than me." *Not that soon*, Andre thought, *remembering how much he loved to sit and listen to Clair play on quiet evenings.* Even before they had fallen in love, Andre had been attracted to Clair when she played a piano recital in the eighth grade at school.

The kids were already in bed, and Andre and Clair talked their way into the night. He was going to tell her about the "chicken and egg" talk he and Hutton had that day, but before he could, he discovered they were sitting too close together which quickly led to the two of them loving each other enough to make up for their time apart. It all happened in the glow coming through their bedroom window and ended with Clair's comment, "I love moon shadows, Andre."

Chapter 26

Ralph and Andre were driving to the Robinson farm. Each day or night they worked, they would meet at various places, one day the Catholic Church, the next at a parking lot, or behind some building, so as to not build a pattern anyone would notice. Hutton encouraged them to switch cars each day as well. Andre had told Ralph about talking with Sheriff Maun at church and they were discussing it again now.

"I saw Jason at the station last night while I was pumping gas. He said he heard I was getting rich building chicken coops. I told him it was just work to me, but I was damn glad I had it, because Bill had cut my hours in half last month," Ralph nodded. "Jason said he knew Bill was going to have to do that because he'd heard him talking about how the gas business was shrinking. Cedarville's village council is even complaining about how much gas Jason is burning in the County Sheriff's car." He laughed, then continued, "Jason said he told the council if they didn't make him serve foreclosure papers on poor farmers, he wouldn't have to drive out there to deliver them. That would save gas. He said the council wasn't too pleased with what he'd said, but it made him feel better."

"I think it's good that we are talking to him about our work. He won't get suspicious as long as we are open about what we are doing. We have to always be ready for that kind of a conversation though, Ralph."

"Yeah, I know. It's kind of like lying to your wife," he grinned. Andre wasn't sure what Ralph had meant by that nor did he want to ask. "Do you think Jason would actually arrest us if he found out we were working with moon, Andre?"

"That is something neither of us wants to find out. Never! Once again Andre added, "Never." Andre could not imagine a way out of such a situation. *That would put me in a predicament I couldn't handle,* he thought. Jason had been one of his best friends throughout both their lives, and one thing Andre absolutely knew about Jason was he was honest. Years back, in the eighth grade, they'd both written some funny, but stupid, words about their teacher on the black board.

When the teacher walked in to the chuckling, one-room class of mixed ages, she knew something was afoot, but not what. Then she turned to the blackboard. She quietly walked over to it and began erasing the words. As she stroked with the eraser she quietly said, "May I ask who is responsible for these words?" The classroom had become instantly silent as she'd begun erasing, and now became soundless as a tomb. Not a sound. She went back to her desk, sat down, opened a book and began reading. This went on for two or three minutes, and then she added, "We will wait for an answer. Those of you uninvolved, who did nothing more than laugh at this foolishness, may read anything you wish. Those of you who are responsible should know that you are now in charge of the day, everyone's day, in this classroom. The rest of us will wait. When you have the courage to honestly own up to your own responsibility for this situation, we'll get on with our normal class day." With that, Mrs. Pauchette went back to her book. Neither Andre nor Jason ever forgot the next ten minutes of fidgeting, sweating, wondering what to do, and especially not the occasional looks they received from other class members who considered themselves innocent no matter how hard they had laughed at the blackboard.

It was Jason who finally stood up at his desk and said, "I did it Mrs. Pauchette. I'm sorry; I meant it to be funny." Andre saw the students admiring Jason for having the courage to be the first to fess up. He wished, as he stood up, he had been first. "It wasn't just Jason, I did it, too," he said with the most embarrassment he'd felt in his entire life. Mrs. Pauchette said, "I forgive you both, and I appreciate your courage in admitting your mistake. Let us have no more of this time-wasting with such foolishness. Sit down now and let's get on with class." Andre always laughed as they grew older, when one of their old classmates would say, "Jason stood up first."

"We can't let that happen, Ralph. Be very careful what you say around Jason. He's no dummy, and he knows us both."

Chapter 27

"Here's what I'd like to do, Andre. I'll put up the money through my clients. It will all be cash to you. We'll build two new chicken coops, big ones that will let you raise lots of chickens and produce lots of eggs. We'll build one on your farm, real visible, out by your driveway. We'll build the other, exactly the same, on Robinson's place, well, it's actually our place now, but I still call it that. At Robinson's we'll build it out front of the barn and house by his driveway. I'll put you in charge of building both coops. That covers your story of part-time work for the next month or so. Now, here's the best part. My client will pay for all the costs of building, buying chickens and feed, everything you need to make this a first-class chicken ranch. You continue to spread the word that you are the manager of both, though you own the one on your farm. You can have all the profits from the sale of chickens and eggs, but once the initial investment is operational and producing profits, you are responsible for all operational costs, chicken feed, labor, and maintenance." Finished with the unveiling of his plan, Hutton smiled. "I told you it would be beneficial to you down the road, Andre."

"I think there's still more to this plan than you've told me, Jim." *These chicken coops should have moonshine in bold red letters painted all over the walls*, Andre thought to himself. "I know you somehow have additional plans I need to hear."

"That's true, Andre, but it will be even safer than the work you are already doing with us."

Hutton went on laying out the entire plan in more detail for Andre, including a schedule, an outline of costs, and an initial dollar commitment of cash Andre could use to get things going. "Remember, Andre, if anyone asks you where you are getting the money to build up your chicken operation, some of it was left over from the loan you took last year to buy that additional property. Now, here's something else you should do. Go back in to see Anderson at the bank. Tell him about expanding your chicken business and ask for a $2000 construction loan for the coops. He will give it to you, because I've already guaranteed it. I had coffee with him last week and told him we were going to hire you to raise chickens on some of the properties we are buying. I did some other business with him, which you don't need to know about. I just want you to know he'll cooperate on the loan. And, do it now, the sooner the better. The word will be out in the County about that lucky Cartier who's expanding while the rest of us go broke. What better cover than that? By the way, Andre, don't tell Ralph about how we worked all this out. Just say you proposed the idea of working with us on chickens and we agreed. Tell him you got the loan from Anderson, which is how you are doing this on your place. You can say my client and I are paying you to manage the chickens on our place with a percentage of profits."

Andre knew he really didn't have any choice. He'd lost his choice the first day he became involved in moonshine. Clair knew it too. But he also knew he liked what he was hearing. It added legitimacy to the surface of things, which would make it easier to manage all these activities with those who knew him.

Chapter 28

Hutton had provided Andre with blueprints of the coops from a draftsman he knew in the Twin Cities. He also hooked him up with a small construction company. They would come in to Andre's place first. Their job was to put in the concrete block basement area beneath the coop, with a concrete floor the full length of the building. They would next string floor joists atop the block walls and cover them with three-quarter-inch boards stretched diagonally across the entire surface. Then a layer of thick tar-paper would be added to help deaden sound and prevent liquid leakage into the basement beneath. Finally, that floor would be covered with inch-and-one-half thick planks, each, twelve- inches wide which would create a wall-to-wall, heavy, and almost soundproof floor at ground level. The basement's existence would be hidden from both sight and sound. Then, Andre and Ralph and a couple of other local carpenters would build the wooden structure of the coop on top of the plank floor. To maintain secrecy of the full basement, the access door in the floor at one end of the coop, would be cut into the floor, in secrecy, after the chicken coop was completely finished. That way no one would be aware of it, or of the storage space beneath the ground-level floor.

Andre had gone to see Anderson as Hutton instructed. With hardly a discussion, Anderson congratulated Andre on his idea to expand his chicken business, handed him the loan papers, and explained the terms in banker fashion. "I like Hutton," Anderson said. "He's a sharp business man. I think you are lucky to be working with him. I have put the $2000 into a new checking account for you. As you know, monthly statements will go to both you and Mr. Hutton," Anderson finished as he handed Andre a new check book. "I hope we can count on you handling all of your new business through us, as you have in the past, Andre. And, by the way, I'm sorry we couldn't go through with that annual planting loan. I am not in charge of everything at the bank. We had to turn down a number of old customers. I hope this action makes up for whatever disappointment you experienced." Andre didn't say anything, just took the papers and checkbook and headed for the bank door, thinking, *Boy, what money can do!*

Andre was surprised at how fast things could happen with money behind them. He barely had time to explain to Clair, Carolyn and Henri, about expanding the chicken portion of the farm's business before things began to happen. Within three days of receiving the loan, Hutton told him to expect a man from the construction company to visit him the next day. He showed up in the morning and he and Andre walked the site by the driveway, took some measurements the guy wrote in a small notebook, as he explained to Andre what would occur during the next week. That was Thursday. Saturday morning, two trucks showed up, one with a crawler type dozer, the other with a backhoe, something fairly new to the construction business. By Saturday night the dozer had dug a ditch some 80 feet long, 40 feet wide, and eight-feet deep, where the new chicken coop was going to go. On Sunday, while Andre and his family were in church, six men showed up to begin framing the forms for footings on which to pour the basement slab. They would mix and pour cement on Monday, so the same men and a few others worked right through Sunday night by light of lanterns getting ready for Monday's cement mixing. Trucks loaded with sand, gravel and cement arrived before Monday morning.

Obviously, Hutton and crew wanted to get this done quickly before others had an opportunity to see it. While cement footing were done Monday, two truckloads of concrete blocks showed up. Tuesday morning, two concrete block layers and two helpers showed up to begin setting block-walls around the entire perimeter of the floor. In three days the walls were up to ground level. On the fourth day, the crew of men stretched floor joists wall-to-wall atop support posts, and began nailing down the three-quarter inch flooring on which the final floor of oak planking and tar-paper would rest. One week after starting the whole operation, the dozer pushed back the excavated dirt against all four block walls making the surrounding ground-level six-inches beneath the oak floor's surface. There was no access to the basement through any of its four walls or the floor. It was as though the basement didn't exist, and the chicken coop floor rested on the footings without even a crawl-space beneath the floor. As planned, no one would ever guess, *Hutton hoped,* there was a full-basement space beneath it.

Friday morning, Andre was walking across the oak plank floor with Ralph, explaining, "You and I and a couple of carpenters I have hired will start building the coop on this floor tomorrow, Ralph."

Ralph belched out excitedly, "I can't believe how fast you put this foundation and floor in. How did you do it?"

"I got lucky. Once Hutton agreed to work with me on chickens, I went to Anderson with a loan idea, and he signed on. I think he did it because he felt guilty about not giving me my planting loan, but I'm not sure. But, once I got the loan I wanted to move fast before anything could go wrong. Hutton said he knew a guy in the cities that did fast work for cash, so I hired him. It's nothing but a rectangle building, just a box to build, but those guys know how to put in footings! I've never seen anyone work so fast," Andre finished.

Ralph was looking at the clean new wooden floor. "It won't take long for this to be covered with chicken shit," he laughed. "It will be easy to work on with the ground level right up to the floor level like this. Ralph had done some carpentry work, mostly odd-jobs, but he had learned the trade pretty well. "We can form the walls on this floor and raise them like they do barns." The building was forming in his mind as he looked around the footings and floor.

"Just months ago, Andre, you asked me at the station, what we were going to do. It looks like you've figured it out. I'm ok for now, with this extra work and what hours I'm getting at the station. I hope you know what you're doing in this chicken business, because I may still need a well-off friend down the road."

"Just remember to keep quiet about the moon, Ralph. That's the most important thing. Quiet", he emphasized, raising his eyebrows. "No one must know about the moon side of all this."

"Well, yeh, but this is chicken business, Andre. I don't have to keep quiet about the chicken business, right?"

"No, Ralph, you don't. In fact I hope a whole lot of folks buy lots of chickens and eggs from the stores in the surrounding towns, because I need to sell chickens and eggs to those stores. Carolyn and I are going to visit a number of them next week to try and gain their business."

As Ralph drove his car down the driveway, Andre thought, *he didn't notice a thing about the floor, and smiled.*

Chapter 29

For the next week, Andre, Ralph, and two local carpenters Andre had hired erected the chicken coop. Weather was dry, and it went together easily as they followed the blueprint Hutton had supplied. The one flaw Andre found in the plan was no running water anywhere near the coop. The ground they had chosen for the chicken coop was higher than where the barn and old coop sat. Consequently, the one gravity-fed water line he used in the barn, which fed from their well on the low hillside just above the house could not be extended to the new coop. Water for the chicken coop would have to be hauled. That was ok, as Hutton had put it; "it will be less suspicious if an agent ever looks at it. Stills need water, and agents always look for it when hunting stills."

They framed the walls of five-quarter two-by-fours. The coop would be thirty by sixty feet, providing 1800 square feet of space on the plank floor. Roger Cartier, Andre's uncle, had told them to build that size, start with 300 chicks and work their way up to the 600 hens that amount of space would handle. When the walls went up, they added the door and window openings. A friend of Hutton's had told him of a lumber company in the cities that had just gone bankrupt and Jim had gotten a real swindle on the windows. They all had heavy-duty screens for summer when the windows were open, and would help keep weasels that loved to kill chickens, and foxes that loved to eat chickens, outside the coop. The two double-doorways in each end of the long coop were wide enough to allow big flatbed four-wheeled carts through to make it easier to harvest eggs and clean the coop. They built the doors of planks and braces and by end of week had only the roof to shingle and ventilators to add along the roof's peak. That left just the outside fenced scratch-yard, attached to the coop to finish. The scratch-yard was the same size as the floor space of the coop. The chicks wouldn't arrive for two or three weeks, so they had time to finish everything.

Part of that finishing was done by Andre and two of the men who had laid up the block walls. Working when Carolyn and Henri were in school, it took the three of them two days to build the hinged floor-door in the end of the coop where chicken feed and supplies would be stored. The fifteen-foot-long door was heavy, but could be lifted by one man using a block and tackle which hung on the wall above it, and then leaned against the wall when open. Beneath the door opening, they built a sloping ramp to the basement's floor, so carts or two-wheeled dollies could transport items up or down the ramp. When they finished it, the door was closed and a pile of remaining lumber was stacked on top to hide its presence. Andre and Hutton were pleased with the stealthily hidden access. Andre explained to him how when erecting walls on top of that floor, it had sounded exactly as though there was nothing but crawl space beneath it. There were no telltale sounds, even when hammering wall frames together on it, and Ralph had noticed nothing but the clean oak planks he'd made his" chicken shit" comment about.

Carolyn was excited about expanding the chicken business. Though she didn't look forward to more work, she did look forward to helping the family earn more money. She was amazed at the size of the new chicken coop. It was fancy in comparison to what she had worked with the last few years. Andre had told her Henri could use the tractor and some other gear to clean the coop as needed. Her job was to feed the chickens, select those laying poorly for harvest and continue to clean and package the eggs to be delivered to stores in the surrounding area. He told her of plans to call on other stores, even suggested she go with him on some of those visits. Andre showed her a letter Jerry had written on the store's letterhead paper about how pleased he was with the Cartier Egg Service, and how he was happy to recommend it to others. "I don't mind helping you and Carolyn get into other stores, Andre, as long as I remain first in line for service," he'd said. Andre assured him he would, as he accepted the letter from Jerry's hand.

Chapter 30

Andre and Carolyn walked out of the grocery store in Balsam Lake. "Good job, Dad," Carolyn beamed. "He said he'd give us a two-week try in August. I'll make those eggs so shiny he can charge more for them. Did you see how beat up and dirty those cartons looked?" They had inspected the store's shelves before meeting with the manager, so knew before the meeting, they had better service. Jerry's letter had a sentence about the cleanliness of the prepackaged dozen-cartons always delivered by Cartier's. The manager said, "Yeh, cleanliness has been a problem at times and packaging from the large boxes to the dozen-cartons takes a lot of time. We'll give it a try. Old man Brown isn't going to be happy to see your eggs in my store though. You've got to be ready to keep up with what I sell if I eventually decide to choose you," he finished, eyeballing both Andre and Carolyn. "You're a lot prettier than Brown too, young lady," he added winking at Andre.

"We've gotten commitments to try our service from four more stores, Carolyn," Andre thought out loud. "That's enough for now. We've got to get the new coop in full production by August. Each time we have enough eggs to add another store we'll do it. When we have the egg production going, we'll go after the fresh chicken business next. Old man Brown has never liked us, but he's going to like us even less now. I guess that's the price of success."

"I don't care Dad. He sells dirty eggs."

They stopped in Cedarville on the way home to gas up. Ralph was working. He filled the tank while talking to Andre and Carolyn. "So, are you two out cornering the chicken and egg business?" he grinned.

"You bet," said Carolyn. "We are going to have the happiest chickens in the County," she beamed.

"How about the ones I eat?" Ralph asked with a serious look.

"They'll be happy to meet you, Ralph," she bantered back, "Our chickens are friendly and sociable, even if you eat them."

"Hutton says he'll have some more work for us next week, Ralph. I'll see you at church Sunday and we can work out driving then," Andre added to the conversation. "Also," Andre said, as he reached into his pocket, "here's your money for the last two weeks for the Cartier Egg Service," as he handed Ralph the envelope.

"I love this cash business!" Ralph patted his pocket after putting the envelope into it. "Hell, I love you, Andre. You, too, Carolyn. I haven't had any cash in my pockets for the last year. Now, because of those damn chickens, I'm feeling rich," he laughed.

"Hang onto it, Ralph. I won't be building a chicken coop every month. Well, I guess that's not true either," Andre said. "They finished the floor on the new coop over at Robinson's this week. I think we'll start building that coop next week. Ok, we've got to get going. See you Sunday."

They talked chicken and eggs all the way home. As far as Carolyn knew, all of the work her dad and Ralph were doing for Hutton had to do with building chicken coops. Andre and Clair had carefully crafted a strategy they would use when Carolyn and Henri were around, to prevent them from ever getting even a hint of Andre being connected to the moon business. They knew they could get by with it, at least for a while, and it seemed to be working. The increased chores she and the kids were doing took more time, kept them busier, which meant less time to be curious. They also had to listen to Henri complain a little more. It took some getting used to, for both Andre and Clair, to make a conscious effort to deceive their kids. For years, their practices had been the exact opposite.

Chapter 31

The curtained grill-window quietly slid open.

"Bless me, Father, for I have sinned," Andre said quietly as he knelt in the dark confessional.

"How have you sinned, my son?" replied the priest.

"I'm not sure I have sinned, Father. Can I just ask you a question?" Andre went on.

"Yes, you may." was the reply.

"Is it a sin to work in some way handling moonshine, Father?" Andre winced. He was speaking quietly to be sure no one else could possibly hear his confession, and also hoping the priest would not recognize his voice.

There was a long pause. Andre thought, *I hope this wasn't a mistake.*

Then, the priest said, "No, it is not a sin. It is illegal, against the law, but it is not a sin. I must add, though, it is very dangerous to involve yourself in illegal behavior." Another pause.

"I am careful, Father. I'm trying not to lose our farm." Andre whispered.

"Christ said, 'Give to Caesar what is Caesar's, and give to God what is his.' What you are doing is not a sin, my son. I offer you this opinion at some risk to myself. Have you anything else you wish to confess?"

"No, Father," Andre said quietly.

"Then, go in peace, my son."

He stood up quickly and exited the confessional, walking rapidly to the church door, looking back over his shoulder to see if the priest stepped out of the confessional to see him leaving.

Father Baptiste stayed within his side of the confessional, knowing anyone asking that questions would not wish to be seen. He knew many in the County were involved with illegal liquor and it was a practice that was growing, because people were so desperate. Frankly, Father Baptiste kept a jar of moon in his own private closet. He had never been a dry, nor did he much disapprove of wets. Christ drank wine with his apostles. In Europe entire religious orders were enabled by monks who brewed wonderful spirits, some world famous. *Prohibition is a strange law that seems to benefit no one*, he thought to himself. He disapproved of bad behavior caused by drunks, or those abusing the use of booze in worse ways, but never of people who simply liked a drink once in awhile. Small farmers were so desperate these days he didn't blame them at all for cooking, bootlegging, or selling moonshine. He knew were he not a priest he would likely be doing it himself.

It was Saturday. Andre had not told Clair or the kids he was stopping at the church for confession, nor did he want them to know. He didn't go to confession often. Since getting involved with Hutton, he'd wrestled with this question, primarily because he knew at some time, for some reason, it would come up from Carolyn, or Henri, should they discover his involvement. It would be difficult when it occurred. He felt better armed with what he heard in the confessional.

Chapter 32

It had been two weeks since Andre and Ralph had cooked or mixed. They had worked full-time on the two coops, first at Andre's, then at the Robinson place. Today, per instructions given Andre by Hutton to pass on to Ralph, they were back in the moon building on the former Robinson farm. The day they were last here, there was over 300 gallons of moon in thirty ten-gallon kegs stretched along the wall opposite the stills. Today they were gone.

Hutton was there, with Andre, Ralph, and Finley. He'd said to meet them there by 9:00 a.m. so they could organize the week.

"Where'd the moon go?" Ralph blurted out, looking at Hutton.

"That is a question I don't want to hear again," Hutton said in a command tone that couldn't be misunderstood. "You don't need to know and you don't want to know, Ralph, and that goes for everyone. Trying to find those things out can make your life more complicated than you want it to be."

Ralph tried to recover with, "I was just curious, Jim, I was just surprised to see it gone."

"Don't be curious either. Curiosity killed the cat, remember? The more you know about cooking, maximizing production, and keeping everything quiet and hidden, the better off you will be. The less you know about anything else . . . the better off you will be. Is that clear?" Jim finished. "Really men, the less you know the better. It can keep you from being arrested. It can get you freed of charges if you are arrested. It can keep a judge from sending you up for a year and a day. The less you know the more innocent you are. Just keep it that way."

Ralph knew from Andre's look he should shut up. So, he did.

Hutton went on, "Ok, fellas, we are going to cook all week. You can see the sugar supply has been replaced," he went on, "the corn seed from last week is sprouted, we're ready to mix some serious mash today."

"Who sprouted the seed corn, Jim?" Ralph stopped mid-question, apologetically, "Sorry, Jim, I don't want to know," he finished.

Jim smiled and then became stern-faced, adding, "It doesn't really matter, does it?"

Ralph nodded.

"We've added 100 more barrels against that back wall, so I want to double the number of mash barrels mixed, cooking in five-day intervals, just like last time. The only difference is we're doing twice as much. Andre, I want you to be in on every decision with Finley. He showed you the ropes on the last batch, but after this run, I want you to be able to set up a station yourself, so you two work together this round."

Finley didn't say a word in response to Hutton's directions, just half-nodded his understanding. He knew the sooner he made Andre and Ralph operational on their own, the sooner he could get back to his family in Stearns County.

Jim left shortly after the discussions. Finley smiled thinking *I'm going home sooner than planned. I've just got to bring these pilgrims up to speed.* He immediately began giving Ralph and Andre friendly orders. "Ok, boys, first we set up five more empty barrels beside the five already filled in each row. Then we stir those already filled, and begin filling the other five in each row. Tomorrow, we'll start cooking. Tomorrow, the first of those five already fermenting, and on the fifth day the first of the new five will be almost ready."

"Great, let's get at it," Andre grinned, climbing the five steps to the upper floor. "We want to make some money."

Andre and Ralph were clearly getting into the routine of things. They were both surprised at how easy making moonshine was once you knew how, and it wasn't bad work. Much of farming was more difficult than making moon.

Hutton and Finley had taken care of that moon inventory Ralph had wondered about from the Robinson operation. Finley had run moon for Hutton out of Stearns, off and on for three years, sometimes cooking, more often bootlegging, and he always got paid. Following directions he received from Hutton via phone, he would pick up a car from a factory parking lot in St. Cloud, Minnesota at a given date and time. He would find the ignition keys on top of the left rear tire. He was told to be within ten minutes of the scheduled pick up time, and often found that the car's engine had not yet cooled by the time he picked it up. No one wanted a car full of moonshine sitting long in a public parking lot, nor the driver seen, if avoidable.

Finley would drive the car to an assigned location in the Twin Cities. It was usually a fee parking lot in downtown Minneapolis. Following directions he received from Hutton, he would pull into the lot, stop at the attendant's booth, hold out his hand with a twenty-dollar bill in it, and say, "I have a reserved spot for E. J. Anderson Company." The attendant would take the money, reach for a clipboard on the desk and hand him a piece of paper with a parking slot number on it. "Around the far side on the right of the lot," the attendant would direct him, adding, "What's your name?" Johnson would then say the name given him by Hutton to use for this specific car and delivery. Finley would park the car in that numbered spot and return the keys to the attendant. The attendant would then hand him an envelope with another numbered parking slot and the exact time of day he handed it to him written on the envelope. Finley, with the envelope, and the attendant, would walk to that spot. The attendant would watch Finley start that car and drive it from the parking lot. Finley was to deliver the car to another parking lot in St. Paul, arriving within a fixed-time from when he'd picked it up in Minneapolis. The purpose of this timing was so the driver of the second car could not wait around near the parking lot to see who picked it up. If Johnson was late getting the second car to St. Paul, he would not receive another assignment to deliver from Hutton. Once signed in with a delivery time in the St. Paul lot, Finley would drive another car back to St. Cloud leaving it, with the keys on top of the left rear wheel, in the same parking lot which he had parked his own car in earlier that morning. The Twin Cities syndicate was organized, had systems, and few bootleggers knew any of the other pawns, what they did, or when they did it. That's exactly how Manny Goldfin and his associates wanted the delivery game of bootlegging to be for them.

Hutton knew Finley's track record, so had singled him out for the first run of moon to be shipped from the Wisconsin side of the St. Croix River to the Twin Cities syndicate. Hutton wanted to direct this first moon delivery from Wisconsin himself, wanting no one else to know anything about it, and was confident Finley could bootleg it to the cities.

A couple of weeks earlier he had visited the ferries that crossed the St. Croix River, one at Sunrise and another at a crossroads above Taylors Falls. After riding both ferries, and having conversations with those who operated them, he decided Sunrise to be the best for his use. It was closer to both the Twin Cities and the Robinson operation, which cut down on mileage and time. The less time moonshine was on the road, the less time it was exposed to the feds. The Sunrise ferry was run by two teen-age sisters by the name of Barnes, who were also helped by their father. Their ferry could handle two cars in a crossing. It was a short trip. In conversation with the girls he found them willing and able to handle crossings any time of the day or night. Hutton explained to them that he earned his living bringing cars up from Chicago to the Twin Cities for resale. Because he wasn't always certain of their legal origin he wanted to bring them quietly into the Twin Cities, sometimes not on the main highways. He asked if they'd be willing to make some prearranged night crossings, which he of course was willing to pay extra for. The oldest Barnes girl said, "That's not a problem. Just tell us what night you'll show up, and approximately what time. Then, just honk your horn once when you arrive. We stay in that little house on the Wisconsin side at night. Our normal fee is twenty-five cents per person. We'll bring the car across for seventy-five cents and," she added, "with no questions." Hutton replied, "Make it $1.00 each and we'll do it." Smiles in both directions finalized their agreement.

For this run Hutton used a car belonging to one of his runners from Stearns County. It had been left for him to pick up in Taylors Falls, so he drove it to the Robinson place at 4:00 p.m. Saturday morning. He knew no one would be there on Saturday or Sunday. It was a 1930 Oldsmobile sedan. The back seat and trunk had been modified to accommodate twenty, five-gallon containers, still keeping a low profile in the back seat as seen from outside the car. He and Finley changed the license plates to Illinois, and loaded the 100 gallons into the car. He covered the tops of the containers with a sheet of canvas, then with a mattress, bedding and a pillow to make it look as though converted to some form of travel-mobile. Finley followed him in Hutton's car.

They arrived at the ferry landing at 10:45 p.m. Before turning into the driveway, Hutton reminded Finley the fee was to be a dollar and switched cars with him. Finley then drove down the driveway. Hutton remained out of sight on the River Road above the ferry landing. No one was there, the river was flowing slowly and the ferry sat quietly, moored against the shore. Finley parked the car on the loading ramp, then, blew the horn once. A light came on in the house and someone came out, The Barnes girls had agreed to drive the car onto the ferry, but seeing Finley at the wheel, they simply guided him onto the barge with hand signals. They had no idea this car was connected to Hutton. They slowly crossed the St. Croix River, listening to the pulley wheels turn on the large overhead cable that guided them across the river while keeping them from flowing downstream with the current. Being an experienced bootlegger, Finley handed the girl $2 saying, "It's a bonus for late night service."

"Thank you," she smiled. "I hope we see more of you."

From his car, Hutton watched as Finley drove the car off the ferry and headed for the Twin Cities, via the route he and Hutton had agreed upon. Hutton would receive a phone call after Finley left the car in the Minneapolis parking lot, and another from Manny's office once they had taken delivery.

Chapter 33

Sampson was reviewing their first week's look around in Stephens County with Agent Brown. It was late June now, and they had both dressed as trout fisherman and driven around the County for the last three days. They used a road map to split the County in half. Sampson took the west half of the County closest to the cities, Brown the other. The plan was to drive the roads, especially the roads that crossed fishing streams, fresh water being crucial to moon production, and they needed to look more like fishermen than Revenue Agents. Sampson had coached Brown on his role as an actor first, agent second, and Brown had worked those two weeks over in Stearns. Brown was anxious to get out there and try out his skills. They both had stream boots, fly rods, fish creels, and authentic well-worn, hats with flies and fish hooks in the hat band.

Sampson told Brown, "Do a little fishing right by the bridges that cross the streams; let people see you fishing; be believable. The best thing you can do is have some fish to show the guys in the gas stations when you fill up." He went on telling him to try to buy just a single jar or two of moon to check out availability. "We need to get a feel for what's going on around here, how big moon is, but don't pry, that makes them suspicious right away. Buy them a drink in the bar, try to get them talking, and they'll volunteer info."

Now, a week later, they were talking in a restaurant in Minneapolis. Brown said, "It's not hard to buy a jar of moon in almost any town in the County, Bob, but finding out where it comes from is kept pretty quiet. Evidently Lundquist sent somebody over here for a while last year, because I talked to one guy who lost his still in a raid last year. He says they loaded his still, and about twenty-gallons he'd cooked onto a truck, then left. He wasn't arrested and nobody ever followed up as the Revenue Agents said they would. He said it took him a month to realize they maybe weren't actually Revenue Agents," Brown laughed. "He'd been robbed! What made him the maddest was that he couldn't afford to get another still to get back in business. Small potatoes though. I didn't find a hint of anything big anywhere."

"The same for me," Sampson responded. "The closer you get to Somerset, the more available moon is. You can buy the stuff in any bar and they aren't even bashful about it. Distribution all over the County seems to be in small quantities via individuals in their own cars who get paid a flat rate per delivery. I fished for an hour on the Apple River with a young guy who makes most of his money running twice a week from Somerset up to Spooner. None of these guys are afraid of being arrested because they never see or even hear of Federal Revenue Agents," Sampson spit. "We are going to change that, but not until we get more information."

They talked for another hour, realizing that they hadn't uncovered anything they didn't already suspect before they started driving around the County. "Ok," Sampson said, "Here's how we'll do it next week."

Chapter 34

Jim Hutton and Andre were walking past the chicken coop on the Robinson place, headed for the stills back in the old building. As they rounded the end of the coop they saw two ducks, mallards, a male and a female, flying toward them erratically. Seeing them round the end of the coop, the green head mallard swerved slightly to its left, the hen, squawking loudly, swerved right.

"Wham!" was the sound of the male smashing into the chicken coop's end wall at mallard speed! Feathers puffed into the air, at the impact area, as the Mallard's broken neck and compressed body flopped lifeless to the ground below.

"My God, Jim! Did you see that?" Andre exclaimed.

"Dammit, Andre! I told Ralph to be careful about dumping the old mash in the same spot!" Hutton was mad, which Andre didn't understand.

"What's wrong?

"That was a drunk duck! Listen, you can still hear the hen squawking and look how she's flying! Ducks usually fly in a long straight line. She's flying like she's loaded and just missed the building herself! Those ducks have been drinking water from that pond Ralph's been dumping old mash into. I told you the story of the drunk cows and pigs over in Stearns County. It's an absolute alarm-bell for Feds that are snooping around! Drunk-wild life means moonshine stills! That old mash is fermented. It has to be buried or spread out over ground that won't drain it back into the pond. That way, the alcohol evaporates into the air. In Stearns, the farmers spread crap over the top of it with their spreaders, to mask the mash smell."

They walked toward the small pond Ralph had been dumping the old mash into. "Ralph said that one of the guys from Stearns County told him the alcohol would evaporate from the sunlight, so he didn't have to worry about it," Andre said.

"That's not what I told him. On a cloudy day the alcohol just mixes in with the pond water and waits for some critter to drink it. We've got to change this situation quickly before the animals and birds have a party that leads the feds right to us," Hutton hissed. "This is the kind of dumb mistake that could do us in."

"I'm sorry, Jim, we thought we were handling the old mash right. What's the best way to fix the problem now?" Andre asked.

"I suspect we need to figure out how to drain the pond. That spreads the alcohol and water out on the surface of the ground it flows over and triggers quicker evaporation. Let's see if we can figure out how to drain the it. You've got to ride herd better on Ralph, Andre."

They saw other ducks swimming on the pond as they approached, and they, too, were squawking loudly, but seemingly without purpose. None were sounding alarm as Jim and Andre approached. They didn't even seem to be aware of them. They were just kind of swimming in circles, squawking, just to squawk, with no apparent purpose in their behavior.

"Look at this, Andre," Jim said.

Moonshine has affected my life in a lot of ways, thought Andre, *but . . . drunk ducks?*

Chapter 35

"Ok, Carolyn, chickens are coming next week," Andre laughed. "More chickens than you've ever dreamed of!" After their chicken coop was finished on the outside they began building nesting boxes onto the wall. Their goal was roughly 175 dozen eggs a week. Andre and Carolyn had found four or five new stores willing to try their eggs, and Andre figured each store would average somewhere around twenty-four dozen eggs a week. He and Carolyn had been doing their existing business with only about eighty chickens. They were going to start the new coop with 300 chickens which should produce their goal plus an extra thirty dozen per week. Then, as business grew they planned to add fifty to 100 more chicks at a time. The coop should be able to handle in the range of 600. All this was based on advice they were getting from the chicken farm in southern Minnesota owned by Andre's uncle. He didn't mind helping Andre because they were not in each other's markets so would not be competing. "I've already made all the mistakes you can make," Roger Cartier told Andre. "There's no point in you making the same ones again. I'll give you all the advice you need free of charge, but remember, advice is usually worth what you pay for it."

"Well, how many are coming, Dad?" she asked again.

"We'll start with 300 chicks, and keep our existing eighty hens going in the old coop." Andre said. "Next week you're going to have 300 cute little yellow peepers! That's why we've been working so fast to get the wall-box nests done. We won't be able to work in here after the chicks are in here. Everything we need for the chicks will be in this week, so we'll be ready when they get here. Roger gave us good advice and we've followed it. We should be ok. The scratch yard was flattened by the dozer. All we have to do there is erect and dig in the bottom of the fence to keep animals from digging under it. Henri will help me do that."

"I told some of the kids at school about the chicks. They want to come over and see them," Carolyn beamed. "What's cuter than baby chicks?"

"Don't forget now," Andre reminded her, "You've still got to care for the other hens and their eggs. We have to keep Cedarville's stores happy. They helped us get those new stores we'll be delivering to next fall."

"Don't worry Dad. I've been doing that for months," she casually said over her shoulder with a grin.

The Cartiers had banded together when Andre obtained the part-time work. Clair, Carolyn and Henri were all busier than before, but it was working. Clair helped both kids with schoolwork at night when they needed help. The most unusual change was that Andre sometimes didn't get home until after dark. Henri and Carolyn were talking about that after school one day.

"What the heck are they doing that keeps Dad working so late?" Henri asked.

"I don't know," Carolyn responded, "I asked Mom, but she said she didn't know either."

"He's probably making moonshine," Henri laughed, "Or maybe he's a high speed bootlegger chasing down the roads with the cops," he grinned watching Carolyn laughing.

"Yes, I'm sure that's it, Henri. Our father, who never takes a drink of anything stronger than milk, is a bootlegger. Hey . . . it could be true, Henri. Billy Sievertson told me in school yesterday, that since they lost their farm, his dad has been working with a still over by the Apple River. He was almost bragging about it. I told him he better keep quiet or his Dad might end up in jail. I've heard more than once they put you in jail for that."

Chapter 36

"After the second cooking, this time we will fill those new charred oak barrels," Hutton said. "We've used one of the favorite recipes used over in Stearns for making Minnesota 13 moon. I had a friend taste our last second-cook, batch. He said it was ok, but didn't have the smoothness, or color, of 13. They get that by storing and aging it in charred oak barrels. They also add oak chips to the kegs and roll the barrels periodically to stir up the residue char that rests on the bottoms inside the kegs. Some even heat the barrels. They say heating makes the moon age twice as fast. In other words if we heat it for a month, it will taste like it's been aged for two months. He told me much of their Minnesota 13 isn't nearly as old as it's sometimes claimed to be."

He was only talking to Andre, because Ralph and Finley were outside unloading barrels from a truck that had just pulled in from St. Cloud. Jim had bought the barrels from a cooperage in St. Cloud with the assurance they were the same barrels used when Minnesota 13 was shipped from Stearns County. The truck had come in before daylight. Now, they wanted to get the barrels out of sight as quickly as possible, so were stacking them against the wall of the lower floor.

"If I've calculated this right," said Andre, "We should have close to sixty ten-gallon barrels after this cooking, Jim. Maybe we should experiment a little with heating, just with a few barrels, so we can see the difference ourselves."

"That's what I've been thinking, too," said Jim. Ok, I'll put you in charge of that, Andre. Think about it a little. Just play around with a half-dozen kegs. I'll get you the info on how they do it over in Stearns. Then, you figure out what our system should be, the timing, how we supply heat where they are stored and some pattern of turning the barrels as they age. You have to keep careful records, because when it works, you want to be able to do exactly the same thing with the next batch. We'll talk again about it tomorrow," he finished, thinking, *I knew I picked the right guy in Cartier. He's just what we need to get the money faucet open. Ralph doesn't think the way Andre can. Ralph's honest, he'll work out, but we've got to get them up to speed. Finley wants to go home.*

"I've got to run now, Andre. I'm closing on another farm on the other side of Balsam Lake. We'll talk again tomorrow. We've got to discuss a new distribution strategy I've been thinking about. Don't mention anything about that to the others, though. You and I are going to know about some things they won't. That's how it has to be. I'll fill you in tomorrow."

With that, he was gone. Andre, Ralph and Finley mixed and stirred all afternoon. Everything was ready to start cooking in the morning.

That night, Andre couldn't sleep. He was surprised to be worrying about how he was going to invent a method of heating moonshine that was stored in barrels. Finley had told him that in Stearns County some farmers actually buried crocs in the ground, covered them with canvas, and then dumped manure on top. The manure pile would generate heat for months as it decomposed and the manure pile discouraged revenue agents from looking within it for moonshine. *Surely, there must be a better way,* he thought.

Andre could feel himself about to take charge of this operation. What was worrying him was that he was beginning to like what he was doing. But still, there was always that little voice in the back of his head reminding him, *you are breaking the law.*

Chapter 37

Andre and Jim Hutton were standing on the wooden floor of Andre's new chicken coop. Hutton had told Andre to make sure no one else was around when they met. "Here's how we do it, Andre. I told you we'd protect you, and that you weren't going to be in danger of going to jail."

Andre had gone along with everything Hutton had suggested, since that first lunch on the beach, at Robinson's farm. He knew he was committed. There was no backing out now. But, so far, all he had done is work as a laborer and a cooker. Today, he knew Hutton wanted to talk about the next step in his plan. It made Andre edgy.

"We are going to start using this coop, Andre. Here's how we protect you. This chicken coop is on your land. You own it. I want to rent the basement beneath it. I'll sign a contract with you, which proves all you do is rent the space. I will use it for storage. I will deliver goods into it and take some out periodically. Though you may get more involved at times, should there ever be a problem with the law, you will be able to claim your only involvement is renting space. Andre, this goes on all the time over in Stearns County, and the farmers renting space never get arrested or go to jail."

Andre had known they were going to make this arrangement. Hutton had given him the money to build the chicken coop, and he knew from the outset why the coop had a full, but hidden, basement beneath it. What he hadn't known, was how the rental agreement would protect him. Andre remembered hearing somewhere, perhaps in Somerset, that you could no longer claim ignorance about who was renting from you. Right now, however, he wanted to believe what Hutton was telling him.

"Judges in Stearns County dismissed charges against farmers who rented space to bootleggers and cookers. They won't send them to jail," Hutton smiled. "This will work ok, Andre. Now, let's talk about the Robinson place. This conversation must remain between you and me, no one else. Understood?"

"Yes, I'm learning to understand the need for secrecy and lies, more than I ever used to," Andre replied with a smirk.

"I selected the Robinson place myself, and still feel it was a good decision. That farm is off the beaten path, and will be given more legitimacy when we add the chicken operation to it. Here's how we put you in charge of the chickens. I've already told Anderson at the bank that I'm hiring you to manage the chicken business. Because you were already in the business at your own place, it made complete sense to him for me to hire you. I have already paid for the new chicken coop. I will finance the initial chicken inventory and all the equipment and I'll pay you a flat monthly fee to manage the business just as you do your own. I will also give you a percentage of the profits. This provides us a highly visible reason to be working together, so no one will question ever seeing us together. It will let you grow that business and it will all be done under your name, Cartier Egg and Chicken Services."

Andre smiled, "It sounds good so far. My daughter is excited and all for growing our business."

Hutton went on, "I will use the storage space beneath the chicken coops, both at your place and at the Robinson's. Our goal is to keep that space as secret as possible from everyone and you and I will try to arrange for all pickups and deliveries from either location to be done when you are off the premises, or in the dark of night. That further protects you should the feds ever discover how we use that space. All you do is manage chickens and rent space."

They talked for another hour. The visible legitimacy of how they were setting up the chicken business eased Andre's mind. It gave him more to hide his other Hutton activities behind. Andre was slowly adjusting to the moon business, but guilt lingered just beneath the surface. He'd spent his entire life being honest, forthright, and legal. In less than three months, he'd broken many rules he had accepted since he was a kid.

Chapter 38

Andre, Clair, and Carolyn and Henri were exiting church Sunday morning when Father Baptiste, while shaking hands with Andre at the church door said, "Andre, could you hang on while I greet the rest of the parishioners? I have some information for you."

"Why, sure, Father. I'll come back up when you've shaken the last hand," Andre responded.

Clair heard the exchange. As they walked away from the church steps she said, "What's that about, Andre?"

"I don't know," he answered. "He says he has some information for me. It will just take a minute. You can wait with the kids."

Back at the church door a few minutes later, Father Baptiste nudged Andre back inside the church, which was now empty. "After our last meeting, Andre, I did some research and thought you would be interested in what I found. One of the Church's teachers, a professor of social ethics at the Catholic University in Washington, D. C. has made public comments on the issue of Prohibition laws related to sin in the Church's perspective." As he spoke, Father Baptiste withdrew a folded sheet of paper from inside the back cover of the Bible in his hand. "Early on he supported Prohibition if it served the common good, meaning the tentative agreement between civil authority and the will of God." Adjusting the glasses on his nose, he then began to read the paper to Andre. "The background of that perspective comes from part of the thirteenth Chapter of Romans, 'Let every soul be subject to higher powers; for there is no power but from God; and those ordained by God. Therefore, he that resisteth the power resisteth the ordinances of God.' The church has used this passage for centuries, Andre, and it means that civil laws are generally binding per se on conscience. Translating from this professor's statement, such as I can interpret, means that the Church would view a bootlegger's actions to be guilty of a grave violation of an important morally binding law."

Remembering his last confession, Andre was focused and absorbing Father Baptiste's words as best he could. Recognizing the look on Andre's face, Father Baptiste added, "I know it's a little confusing, Andre, but hang on for a moment and it will be easier to understand."

Then, he read on, "The very same professor, who initially supported Prohibition, however, later reversed his findings. He was always unhappy with the Volstead Act, which forbids the making of moonshine for one's own use and to share it with friends, or to carry it from one place to another. Just three years ago he reversed his position and thus, to some degree, the Church's, by declaring; 'The control of alcohol for the common man's good has not worked and the 18th Amendment is not the best way to control liquor. The evil consequences of national prohibition have shown to all who have eyes to see, that it is not only not the best but probably the worst method of dealing with the liquor problem. Therefore, I do not think that the national prohibition laws are any longer directly binding on conscience.' Father Baptiste looked at Andre again, and then added, "A priest such as I, can interpret his statement to mean that, under the laws of the land, involvement with moonshine is unlawful, but in the eyes of the Church, it is not sinful because it is not binding on conscience. I was grateful to find this information on the church's perspective, because it supported the answer you were given when we last spoke. I hope it helps you with whatever you were wrestling with, but I again urge caution in anything that might be interpreted as unlawful."

Father Baptiste smiled and handed the piece of paper to Andre, as he escorted him back out through the Church doors.

"Thank you, Father. It helps to know this," Andre said, sincerely. Then, thinking back to a few moments ago when Father Baptiste stopped him at the church door, Andre thought, *he's known it was me since I went to confession.*

Chapter 39

Hutton had more background in the moon business than anyone in Stephens County realized. He had shown only what he wanted known about himself to those currently working with him, like Andre, Ralph, Anderson at the bank, and Bill at the gas station. Anyone else in the County who had met him knew him as a real estate agent from the Twin Cities.

In fact, Hutton had been active in the moon business of Stearns County for over five years, and knew the business well. He was connected with the syndicate in the Twin Cities and had been one of their prime suppliers for years. He was actually in charge of his own business in Stearns until just five months past, when the feds became a little too active over there. He still owned operating stills in Stearns County and was still connected to bootleggers who ran much of his moon to the Twin Cities syndicate for distribution. He was, however, rapidly shutting down the stills. Hutton didn't actually work for clients in the Twin Cities. He and Manny operated almost like partners, and had been doing so for years. They had worked together on many moon projects, just as they were doing now in Stephens County. Hutton wanted none of that known by those in Cedarville. Now that he was operating in Stephens County he hoped to be totally shut down in Stearns within two weeks. He needed just one more cooking setup here to replace revenue which used to come from Stearns County.

He had a long list of smaller bootleggers who transported bulk-moon via specially-adapted automobiles with horse power, speed, and clandestine methods of carrying booze in their cars. He also knew larger transporters who had invented ways of transporting bulk-moon in disguised ways to avoid Revenue Agents. Hutton intended to use only a few of the same people he had worked with in Stearns because he intended now to compete with Stearns without anyone in Stearns knowing about it. He would work with only one trusted element of the syndicate he had special agreements with in the past, Manny Goldfin.

His first test of the new plan was the 300 gallons of moon from the Robinson place, the same 300 gallons Ralph had asked about.

Secrecy was an essential element of moonshine trafficking, which is why he lectured Ralph after his question, "What happened to the moon?" Hutton knew that though there were few Federal Agents currently around Stephens County, they would be coming. Agents would go where they found action, just as they had in Stearns. He also knew when that occurred Feds would watch the bridges that crossed the St. Croix in Hudson, Stillwater, Osceola, and Taylors Falls.

Right now bootleggers could still use them, but due to the increase in agent activity, he knew time was limited. Agents loved to set up snare-raids at bottlenecks like bridges. When that time came, Hutton planned to use ferries to cross the border river and avoid detection. Smaller deliveries usually went out in five-gallon crocks, which were better suited for loading onto the ferry via car, so he was going to continue using the ferry now. The best part was that the Barnes girls who operated the ferry thought he was an auto dealer delivering hot cars from Chicago to the Twin Cities and so only wanted to cross the St. Croix River late at night. They normally received twenty-five cents per car per trip. Because they were willing to quickly respond to the honk of a horn from the Minnesota side of the river in the middle of the night, Jim had agreed to pay them one dollar per car.

Chapter 40

Sampson and Brown had driven around Stephens County for nearly two weeks, mostly Brown actually, because Sampson had concentrated on the Somerset region. Today, he and Brown rented a small boat on the St. Croix River. Disguised as fishermen, they were exploring the shores of the river between Taylors Falls and the town of Osceola, seven miles south. Agents knew it takes water to make moonshine, water to make mash, and water to cool the worms of the stills to cause steam to condense and drip as moon. Consequently, cookers liked to have a handy fresh water source close to their stills. The shores of the St. Croix River were likely still-havens. Not wanting anything to do with rowing upstream, they had rented their boat in Taylors Falls and were drifting with the current downstream towards Osceola.

As they drifted, both had fishing lines trailing. They were looking for anything suspicious on either shore - pipes that could suck water from the river, buildings that might house a still, signs of activity hinting of moonshine and any such things that appeared to be hidden, but even if they found something they weren't going to explore it. They just wanted to know where it was for a later visit. They still did not want anyone to know they were from the Revenue Department. The more they could learn of different operations, before the first raid, the better off they'd be. Once moonshiners knew feds were around things quickly went quiet.

Sampson was remembering some of the stills he had discovered down around the Chicago region. Most of them were found on farms, especially farms with fresh water of some nature - lakes, ponds, rivers and good wells. Cookers liked to hide the smell of cooking behind the stronger smells of farm animals. His squad had found stills on farms covered by brush piles, hay bales, loose hay, garbage, and more than once surrounded by manure piles. Agent strategy was, look in the last place others would look. Experience had taught him to look in the places most agents would avoid, due to smells, manure, mud, difficult terrain and brush. He'd once found a farmer's bulk gas tank, which stood on ten-foot legs to provide gravity feed of gasoline, to be divided with a partition inside the tank that couldn't be seen from the outside. When you lifted the top access lid, you smelled gasoline. With more thorough inspection, when he found another hidden valve on the bottom of the tank, it poured moonshine from its bottom half. Because there were more agents inspecting around Chicago, the shiners had become good at hiding their operations, but once an agent began to think like they did, it wasn't too difficult to dream up where something as large as a still might be hidden. Stores of moon were easier to hide, and consequently harder to find, but the same routine of thought could ferret it out. Up here along the St. Croix, because there had been fewer Agents, he expected it to be easier to find stills. After two weeks of snooping around, he was changing his mind. He remembered how he had underestimated those over in Stearns County. They were much better at both cooking and hiding than he had thought while still in Chicago. *Never underestimate your adversary* he thought as they drifted down the St. Croix.

By mid-day, he and Brown had found little. Either there weren't many stills along the river, or those using them were better at hiding than he thought. Twice during the day they watched a paddlewheel boat pass them, one headed upstream, the other down towards Stillwater. Sampson thought, *someone could transport booze on one of those* and concluded, *we'll have to check out the boats.* By the end of the day, he and Brown had all but written off the shore of the river for potential still raids. Sampson had pretty much made up his mind that the bulk of moon activities were around Somerset. That's where he and his new squad would make their first raids. He wanted to have three or four targets identified, before bringing his men over. He wanted his new squad impressed with what he and Brown had found by themselves, and also to impress Lundquist by making several arrests in a short time once he started.

Chapter 41

Carolyn handed two small yellow chicks to Molly in the chicken coop. "Have you ever seen anything cuter?" Carolyn smiled. "There are 300 of them in here with us."

Molly smiled and caressed the chick's back with her finger tips. That was the first time Carolyn had seen her actually smile since that time she'd cried all day at school after her parents lost their farm. They had moved onto the farm of her uncle, and were sharing their house now, while her father continued, unsuccessfully, to look for work. That allowed her to continue to go to the same school, which had brought the girls closer together. Carolyn seemed to be the only one who seemed to care for Molly. Molly wrongly carried the loss of their farm and home, as partly her fault, though she could not explain why.

"I wish I could have done what you're doing, Carolyn," Molly said. "Maybe I could have brought in enough money with chickens and eggs to help Dad keep the farm. I'm so afraid now. Mom keeps crying all the time. My aunt tries to comfort her, but nothing seems to work. Dad's drinking too much. My uncle was hollering at him yesterday about drinking and not finding work. I don't know how long he's going to let us stay there."

"Don't be discouraged, Molly," Carolyn urged. "Maybe when these peepers grow up and start laying, we can hire you to help us here. I'll ask Dad about that. It's not your fault about the farm, Molly, you mustn't blame yourself," she finished with a hug. "Here, sit on this bench, push out your knees a little and I'll fill up your skirt with some yellow happiness. Have you ever seen anything cuter?"

Molly smiled again and this time it lasted longer.

Andre and Ralph had finished building the nest boxes, and had the coop completely finished before the peepers arrived. The move-in had been uneventful, without losing a single chick. They had small-wicked heaters and water-bottles with troughs around their bottoms. Chicks could drink whenever they wished. They could light the heaters in the evening, but June was a warm month, so they weren't needed much. Andre had ordered the 300 chicks from the local grain elevator, which sold chicks every spring. He wanted to keep the business local, which he always tried to do and he wanted word to spread about the growing Cartier Chicken Service. The elevator men had been surprised to get such a big order. They had cut back on their normal inventory because everyone was so short of money.

"The bank wouldn't give me the spring planting loan this year, but were willing to finance expansion of my chicken business. Without my chickens, I'd be out of business. If this works out I'll be ordering 300 more next spring."

Henri was out in the pasture with Molly's brother, Dan. He and Molly had come over together. Henri had to move the beef cattle into a fresh-grown pasture, so Dan was helping him. "So, do you have chores to do at your Uncle's place, Dan?"

"Yeh, he milks about twenty-head, so I help with that in the morning and at night. My Dad was going to do it, but he's been so busy trying to find more work, that he hasn't been able to help with milking," Dan finished, thinking *I don't want him to know about Dad's drinking. It's hard enough to admit living with my Uncle.* "That's about it, though. I just try to stay out of the way. They say they are happy to have us there, but there are some hard feelings between my Dad and my Uncle. I don't really understand it, but I for sure don't want to get in the middle of it. My Uncle's daughters have been nice to us and my Aunt keeps saying nice things. I just feel like I'm in the wrong place, Henri, I don't know . . . it's just so different."

Pointing at a head of beef that was running to avoid being herded, Henri said, "Run after that rambunctious one over there, Dan; he wants to go to another pasture. Rambunctious, that's what Dad calls that one," Henri laughed. "He's dumb as a bale of hay!" Thinking how sad Dan looked Henri said, "Let's go back and see Molly and Carolyn, Dan, before you have to head back to the farm. Have you ever seen 300 peepers? What a riot."

Chapter 42

Now, after a month of cooking, Andre and Ralph had become proficient at the task. Andre easily qualified as a foreman in the Robinson operation, and Ralph was happy to stay busy at the daily routines. What last month had been a mystery to them was now understood. Andre was demonstrating this in his summary to Hutton as they stood beside one of the stills. Two weeks earlier Hutton had talked to Ralph, Andre, and Finley about work assignments for each of them. He put Finley and Ralph in charge of producing mash and all of the necessary work it took, as well as maintenance of the building, stills, and container packaging. He put Andre in charge of cooking and maintaining inventory of everything needed to produce mash and moon

Hutton said, "So, Andre, what do we have to do to increase production?

"According to my records, Jim, each barrel of mash we stir produces about eighteen gallons of first-cook moon. Each cook of 250 gallons uses about eighteen gallons of gas and takes about six hours to condense into moon, just as you pointed out to us earlier. All I've done is to confirm your estimates. We've only been cooking two days a week, but with the amount of mash our barrels currently can handle, if we cook five days instead of two, we can produce about 1000 gallons a week in this building. That's the short story. To do that, we've got to invent ways of bringing in truckloads of sugar, kegs, cans, and any other containers. I know how to handle gas deliveries, and I know where we can get some more help that we can count on. I need three more people to make this happen. If you agree to what I've figured out, I think we can be up to that level of production in about two weeks if you can help us figure out some of these details." Andre finished.

Now talking to Andre, Ralph and Finley, Hutton said, "Mr. Finley, who has kindly helped us get up to speed here, wants to go home to his wife and family. I'm trying to coax him into remaining two more weeks. Andre, you and Ralph have to learn all you can from him before he leaves. My plan is, when he leaves, you, Andre, take over the whole operation."

Ralph's eyes expanded when he heard of Andre's promotion. He'd been working doubly hard to make up for his mistakes. This announcement made him wonder if he ever could make up for them in Hutton's eyes.

"We're off to a good start here guys. Let's keep it going. Ralph, you and Finley can get on with mash mixing here for now. Andre, I want you to come with me up to the new chicken coop. I have some other things to go over with you there," Hutton said. "Let's go."

Chapter 43

Leaving Ralph and Finley to work on mash, Andre and Hutton returned to the new coop building at Robinsons. They walked the perimeter of the building outside, then, went in. It was identical to the one on Andre's place, complete with the hidden access to the lower level.

"Ok, Andre, what are the details you need help with?" Hutton asked.

"Well, like farming, Jim, producing moon requires planning and scheduling. You've had a lot more experience than I have, so I'd like to sit down with you and plan our production for the next three months. I need to know where you want to get the needed inventory for mash, proper containers for storage or transporting, and I need to know how you expect it to be packaged, so I know what containers to buy. There are other things we have to fix or upgrade too." Andre ended.

Hutton said, "Tomorrow I'll give you an order, Andre. It will tell you how much I need, when I need it, how I want it packaged. Pickups and delivery will be set up verbally between you and me, nothing in writing. No one besides you and I will ever know when we are transporting moon, no matter how it's packaged, not even Ralph. No one but you or I will know when it is to be picked up, by whom, or where it is going. I want you to go over your numbers again. Be sure they are correct, because I'm going to be asking for maximum production while I think we can get away with it. Things change fast in this business. When the feds start sniffing, you can be shut down in one place and open in another really fast. That's one of the reasons we don't store more inventory near the stills than needed for one or two cooks. I once shut down an operation in Stearns, moved the stills to a new location, and was back in full production in three days." Jim grinned. In this business you have to be ready for quick moves . . . it keeps you out of jail," he laughed.

Andre paused for a minute, then went on, "Here's what we need to fix up or improve. To keep up with that max-production you keep asking for, I have to increase the cool water supply to cool the worms so they condense. We have to keep the cook temperature under 212 degrees in the cooking range and we have to maintain that cool water around the worms. We have enough water in that pond to do it all, but I need a bigger pump to increase the flow. Existing plumbing will work; I just need the bigger pump. The stills are adequate, with more water. I need a bigger, elevated, gas tank, so we don't have to keep screwing around with all these gas cans. Those cans waste a ton of time. I talked to Bill as you suggested; he's fine with night deliveries and will truck out gas whenever we need it. I said we'd pay his going rate. He was fine with that. He thinks it's all for the chicken business. In fact, Ralph may end up driving the truck. Bill's having Ralph do more bulk deliveries to fill up his half-time work. This will interest you too, Jim. Ralph says he's learning where more small stills are operating because of the gas deliveries. You should talk to Ralph about it." he finished.

"Go ahead and buy what you need, Andre. Just pay for it out of your Cartier Egg Services checking account, and make sure you don't buy anything that would make anyone suspicious of moon, locally. The more people see you involved with the egg business the better. Anything you need that could smell like moon, tell me. I'll buy it in the cities. Let me know the amount you spend. I'll pay it to you in cash. Remember, as we've discussed, be careful about large amounts of cash. Either hide it, or put it in one of those accounts in the cities, not locally," Hutton went on, "And only use the accounts I've given you. "My order this week will specify what size containers I want to take deliveries in. Let's talk about that a little. I'm going to hook you up directly with a container supplier I worked with for years up in St. Cloud. That has to be handled carefully. I'll explain how we go about that."

"One more thing, Jim," said Andre. "I'm concerned about Ralph feeling down because of everything that's happened to him in the last month. He makes mistakes now and then and needs some direction, but he knows that. He's working damn hard to make up for it. Now, if he gets shut out of managing some of the activities around here, he's going to feel worse. I need him around here and I want him feeling good."

"I understand that, Andre, and I saved this idea for you. I wanted to make sure you agreed with it, and that, you, did it. I think when Finley leaves, and you take over, your first move should be to make Ralph operations foreman under you," Hutton grinned. "That will make Ralph feel good!"

Andre was relieved to hear that. After seeing Hutton angry about some of Ralph's errors he'd not been sure how Jim was thinking about him. "That's great, Jim, and it will work. I know how to handle Ralph. I will make him a valuable part of things. Thanks for that freedom."

Part III

The Feds are here!

Chapter 44

"On a hill far away . . . stood an old rugged cross . . . the emblem of suffering and shame," the small voice sang on. The four-year old boy was singing, at his grandmother's request, to a gathering of the Women's Christian Temperance Union. Though he sang well and much to the satisfaction of the women gathered there, especially his grandmother, he looked like he'd rather be anywhere else. He sang on, dressed in a white short sleeved shirt with a stiff collar that scratched his neck as he sang, "I will cherish that old rugged cross . . .," he sang, holding the collar from his neck with his fingers.

The WCTU had existed long before Prohibition came into play with the Volstead Act of 1922, but had gathered strength steadily since Prohibition was enacted. Women met monthly, sometimes weekly, and often at special meetings called to encourage efforts to support the dry philosophy. The WCTU was also one of the first national organizations aimed at stopping, and/or preventing women from spousal abuse. They were a force to be reckoned with and had done much good for women. Today's meeting was held at the Cedarville Town Hall, and was directed by Clair Cartier's mother, the widow Girard, who had lived in Cedarville for the last fifty-five years, the last ten alone, since her husband's death. Mrs. Girard was a long-standing member of the Cedarville Protestant Church, and a long-time member of the WCTU, which is why she was today directing the WCTU meeting she had scheduled. Mrs. Girard wanted to encourage support of new efforts to enforce Prohibition in Stephens County, and to grab a headline for the WCTU's work. She knew that following this meeting, there would be an article in Thursday's edition of the Cedarville *Gazette*, bearing a headline like, FEDERAL REVENUE AGENTS ASSESS ILLEGAL LIQUOR IN STEPHENS COUNTY, which would get the attention of most County residents. What she didn't know was how Agent Robert Sampson, currently assigned temporary duty to the Midwest Revenue Department, would feel about that headline appearing.

The boy finished singing to polite, loud to him, applause, while receiving an embarrassing hug from his grandmother in front of what he felt were too many ladies. Mrs. Harold Girard stepped to the podium, where she began issuing calculated WCTU rhetoric from stern lips, which alcohol had never touched. "That fine rendition of, 'The Old Rugged Cross,' was sung by Philip Peterson, at the suggestion of our member, Rella Cathcart, his grandmother. Isn't it beautiful to hear such pure music sung by lips never seared and brain never warped, by alcohol?" she beamed, leading another round of applause by her own clapping. As quickly as his grandmother released him from her hug, young Philip ran from in front of the audience, not stopping until he reached his grandmother's car, where he immediately crawled into the back seat and closed the car door. His objective was to try and get a deep breath, which he had seemed unable to do from the moment his grandmother sat him in the front row of seats beside her.

"It is my pleasure today to advise you of the progress of WCTU work in our unending fight against the sins of drink. One of our Twin Cities WCTU affiliates brought to my attention last week that the National Revenue Department, which enforces Prohibition, has assigned some additional Revenue Agent attention aimed at illegal activities within Stephens County in the coming months." Her statement brought abrupt applause and more smiles. "My associate from the Twin Cities actually asked me not to announce it until they arrived, but I simply could not contain such inspiring information beneath a bushel basket. Our members need to know of progress being made through the constant WCTU efforts of our member's towards virtues of temperance." She was proud to be director of her County chapter, and it made her feel righteously superior to non-members when she could publicly alert them to the success WCTU was enjoying at the expense of those sinful participants on the wet side of the law. She was also convinced any additional attention by Federal Revenue Agents would never occur without unending pressure applied by the WCTU and, was likely, right.

The meeting finished with a luncheon and interview with Mrs. Girard by a writer from the Cedarville *Gazette*. Girard waxed on eloquently on how the WCTU motivated the Revenue Department to apply more intensive enforcement within Stephens County, which local, and County, enforcement seemed unable to effectively do. The weekly issue of the Gazette would be out Thursday, containing this interview.

"I also want to compliment our members and local law enforcement," she thought *she better throw local law a bone* after her last comment, "They have been doing a better job of making sure the weekend dances at the village halls are attended by dance inspectors. That is a high priority of the WCTU, to help protect our young people from the ravages of alcohol," Mrs. Girard glowed. She loved limelight and social atmosphere, especially when those present were listening to *her*.

Dance inspectors, under authority granted them by the County Sheriff, attended weekend dances throughout different Midwest counties. Their job was to see that no one brought moonshine or beer into the dance halls, and also to ride herd on those brown bags stashed outside in snowdrifts, under cars, and at the base of fence posts adjacent to the halls.

When the music stopped between dances it was common for one dancer, to say to another, "I'll meet you outside, west side, post 7." Dance inspectors were supposed to curtail such activity, but weren't actually very good at it. Most made one early round of the parking lot, before the revelers had much time to drink. After ten, inspectors mostly prevented booze from gaining entry to the dance hall, because the later it got, the more dangerous it became to hunt booze outside. More than one inspector found himself with a black eye the morning after a dance. Most explained it as, "Yeah, I fell down outside in the dark," rather than explain they had challenged someone, who already had a snoot-full and wasn't about to see their moon taken, especially by an unarmed pseudo-deputy appointed by the Sheriff and endorsed by the WCTU. Dance inspectors were a joke with dance regulars, but not with the Women's Christian Temperance Union, which helped raise funds to pay the inspectors. To the WCTU, inspectors were the last line of defense between the young and innocent and the evils of moon.

Chapter 45

Sampson was talking to his squad during a training session. "I'm told you two have learned effective tricks-of-the-trade in Stearns County over the last two weeks. That's good. You'll spend next week with Brown and me over in Somerset. One more week of surveillance, then we go into action. We have found nearly ten stills and a substantial list of bars selling moon. Another week will turn up more. Then we start putting them out of business. We'll work in teams of two, three on bigger operations, four if big enough, so we catch more in the act and prevent anyone getting away. Once we start raids the word will go out and they'll start hiding things. We've got to have evidence on every raid, or we have nothing to convict with in court."

"How are we going to handle the evidence?" one of the men asked. "Each agent I worked with over in Stearns does it differently. One was axe-happy. He broke every keg, crock, or can, made the biggest damned mess you've ever seen, and loved doing it. Another one confiscated all the booze. He made us load it all up and hauled it away himself, said it went to a holding warehouse," which immediately got Sampson's attention. "Do we have a warehouse, or should we bring an ax?" the man finished, grinning.

Sampson looked stern. "Here's how we do it." He thought to himself, *do this right Sampson. This is why you wanted to come up here on assignment. You can earn your retirement in just the next year with this opportunity.* "I want this to be clear to all of you. I got burned a few times down in Chicago due to lack of adequate evidence. That will not happen to any of us. Understand *that* . . . it will not happen," he paused for a few seconds, eyeballing each of the Agents, one at a time. "I have rented a place we can safely place evidence from raids. Each of you will handle evidence two different ways in each raid. First, whether moon is stored in kegs, crocks, or bottles, you will destroy on premises, ten to twenty-percent of what's there. Destroy it in a demonstrative way, using axes on kegs, cans, or bottles, and make a big display of it, and make as big a mess as you can. We want them to remember the raid and see how much Federal Revenue Agents like to destroy the stuff. We want broken containers and smelly moon all over the site. Ok, everyone got the first step of evidence handling?" he asked.

All nodded affirmatively with smiles.

"Be sure to have someone take pictures of you swinging the axe."

Holding a picture up in front of them, "Pictures like this." The picture showed an agent's axe staving in the middle of a keg and, pressurized by the axe-head's impact, moonshine, spraying into the air. Around and behind the axe-swinging agent were smashed kegs and puddles, and the agents feet were half-covered with liquid. "Second, after you have destroyed that ten to twenty-percent, move any of those arrested or involved in the operation away from the destroyed evidence. Put them in another room, a different building, somewhere out of sight of the remaining evidence. One agent stays with those people where they cannot see what is going on, until the other agent or agents have loaded and moved the rest of the undestroyed moon off the premises and on its way to our storage facility. We do not want any of those raided to see what we do with the balance of their inventory. If the cars we use in the raid are not big enough to carry all the evidence, your options are to make more than one trip, or to get word to me to have our truck sent over to you for loading. If we expect a large inventory from a raid, we will have the truck standing by, and close enough that it can be there quickly."

"What if the people who work the still don't want to stay put while we are wrecking the kegs?" one of the agents asked.

"You are a Revenue Agent. Take charge, be in charge, and take no crap from anyone. If you have to scare them pull your pistol and wave it around. You've been trained in arrest-handling; you know how to man-handle people when it's needed. Do it! It you have to get tough . . . get tough! I don't want these people to like you . . . I want them to fear you. Make sure they do. Once fear is established you won't have any trouble. If you tell them to sit on a chair, while we take two hours to remove evidence, I expect them not to move from that chair. You are a federal agent . . . act like one! Hell, every now and then in Chicago, we'd shoot one. You'd be surprised how the rest shut up and settle down when they see someone get slapped with a pistol," he grinned, thinking, *I miss that action. I haven't had any arrest fun for over a month, not much with women either. That's going to change.*

"Now, there's a third step with evidence. You each have a camera and I expect you to use them. I want pictures of the people arrested, both as a group, and individual pictures. You remember your arrest training, and you all saw this practice in action when you trained over in Stearns. After those arrested have been removed from the evidence scene, take additional pictures of the evidence being destroyed, and the leftover mess. Make those pictures look big. Spread out the destroyed kegs, cans, and bottles to make it look like more. Be sure to pour the moon around so it shows in the photos as puddles. We used to even add plain water to make the puddles bigger. Broken glass, twisted and punctured cans, and splintered kegs, sitting in puddles of moon is what we are after. Take pictures only of what you destroy, but make it look like you destroyed everything. Any questions?"

"Why all the destroyed evidence pictures?" agent Eggert asked.

"One of our squads in Chicago made a raid and confiscated over 300 gallons in ten-gallon kegs, but didn't take any pictures of the kegs they destroyed. One of the local newspapers wrote an article accusing the agents of stealing and selling what they'd confiscated for personal profit. Without pictures of some destroyed evidence they didn't have a leg to stand on. I learned from the problems that followed, that we don't want any problems like that up here. I had the top arrest record, with fewest follow-on problems, of all Chicago Federal Revenue agents," Sampson went on, "Just follow my suggested procedures and you won't get tangled up in unnecessary problems." Sampson wanted to move on. *I don't need them thinking about this stuff now. I need to keep them focused on finding stills to raid.* He also didn't want to explain any more details about the evidence they stashed.

"What happens to the evidence we accrue in that warehouse?," asked agent Eastman"

"You'll get in on all that activity later on," Sampson said forcefully, "We don't have much time today. I want to cover the rest of raiding details in the next hour, so let's get on with it now," he finished quickly, in a no-nonsense manner, that agents understood.

"Next week we are going to hit Somerset," Sampson declared. "We've got three to six stills targeted and a half-dozen retailers we can land on, perhaps more by then. There's also one house that I'm told has a whole basement full of booze. Somerset hasn't been raided since last year when those agents came over from St. Paul. I want to accomplish something for Lundquist in this first raid, so we are going to concentrate on Somerset all week. Keep quiet about it. No one in Stephens County even seems to know we are around, and Somerset is the same. Next week is going to impress Lundquist and scare the hell out of Stephens County. Usually, right after raids, moon shipments pick up, because they want to sell it before we find it. Right after we hit Somerset, we're going to watch the bridges for a week." Sampson finished.

Agent Eastman asked, "Do we work the bridges the way they do over in Stearns?"

"Ok, let's talk about that next," Sampson went on. "They've had it pretty easy in the Barrens for the last year. Now, they're going to know the feds are here."

Chapter 46

Hutton arranged for Ralph to deliver the next car load of moon from the Robinson place to the Sunrise ferry at 2:00 a.m. Jim drove the car back from Taylors Falls, where he met one of his runners from the Twin Cities. He wanted to see how Ralph would work out on short deliveries to the river. He would only allow experienced runners to take deliveries from the St. Croix River into the cities. Hutton was still concerned about Ralph and was rationalizing as he drove. *How much can go wrong between the Robinson place and the river? It's only twelve miles. Ralph should be able to handle that.*

Ralph met Hutton at Robinson's at 1:00 a.m. "Well, Ralph, now you're going to see what happened to the other moon you asked about awhile back. But I want you to forget it just as quickly. From this moment on you don't remember a thing about today's activities."

Ralph nodded his understanding. This was the first car modified to carry moon he'd ever seen. It was an Olds, similar to the one he'd seen Jim drive into the gas station, but really different on the inside. The back seats were removed, and you could see right into the trunk compartment. He and Hutton loaded twenty, five-gallon, crocks into that space in back. Each crock was wrapped in burlap to prevent breakage. Those twenty crocks precisely filled the available floor space of the back seat and trunk. Hutton explained the rubber belting beneath the crock's bases kept them from sliding around, which could cause breakage. They had 100 gallons of moon in that Olds. Then, they covered the door-to-door flat-top load, with a mattress and blanket, adding a pillow to make it look like a sleeping compartment behind the driver.

This was a chancy move on Hutton's part. He'd been much more careful over in Stearns where there were Revenue men all the time. Bootleggers who hauled where Feds were active went to great extremes to hide their cargo. Jim had seen cars with two gas tanks, one for gas, one for moon, and twin-tanked Model-A and Model-T Ford trucks, as well. Bootleggers made containers of inner tubes and hid them within doors, car tops, and behind and under seats. Some of the high-speed cars had the ability to pull a wire within the car so when chased by Feds they could empty the moon tank onto the road. No evidence, no arrest. Jim was less concerned in Wisconsin, because there were seldom any Revenue Agents over there. When he spoke to the Barnes girls at the Sunrise Ferry, they told him they had never seen an agent. For the time being he was going to risk shipping in this manner. When Feds showed up in the County he would adjust his stealth to match, but until he got production higher he would use this method.

"Ok, Ralph. You know what you need to do. Drive from here down to river road on the St. Croix and north to the Sunrise Ferry as I showed you yesterday. Drive as much of it as you can with no lights on. The Barnes girls stay in that small building on the Wisconsin side. Park just off River Road, on the ferry drive and if nobody is obvious, just toot your horn once to signal you want to cross. The girls will come out and direct you onto the ferry. After crossing, leave immediately. Tell the girls you'll be back for the return ferry trip in about ten minutes. Drive up the road to the first crossroad. It's about a half mile. There will be two men waiting there in another Olds. Stop behind their car. One of them will tell you he is picking up your car for *President Lincoln*. That's how you know they are the right people. Give the car keys to them. The other man will drive you back to the ferry. Now, let me hear what you say if you are stopped by anyone else," Hutton finished.

"I was asked by a man in the gas station in Cedarville, to deliver the car to the Sunrise Ferry and give it to another man who would meet me in Taylors Falls on Main Street. He drove in to the gas station this afternoon, filled it with gas, said he'd just driven it up from Chicago, but had to hurry back in another car that was waiting for him. That car filled up at the same time. They offered me $10 to deliver the car, and paid me in advance. I agreed. It's the first time, the only time, I've ever done it, but $10 is $10. I just happen to work in that gas station. Hell, I'd like to do this every day."

"That's good Ralph. Beyond that, you know nothing. You drove the car from the gas station to the ferry. I am sure you will have no problem, and will see no one else to ask you questions at 2:00 a.m." Hutton added. "Remember to call me as soon as you get home."

With that, Ralph hopped in, started the Olds, after Jim showed him how to do it, and drove out the Robinson driveway. He was going to use the phone at the ferry dock in the Barnes girl's house, to arrange a ride home.

Chapter 47

The clear sky and moonlight made it easy for Ralph to follow the roads from the Robinson place down to the St. Croix River Road, and north to the Sunrise Ferry driveway. He drove all the way without lights and never saw another vehicle. He was feeling pretty cocky behind the wheel of the most expensive car he'd ever driven. He was also feeling he'd taken a step upward in Hutton's opinion of him. Driving a load of moon was a big deal, and he was especially glad Hutton picked him to do it.

He pulled onto the flat at the top of the Ferry driveway at 3:00 a.m., turned off the engine, stepped out of the car and watched a couple of minutes for signs of life around the building the girls stayed in. There were no sounds from the house, but the porch light was on. He reached through the open window of the Olds and pressed the horn button, one-short-push. The toot produced an expensive sound, as only a high-priced and fancy car would. A light came on in the window of the building. He waited another three or four minutes then, saw the door open as one of the Barnes girls stepped out. *Everything according to plan,* Ralph thought. He walked down the slope toward the Ferry Landing to ask her what he should do next. He was surprised that she looked like a teenager. It turned out she was.

When just a few feet from each other, the Barnes girl's face went white and tensed with fear, as she pushed him to the left, screaming, "Look out!"

Ralph half-moved and was half-pushed to his left by her. As he turned, he saw the Olds rolling down the Ferry driveway, gaining speed as it approached! It looked as though it was following the two tire tracks worn into the driveway's gravel surface. Thinking he could do nothing to stop the car, he remembered, *I didn't set the brake! I don't even know where the brake lever is!*

As the car rolled past, Ralph quickly tried to open the passenger side door. It wouldn't open. As he released the handle, the car was now only some thirty feet from the Ferry's ramp, and began to veer to the right, off the driveway. It missed the ferry's loading ramp by less than a foot, and splashed into the St. Croix just to the right of the ferry's hull, and stopped. Its front tires sank into the soft sand on the river bottom, with water up to and running over the tops of the front windows into the car.

Ralph felt the world disappearing from beneath his feet. *My God,* he thought. *What have I done? That car is full of moonshine, sinking, and stuck in the mud-bottom of the St. Croix!*

"Oh good!" said the Barnes girl, with a smile. "I was afraid you were going to hit the ferry! You aren't the first who's done something like this," she said, "and likely not the last."

"Oh, but this is serious business young lady. I was just delivering that car for a man from Chicago. Now what the hell am I going to do?" Ralph almost shrieked.

"Oh, don't worry, Mr. At daylight, I'll hitch up a team of our horses. We can have you out of there in no time," she smiled.

"But I'm supposed to meet someone on the other side in about a half hour. If I'm not there they're going to think I stole the car!" Ralph said excitedly.

She could see Ralph was about to wet his pants, which actually seemed funny to her. She was a veteran of such ferry incidents. Still calm, she smiled at Ralph and said, "Well, is it the car, or what's in it that's important? We get all kinds of things crossing here."

Thinking, *he'd better find a way to dig himself out of the very deep hole he'd just dug himself into with a brake lever he couldn't find*, Ralph decided to risk more info.

"The guy who hired me said he didn't want anyone to know what was in it, so I suppose it's important. Do we have to wait until morning to get the horses? Can't we do it now?"

"Nope. My dad won't let us use the horses, without his helping with the harnessing, and I'm not going to get him up in the middle of the night." she declared. "You'd be sorry if we did. Let's take a look at your load. Maybe we can just move that across, and then do the car in the morning."

"Ok, " he said, then, remembering how Hutton had asked him and Andre *if he could count on them to keep quiet about what he told them, even if they wound up not working together*, he added, "But, can I count on you to forget what we find?"

"Oh sure, that happens to us all the time. We never remember anything like that. That's why we have such steady customers," she grinned.

Ralph was beginning to feel a glimmer of hope.

They walked down to the car. Just before they reached it, Ralph said, "I'm betting it's moonshine."

"Why didn't you say so?" she grinned. "That's what I expected anyway. Cars, as fancy as that Olds, are usually carrying something like that. OK, here's my suggestion. Let's just load the moon onto the barge. We'll take it across and hide it under a canvas on the other side until we get your car out in the morning. We've never had a revenue agent here before, but there's going to be a few people looking at that car in the river come morning. We won't be able to hide it then."

"Ok," Ralph answered, "Thanks for the help. Let's get at it before it gets any lighter out. We've still got another hour of darkness, but it took us an hour to load it," *he regretted saying, before he could stop himself. He realized he just declared himself as doing more than simply delivering a car for someone and could tell by the Barnes girl's expression she'd heard him.*

As he, the Barnes girl, and her sister, another teenager who had gotten out of bed to see what was going on, loaded the twenty containers from the car to the ferry, the headlights of a car came down on the other side of the river. The car stopped by the ferry landing. A man got out and shouted, "Are you coming across?"

The Barnes girl shouted, "Yeh, we'll be there in about twenty minutes.

The man on the other side shouted, "What's the car's driver's name?"

Ralph thought, *well I can't do too much else wrong tonight.* Then, shouted, "Lincoln."

The man waved, then walked back to his car, backed it up the road a ways and parked.

Ralph and the Barnes girls brought the twenty crocks across unloading them on the other side. He and the man picking up the load for President Lincoln had a brief discussion. The car he was driving was similarly modified to haul, and had room for the hundred gallons, so they quickly loaded and he left for the Twin Cities.

Ralph went back across with the Barnes girls, then, used their phone to call Hutton.

"Jim, you're not going to believe this, but I thought I'd better call you." Then, Ralph went on with the explanation he hoped would not cost him his job.

Chapter 48

Hutton was incensed at the outcome of his own decision to test using Ralph for short deliveries. This one error could have put them out of business. He was so angry, that when Ralph asked him to arrange a ride home, he simply said, "You figure that out yourself, Ralph." Hutton regretted that later, *feeling his own behavior, totally out of character, that he should have picked him up.* Hutton broke one of his own rules of trusting his own judgment first, when he picked Ralph for this task, but he'd been encouraged by Andre to do it. "Ralph can be counted on to do what he's asked," Andre had said. "Just keep his assignments simple at first." Jim thought he'd done that. He remembered thinking *something like, How much can go wrong? It's just twelve miles to the St. Croix.*

After the Oldsmobile's night plunge things got even worse in the morning. Ralph spent four hours sitting on the ferry, before one of the Barnes girls showed up with a team of horses. She had promised to be there by 8:00 a.m. and was almost three hours late. Since she knew the moon was gone, she didn't want to push her father to get there by 8:00a.m. She drove that team as though older than a teen. Her father just watched. Hutton, not wanting to be seen or connected in any way to this whole mishap, had told Ralph to take the Olds across and leave it on the Minnesota side with the key in the ignition after they hauled it from the river.

The team of horses was quickly hooked to the car's rear bumper by the Barnes girl's sister. They easily pulled it from the river, positioning it to roll onto the ferry platform. Ralph got into the driver's seat before the car was out of the river so he could steer the front wheels as the car was pulled backwards up to where the sloping driveway began going uphill, by the team. The horses pulled him about fifty feet and stopped at the girl's command. The drive was flat between there and the ferry, so in case the engine wouldn't run they could just push the car onto the ferry and off on the other side. Everyone was surprised, including Ralph, when the Old's engine started.

"Just drive right on and we'll take you across right now," the Barnes girl shouted.

Ralph shifted into first gear and let the clutch out. He drove slowly onto the barge. Rolling forward almost to the end of the ferry's deck, he stepped on the brake pedal to stop shy of the end. The car continued to roll . . . there were no brakes! Sitting in the river all night had soaked the front brake pads beyond functioning. The Olds rolled forward until the front wheels dropped off the end of the ferry! Then, it stopped as the bottom of the frame behind the front wheels came to rest on the ferry's deck. Ralph had nearly lost the Olds to the St. Croix River again! The Barnes girl told him to just sit in the car to keep it stable till they reached the other side. "This has happened before too," she grinned. One guy drove right off the front end and totally sank his car. It took us half a day to get him out. Just sit there," she smiled. "We'll be across in a few minutes."

Ralph *felt sick*, but did as he was told.

On the other side, the girls put jacks on a plank resting flat on the sandy river bottom beneath the front axle of the Olds. They tied the ferry to shore with a length of rope, and then jacked up the car until its frame no longer touched the ferry. Then they untied and backed the ferry out from under the car's rear wheels, letting them come to rest on the ferry's on-ramp planks that sloped down towards the sandy bottom. When just the ferry's on-ramp was under the rear wheels, they lowered the car's front end and drove it off the ramp onto the shore. The man who answered to "Lincoln" the night before met him, grabbed the keys and, unhappily, climbed onto the wet seat. "Tell them not to send you next time," were intended to be his last words as he drove west up the hill, until Ralph hollered.

"Don't forget there are no brakes!"

The man shouted back, "There will be after I drive it for a mile with my foot on the brake pedal. It'll cook them dry." With that, he drove out the ferry driveway towards the Twin Cities.

Ralph, after thanking the girls profoundly by giving them each a $5 bill, slowly walked up the Ferry driveway on the Wisconsin side. He was wondering *if he still had a job.*

Chapter 49

Agents, Sampson, Brown, Eastman and Eggert were all parked on the hill above Somerset. Each had a car and Sampson had arranged for two stake-bed trucks to also be with them. Eastman and Eggert were surprised the trucks were not driven by Revenue Agents, but instead, by two men unknown to any of Sampson's squad, but Sampson.

"Ok, we have two-man teams and each has a target assigned. You know the routine and what I expect. These two trucks will be parked just off Main Street. The drivers will be standing outside your targets. If you need their help to haul evidence, one of you just step outside and wave. They'll come in and follow your directions. The first truck will be with Eggert and Eastman, the second with Brown and me. As soon as the first raid is complete, the people arrested and delivered to the police station and the evidence loaded, go back to where we were parked this morning. Once both teams are together again, we will do raids three and four. Now, listen up men, I want four, not three, not two, and sure as hell not one, but *four* successful raids! We all have to answer to Lundquist after today. Don't screw up!" Sampson finished, with a look on his face that had each agent thinking, *don't screw up!*

"Remember, we selected these four sites in town, because we want people to think we are trying to capture product rather than destroy stills. Federal agents normally just go after stills, not speakeasies or saloons. If we take out these four distribution points right here in town, I think most of the stills in the County will get more active, wanting to get rid of anything they might get caught with in a raid. We'll spend the next week concentrating on bootleggers. The following week it will be the stills," He finished. *He had been craving action for the last few weeks. This was the part of being a Revenue Agent he liked best.*

Chapter 50

All four places were targeted through tips Sampson and Brown collected over the last month. There were so many places in Somerset involved with moon they had to eliminate a number of them as too small to warrant a raid. Sampson and Brown raided a neat old home on the edge of downtown Somerset. They'd been told it had a storage center in the basement. It was the home of Mr. and Mrs. Harold Naab.

When Sampson knocked on the door, Mrs. Naab opened it, with a look of surprise on her face. Before she could speak, Sampson held up the shield in his wallet and said," Mrs. Naab, we are Federal Revenue officers and this is an authorized raid looking for illegal alcohol products forbidden by Prohibition law. Is anyone else at home in the house at this time?"

Flustered, she hesitated, then, said, "Just me."

Sampson continued, "Mrs. Naab, we can do this the hard way, which makes a real big mess of your home, or we can do it the easy way, which doesn't. Which would you prefer?"

"The easy way," she said. "That crap has smelled up my home for the last year!"

Sampson nodded at agent Brown, "The easy way." Brown nodded in response. Sampson then added, "Where is the moonshine stored on the premises, Mrs. Naab?"

"In the basement, come in, I'll show you."

Brown held one of the fire axes, so famous in newspaper photos about Prohibition raids. "You won't need that!" she shouted. "I want no more mess made in my house!" looking at Sampson, sensing him in charge, she continued, "You can just take it all out the basement window, the same way it came in." "Follow me."

To Sampson's amazement, there were 50 ten-gallon kegs stored in organized fashion throughout the basement. Based on what he had seen while working with the Stearns County Federal Agents, Brown expected they would immediately start bashing kegs with the fire axe. He didn't expect Sampson to be dissuaded by her statements about, "No mess," or "the basement window."

Sampson, on the other hand, had found exactly what he wanted: *evidence,* and more than expected. "Ok, Agent Brown. While I fill out some papers upstairs with Mrs. Naab, you wave down the truck and get the driver in here to help you. Pass the kegs through the basement window and load them up. Leave two kegs on the front lawn, with about five more standing behind them, the way I showed you last week. I'll join you as soon as I am finished. When I come out, I'll shoot the photos for you." He then went upstairs with Mrs. Naab. They sat down at the kitchen table and had their discussion with coffee.

While Brown and the driver loaded kegs, Sampson got all necessary information from Mrs. Naab. Her husband would not be home from his on-the-road salesman's job until the next day. Sampson explained to her there would be an arrest of at least one of them, but because of her cooperation she would not be jailed at this time. He instructed her that he would notify local law enforcement of the raid, the likely arrest, and that he would get her more information the next day. In the meantime, neither she or her husband were to leave town and her husband was to check in with the local police chief as soon as he returned.

Sampson had Brown break up the two kegs left in the front yard of the Naab's home, and took pictures himself of Brown in action with the fire axe. Splitting those two kegs in front of the others behind them was a ploy. It made the flying spray of moon look like they destroyed all kegs in the photo. He would release those photos to local papers later this week. Photos of Federal Revenue agents destroying kegs and stills helped keep people from being too curious about evidence and made them fear the visit of an agent.

The other three raids were each successful, but not as productive. They found a total of twenty gallons of moon in five-gallon crocks, and two small stills at the next two places, but neither was in action. The third had four wooden cases of expensive Canadian whiskey in bottles. Only the wife was home, and she had no idea where it came
from, why it was there, or any other information. She only knew her husband liked to drink it and did so often. They confiscated the booze and announced they would check back with her husband the next day.

A writer from the Somerset newspaper caught up with the last two raids, but missed the first two, as well as the trucks full of evidence as they drove out of town.

The morning after the Somerset raids, the truck was parked in a parking lot behind a building in Stillwater, Minnesota. It was on the edge of town and the lot was behind the abandoned building, so could not be seen by anyone driving by. The building had been abandoned when the company went out of business. Sampson found it when talking to a Stillwater real estate agent. He drove out alone to look it over. It was isolated with nothing happening nearby. The building was locked up, and the agent said no one was even looking at it.

The drivers of those trucks had been talked into driving for Sampson just a few weeks before. They had been working a small still southeast of Osceola for the past two years making a small amount of moon. They had been visited by Sampson a month before the Somerset raids when he was tipped off to its location. Sampson surprised them at the still one day when they were cooking. When Sampson flashed his Federal Revenue Agent credentials at them it seemed to them it would not be a good day. They shut down the still and had a somewhat one-sided conversation with Sampson, during which, he outlined how they could avoid being arrested. The long and short of it was, if they occasionally did some driving for Sampson, per his instructions, no one would ever know of this raid. They would not only get off with no arrest, but could continue operating as though they'd never been discovered. It was a small still Sampson felt would not likely be discovered again. He would never have found it without the tip.

Chapter 51

"Those dumb moves Ralph made could have put us out of business, Andre," Hutton said.

"I know, Jim, I couldn't believe it when I heard about it. But still, I know Ralph's a good man. Yes, he screwed up, but did either you or I ask him if he knew how to set the emergency brake?" Andre questioned.

"That's bullshit, Andre. A high school kid knows enough to set the brake. From now on, we'll keep Ralph busy, but nothing outside of the stills and cooking."

"OK, Jim, you're the boss. I just don't want Ralph to start feeling worthless around here. We need him. Ralph is my friend and I am on his side. Why didn't you ask me to deliver it?" Andre finished.

"Because I don't want you seen by anyone that could in any way connect you with the moon business. The perception of Stephens County is that Andre Cartier is a farmer and in the egg business. I want it to stay that way, Andre, and by God that's the way it's going to be!" Hutton declared, forcefully. As far as Stephens County goes, you are in the chicken business! Friend of Ralph's, or not, you are going to have to play by my rules."

"Ok, Jim, let's move on. We survived this one, and only better planning will allow us to continue. I have always agreed to your rules. What's' the plan?"

Chapter 52

"Happy birthday to you." they sang. It was Henri's fifteenth birthday. John, Clair, and Carolyn had carried a cake out after clearing the dinner table. Fifteen candles burned on top. Henri was totally surprised. He'd forgotten his own birthday.

"Happy birthday son," said Andre in harmony with Clair.

Carolyn said, "I was sure you would guess what was going on in the kitchen. I couldn't get some of the candles to light."

Henri laughed and everybody gave him hugs. Birthdays were not big deals since the Depression. Gifts were rare, unexpected, and most often home-made.

"I'm proud of you, son," Andre exclaimed. "At the rate you're growing you'll look to be twenty by spring."

Clair added, "Yes, you are starting to look older than your sister, who is older than you!

"But we all know who was first born, don't we?" Carolyn smiled. "He's my *little* brother!"

"You'd better take another look, Carolyn. I think you meant to say . . . *big* brother." Henri laughed.

They ate birthday cake and chuckled on through the evening. About an hour later, Andre said, "Ok, let me have your attention everyone. Having such a fine, strong son, it being his birthday, and the fact that I've been earning money again for the last few weeks, your little sister, your mother and I have found what we felt was the perfect birthday gift for such a handsome young man." With that he went into the next room, returning with an attractive wooden box that appeared to have been professionally made. On its cover was the word "Buck."

"You have our promise, Henri, that this item will make you attractive to girls, and envied by the boys," his father grinned.

Clair and Carolyn had not known of the gift, so were both surprised as Andre handed the box to Henri.

"What does "Buck" mean? Is there a deer, or a dollar, in here?" he asked.

"Open it and see, little brother," Carolyn laughed. She didn't know for sure either, but the box looked like it might be valuable.

Clair knew what it was, and could barely believe Andre was parting with something that had meant so much to him for so long, as a birthday gift. Then she was quietly ashamed of herself for an instant . . . *of course he would*, she thought.

Henri opened the box and lifted out the first quality hunting knife he'd ever owned. It had a polished bone handle, and a blade of about four inches inside an elegant leather sheath. It was obviously old, but had been well cared for.

"Wow!" was Henri's first word, as he began to withdraw it from the sheath.

"Be careful, it's sharp, and that metal really holds an edge," Andre said. "It was my father's - your grandfather's, Henri - and he will be very pleased to know it is now yours," he smiled.

Henri answered, "Man, Dad, thanks."

Clair wiped a tear from her eye at the expression on Andre's face. *Like father like son*, she thought.

Later that night, Clair said, "I know what that knife meant to you, Andre. You should have told me you were going to do that."

"It just seemed like the thing to do. I've always planned on him having it. I'm damn proud of him."

"I'm glad you did, Andre. I can't remember seeing him that happy. I also noticed Carolyn looking at it rather fondly. Her birthday is in February," she warned, laughing.

Later in the evening, Andre was talking to Clair. "You and I have to figure out what to tell the kids about my renting some space to that Twin City Company. I'm going to allow them to store some things here, and some deliveries and pick ups will begin pretty soon. As you and I discussed, most of them will be at night, likely in the middle of the night. I haven't really figured out how to explain that to them."

"I think it's time for some truth-telling, Andre. They'll never respect us for lying to them, and they will find out sometime. We need to respect them, Andre, with truth."

"I knew you'd say that. I just haven't figured out which truth to tell them. Their father is now a criminal by definition of the Volstead Act; he manages a high volume moonshine-still operation and if caught could end up in jail? Or I could start with the fact that our new chicken operation is all paid for by a gangster syndicate from the Twin Cities, and is a front to help hide the illegal liquor operations that will now begin taking place on the Cartier farm?" he said, shaking his head.

"Andre, I think you might be surprised at their reaction. They're part of this family. When they know the truth, they will handle it. The truth is what they need. Anything else will destroy our relationship with them."

"I know that's right, Clair. By the end of the week, we'll tell our children the truth." His thoughts went on. *I hope we know what we're doing.*

Chapter 53

Officer Needham, the Cedarville Police Officer, greeted Sheriff Maun as he came through the door to the office. "Morning, Jase. Did you hear about the raids in Somerset?"

"No, What happened?"

"The feds raided four places in downtown Somerset yesterday. Horace, at the Cedarville *Gazette*, said he got word from a relative in Somerset. They destroyed 130 gallons of booze, and arrested three people. That's the first raids or arrests over on this side of the river since last year. I hadn't heard about any action coming down, have you?"

"Not a word," the Sheriff answered. "Let's try and get some more information. I'd like to know the names of any of the Federal agents. If we can get names I can dig up more information on them. If there's going to be more raids in western Wisconsin I'd like to know about it."

Needham responded, "Bill, over at the gas station, said a month ago he was suspicious of two guys that kept driving in to gas up their cars every day. They wore fishing gear, and claimed to be trout fishermen from Chicago. He said they were friendly as hell and kept inviting him over to the saloon in the evenings wanting to buy drinks. They claimed they wanted fishing info, you know, where the big ones are and that kind of crap. But Bill didn't buy it. He said none of their fishing gear was dirty, the flies in their hats looked new, and they didn't appear to really be fishermen. The one night he let them buy him a drink, they kept asking where they could buy a jug of moon, said they were tired of fishing and wanted to party. Bill just kept telling them Somerset. He told them the only place you can't buy moon in Somerset is the church." Needham laughed. "He said after that night he never saw them again. He thought they might be scouting agents, or something like that."

"Yeh, it sounds like that could be the case" Maun added. "I would like to get more info. Why don't you see what else you can dig up? I'll do the same."

Chapter 54

Manny and Hutton were talking in Manny's office in Minneapolis. "I did a little digging for you, Jim. Those Somerset raids were instigated by a temporary-duty Chicago agent, who's been assigned to Chief Lundquist and the feds for the next year. Lundquist has assigned him to work the east side of the St. Croix River, between Somerset and the Barrens, up above St. Croix Falls. One of our guys works for Lundquist up in Stearns. Lundquist, of course, has no idea his man is connected to us. Lundquist had his agents train some new agents for this guy for two weeks in raids around Stearns. Then, last week, all four of them moved over to Wisconsin. Our guy says Lundquist doesn't want Wisconsin to flare up the way Stearns County has. That's why he's stationed them there."

"So, we better expect a little company for a while, huh?" Hutton asked.

"Yeh, you'll have to step up your stealth, but my guess is those four can only accomplish so much. I'll bet they concentrate on small stills and go for lots of raids, rather than search out the big ones." Manny continued. "Being a new team, they'll want to impress Lundquist. I can help you some. Our guy keeps us informed. We almost always know a raid is coming before the feds arrive in Stearns. Some of our guys have even been tipped off by the county-sheriff. He doesn't have much use for the feds. Our guy will stay in touch with Lundquist's agent Eggert, who trained with him in Stearns for a couple of weeks. Our man says when he gives Eggert a little info on what's happening in Stearns, Eggert empties his mind on what's going on in Wisconsin, even asks for advice on how to handle it. We knew there was some kind of a raid coming in Somerset. I didn't say anything because it didn't involve you or any of our operations. We're better off if they continue to concentrate on that area and stay out of the Barrens. We even feed tips to them now and then," he laughed. "That helps keep them down in the Somerset area."

"Ok, Manny. We're ready to start warehousing and aging moon in Cartier's new chicken coop. I want to keep inventories low at the Robinson place, just in case we are raided. Andre Cartier is developing the chicken and egg business both at his place and at the Robinson farm, which gives us something legitimate to hide behind at both places. I'm also keeping track of where other small stills are in Stephens County. Also, you should know about this. I think I've located a really big operation up in the Barrens. One man hinted about it to me, and said he'd heard it was run by Chicago people. I was asking him about that farm, you know, looking for real estate, and he said, 'stay away from there.' Nobody wants anything to do with those Chicago guys," Hutton finished.

"Keep an eye on it, Jim. We might be able to use that info later on if the Fed's agents put pressure on us. I wouldn't mind turning in Chicago competition to take heat off us," Manny grinned.

"One more thing, Manny," Hutton went on. "Even though we are transporting via the Sunrise Ferry, I'd like to keep an eye on the bridges between Stillwater and Taylors Falls. Hearing of raids in Somerset I want to know what those Revenue agents are doing. I don't have enough help right now. Have you got someone who could do that for us, and keep us posted? If I knew when the Feds were watching the bridges, that would be a good time to cross by ferry."

Yeh, I do, Jim. I'll put someone on it for the next two weeks. Just call me when you are ready to make a run. We have to coordinate our bootlegger on this side of the river anyway, so just call me a couple days before you move. We'll watch all the bridges for a couple of days before."

"Ok, Thanks, Manny. We've still got two production months before the November snows arrive. Besides shipments to you, we are going to build inventory of moon in the coops, so we can do some aging as well. The better it gets, the higher the price you can get here in the cities."

"That's right, Jim. Minnesota 13 still holds the top quality reputation and price. I want to get the quality up there so we can compete." Manny ended. "I'm hoping you'll have that for us by November."

Chapter 55

Andre and Clair planned to talk to Carolyn and Henri after dinner. They had agreed Andre should talk first. He was more concerned about the kids' reactions than Clair. She kept telling Andre he didn't realize how mature they really were and how she thought they would understand why Andre, not just Andre, what they all were now doing to keep their farm. Andre didn't realize how much he was wrestling with his own conscience, as he tried to figure out what to tell the kids.

As they were clearing the table, Andre said, "I need you all to gather round the table after dishes. We need to have a serious discussion and it affects all of us. I've got to run to the barn to shut the water off, but be ready when I get back. I want to get this over with." He quickly walked out before questions could be asked.

"What's that all about, Mom?" Carolyn asked, as Henri listened for her answer.

"Dad's not sick is he?" Henri added.

"No," Clair said, then, hesitated a few seconds looking at them both. "It's about his jobs and where he's working, but it is serious, and we will need the support of both of you. I want him to tell you about it, so just wait for your Dad. No more questions."

Carolyn and Henri looked at each other, remembering that last conversation they'd had. *Here comes more chores,* Henri thought.

Andre came back in to find the table cleared, the dishes put away and the three of them quietly seated at the table waiting. He grabbed a glass of water and sat down at the table, with it in front of him. He looked carefully at each of them for a few seconds, then cleared his throat, and began talking.

"Carolyn, you and Henri know your mother and I have been worried about money for some time. Neither your mother, nor I, or most farmers in the County expected crop prices to bottom out as they have today, and we couldn't imagine the banks ever refusing spring planting loans. It's still hard to believe, but it's real. Three months ago, we were in danger of losing this farm and home I inherited from your grandfather. When I expanded our acreage last year, I incurred more debt and got a new mortgage, not knowing I wouldn't be able to continue farming. We just couldn't believe the bank turned us down this spring."

He stopped to take a drink of water, and made eye contact around the table. "That was the first time in my life I simply did not know what to do. Your mother didn't either. He looked at Carolyn and Henri, "Molly's family lost their farm, and there's been more foreclosures since. Your mother and I knew we had to do something . . . we just didn't know what."

Andre took another drink, and looked at Clair. Her eyes and slight nod said, *you're doing fine Andre, just say it.*

"Oh God, Dad! Are we going to lose our farm?" Carolyn cried.

"No, Carolyn, we are not, but we are going to do some things to keep it that you'll find hard to believe," he went on.

Clair reached across the table to grasp Carolyn's hands, as tears wobbled on the bottoms of her eyelids. The expression on her mother's face told her, whatever was happening, would be ok.

Andre looked at Henri. "We are going to be ok, because of the new work I found. With your help, all three of you," he circled eyes again; "we are going to make it." He said "all three," because, if the kids were going to blame anyone, *he wanted it to be him, not Clair.*

"Now, let me go on, and please don't ask any questions till I finish. Henri, you and Carolyn are sworn to secrecy. What I am about to tell you, you cannot tell anyone, no one, without my permission. I can tell you no more without your agreement. I am speaking to you as adults. To know adult information, you must commit to it in an adult manner. Do I have your agreement?"

Carolyn and Henri first looked at each other, then their mother, who nodded affirmatively, then at their Dad.

"Yes," they harmonized.

Andre took a deep breath, looked at Clair, who again nodded and stared, *yes, Andre, keep going.*

"Your father is in the moonshine business," he declared, trying hard not to react to the expressions on the kid's faces. "A man offered me a job, when I was desperate for money, and I took it." Andre swallowed again, took another breath, and continued, "I first discussed it with your mother. She and I agreed it was our only option, and that we should do it. I am not going to tell you much more than that, because I don't want you to know more than that. You are safer without more knowledge of what I'm doing. I don't want you to worry; it is not dangerous, I will not be injured; I will not be arrested, or go to jail, and my work is going to keep this farm and our home. Here is the most important thing for you both to understand," he stared at Carolyn and Henri. "You must now forget that I have anything whatsoever to do with the moonshine-business. Completely block it out. Don't even talk to your mother or me about it!"

Clair quickly added, "I supported this decision kids and am in full agreement with your dad. We were about to lose our home. This is something your father and I felt we had to do, and we now need your help, too."

"Help?" Henri exclaimed, "Why'd you even tell us? Now you want us to forget about it?" he tensely queried.

"Here's why, kids," he said, as his face calmed. "We couldn't lie to you. We considered it, but only to spare you any anxiety knowing about it might cause. We just couldn't lie to you. Two days ago, we asked each other if we could keep you in the dark on all this. We both said, "no." That's why we are sitting here right now."

"We couldn't let your grandfather's farm be taken from us, or from you. Your father and I felt we had little choice. Given time to consider all this, I think you will understand." Clair finished.

"What we need you to do right now," Andre continued, "is just keep what you know a total secret. Be ignorant about it. You've never heard a word about it. There is little danger to me and my illegal activities unless it is discovered. The only way it can be discovered is if one of us says something about it. The four of us sitting here right now can't let that happen. Each of us has that responsibility to the rest."

He paused, looking a few seconds at each. "Ok, that's it. You two are now in, neck deep, with your mother and me. I want you to think about this tonight. For tonight, you can talk about it together. After tonight, you cannot. I don't have to go to work tomorrow, so I will be here all day. I want us to talk about it again in the morning. I will ask you for your commitments to secrecy again, then. One last thing . . . what I have done will keep this farm. Your mother and I have no greater loves than the two of you. That was foremost on our minds when we made this decision."

Andre stood up from the table.

"I'll take care of the barn chores tonight. You three can talk." He placed a heavy hand on each of their shoulders before walking out to chores.

Clair added, "This is something we are forced to do during these times of depression. It is not forever, it's a temporary situation. Building the chicken coops was legal work, and when we can make ends meet again without this other type of work, we will quickly go back to only farming and raising chickens," she said firmly, looking directly at Andre.

None of the three said anything for a couple of minutes. Clair immediately got busy doing something in the kitchen. Henri and Carolyn glanced at each other about every thirty seconds, with questioning expressions, but neither knew what to do right then. They didn't know if they should ask their mother anything. What they were wrestling with right now was their dad's statement, "Completely forget it. Not even talk to your mother or me about it." They weren't sure if they should remain quiet, talk, or find something else to do.

Clair said, "I know you have a lot of questions on your minds. So do I. I don't even know what your father does when he goes to work. The reason he won't talk about it is for our protection. I have a lot of questions I'd like to ask, but I don't want to give him any more to worry about. We just have to help each other through these times. It will work out. You've been a tremendous help with the chores since your dad started this work, your schoolwork is going well, and now we've got those 300 cute little peepers. Just keep going and trust your father and me. You always have, and we've never let you down. This is a temporary state of things."

She walked over to them, wrapped an arm around each, and said, "Just give it a little time and I think he will begin to share more information with each of us. He has to be sure he's not endangering us."

Chapter 56

"Ok, Andre, that's good work. Are you confident they'll keep quiet?" Hutton asked.

"Yeh, I am. I've known these guys for years. They're in the same trouble everyone else is. They've been trucking beef and pork to the cities for years, and they've all got payments for and maintenance to make on those trucks. As the price of meat has declined, they've had to lower their rates to the point they are barely making it. When I offered them a steady way to make money by not coming home empty, they couldn't stop grinning. They know they have to keep quiet, and the way I've set it up for them there's little risk." Andre finished.

"Tell me the details," Hutton questioned with his eyes.

"They tell me in advance when they are making a haul to the cities. I coordinate a load for them to pick up on the way home and give them the info. They love back-hauls, which prevent them from coming home from the cities, empty. We are going to need combined loads of sugar, yeast and containers, three or four times a week, Jim. Their return trips will all be at night. These three guys don't want to risk their trucks, so they will never go to where we cook, and won't know where it is. They will pull off the road by the old sawmill parking lot, west of town, usually after midnight. They will leave their truck there, and drive home in a car we leave. The saw mill parking lot is hidden by the old buildings, so no one can see what is parked behind them. Two of our guys pick up the truck, and based on my instructions, drive it to either the chicken coop at Robinson's and unload for storage, or straight to the cooking at Robinson's, for immediate use. They then return the truck to the parking lot. These guys can then pick up their trucks anytime after 6:00 a.m. which gives them plenty of time to coordinate Twin City bound haul-jobs the next day. We leave envelope of cash hidden in the truck for the delivery fee."

Hutton was smiling as he listened to the way Andre had set up this system. It was well thought-out. The truckers just went where they were told to go for pickups, just as truckers normally do. Then they hauled it back to the saw mill parking lot and left for home. They never saw anyone pick up their truck, had no idea where it went, or who finally received the load. The next morning they retrieved their trucks, and their cash fee, never knowing where it came from. This method kept things secret and made for happy truckers.

"So, what about paying for all the sugar, and stuff?" Hutton asked.

"I am hoping you can arrange to have that all handled by your contacts in the cities. I would like each shipment paid for before the truckers pick the stuff up. That way, the truckers can be given an invoice without a buyer's name on it, and do not have to be in any way involved with money exchange. Their responsibility is just driving the trucks, the same way they do for everything else they haul. Can you set that up for us, Jim?" Andre asked.

"Yes, I can. We did similar things over in Stearns. I'm going in to the cities tomorrow. We'll have a system of money transfer set up by the weekend."

"Great," said Andre. "This way, the only hauling to my place will be kegs of moon for storage and aging, and we can do all those at night. To keep the chicken business more visible, I'll have truckloads of chicken feed, eggs and fresh chicken deliveries done both to and from my place and Robinson's, in broad daylight. That lends us more legitimacy. If we ever find Federal Revenue Agents up here I will parade those trucks past them hoping to be stopped." Andre laughed. Deluding the law was beginning to have a *fun side* to Andre. *He was amazed at how quickly and significantly he was changing, and, it worried him.*

Chapter 57

The Monday following the Somerset raids, Sampson was handing pictures to Brown, Eggert, and Eastman. "Do you see how these pictures look like everything was destroyed? We will use some of these photos for news releases to some newspapers. Seeing you guys swing those fire axes on moon kegs scares hell out of people. When they are scared of us we get more cooperation, more tips, and we find more stills. Make sure you get photos like this at every raid. Also swing those axes at the stills. Hole every copper kettle, break the worms, and if there are empty kegs and crocks, bust them up too. Each of you has been issued a camera, good Leica Model Ds, with automatic focusing. I want them used. Newspapers love photos."

"Where did the moon we hauled away in the truck go?" Eastman asked.

"I have set up a warehouse down by Hudson, where we'll put evidence temporarily. Later, it goes to the main Revenue building in Minnesota, the one the Stearns County boys use. Now, the word is out, men. *The feds are here!* These raids will trigger action. I expect people to be trying to move their moon, so they don't get caught with it, should they be raided. All this week I want us to haunt the bridges, and I mean haunt, around-the-clock surveillance is what we need. Eastman, you take Stillwater, Eggert, you take Osceola, and Brown, Taylors Falls. Take notes, take photos, and pay attention. We had this down to a science in Chicago, and that's how we earned such a high arrest record. We are looking for big, high horsepower expensive cars. The kind modified to carry 100 gallons or better, the kind with the big engines that can outrun Revenue Agents. This week, we are not going to be making stops or arrests. We're just taking inventory. Look for the same cars crossing back and forth, keep records so you recognize repeat or suspicious behavior. There are gas stations near each bridge. Keep track of whether those cars gas up or not, and if they do, is it when heading east or west across the bridge. Bootleggers normally don't stop when full, only when empty. This detailed surveillance will help us figure out what's going on with deliveries. You can hire a helper to watch the bridges, so you can follow suspects through town. You've each got $2 a day cash for help. I want each of you to check in with me via phone twice a day. Those gas stations have phones you can pay to use. While you three are on the bridges, I will be doing some work in the Minneapolis office." He was actually thinking *of making a matching welt on his paid girlfriend's other cheek. She didn't seem to mind the rough stuff last week.* "You can call me there. If you can't reach me I'll call each of you in the evening between 7:00 and 8:00 p.m. all week."

Being new agents, all three were anxious to get on with this next assignment. All had been inspired by the first raids they'd done on their own. Each had behaved like their Stearns County trainers, and added some of the attitude Sampson had demanded of them. They felt accomplished, and wanted to feel it again.

Chapter 58

Clair brought a platter of pancakes and joined the family at the breakfast table.

All could tell Andre was about to say something, but before he could, Carolyn and Henri nodded at each other and said in unison, "We're in Dad."

Andre looked surprised, glanced at Clair, who was smiling, and said, "That's it? You're in? No questions?"

"We don't want to discuss it. We have no questions. We've forgotten it," Henri said with a stern face. We think you should have told us sooner, though." Then, he went quiet.

He and Carolyn had agreed the night before to make Henri the spokesman. They had talked for a couple of hours into the night. They realized what problems had driven their mom and dad into such drastic action. Carolyn's last comment before going to bed was, "Well, it's just like the last time we talked, Henri. We'll figure out ways to help."

Andre said, "Well, ok then, let's eat. I'll provide more information when I can. Thank you," he finished, reaching for the platter.

"Carolyn, didn't you have some questions for your dad about the peepers?" Clair asked.

"Yes, I do. I think everything is ok, but will you come down to the new coop with me this morning. Those little peeper heaters we light are working ok, so they don't seem to be cold at night. They have plenty of food and water, so it's hard to know if anything is wrong. All they do is peep all day long. But, this morning, there were two dead chicks on the floor. I don't know why, so maybe you'll know," she finished.

"Ok, right after breakfast," Andre responded.

Henri added, "I need some help too, Dad. Last week, I fixed that old gate out in the pasture, but that one dumb-as-a-bale, rambunctious critter tore it half apart again yesterday. I don't know why it is so damn important for him to get into that other pasture, but I need help fixing it."

"Ok, as soon as Carolyn and I are finished, we'll go out there and take a look. I'm sure glad you two are off school for summer vacation. We'd never have kept up with all this. We'll spend part of this afternoon working out schedules so we can keep up with things when school starts again in a month."

Clair gave Andre one of those, "see? . . . everything will be all right," smiles, and passed the bacon.

Later, as the kids cleared the table, Clair slipped an arm around Andre's waist

and walked with him out into the early morning sun. They both exhaled in relief.
"That went even better than I anticipated, Andre."
"Thank God," Andre said. "Now, we just have to make it all work."

Chapter 59

"I don't know why it's so hard to find out anything about those Revenue Agents in Somerset, Sheriff," the local lawman said. "I called the Chief of Police there, and he said he didn't know who they were. They are out of the Minneapolis Revenue office, but on the arrest papers they left with the chief down there, there are no officer names, only numbers."

Sheriff Maun was automatically curious about raids happening near his territory. Specifically, he wondered *if there would soon be raids in Stephens County and, why numbers instead of officer's names on the arrest records?*

"They said there were four arrests in four raids; one was the man at the house where they destroyed 100 gallons of moon that was in his basement, I guess. There were two other raids where they tore apart stills that weren't in use, and each was charged with possession, but each was small. The last one turned out to be illegal Canadian booze in a guy's house," the town constable finished.

Councilman Teggart entered the office door. "You got a few minutes, Sheriff?"

"Sure, Councilman, what's on your mind?" he answered.

"Officer, will you give the Sheriff and me the office for a few minutes for some official business?"

The town cop nodded and left the room, as Teggart closed the door. Maun was alerted and curious. No one ever closed the door.

"Sheriff, Anderson's bank officer, Corbit, who handles the bank's foreclosures, complained to us during last night's council meeting, about the way you handled the last foreclosure you served a few weeks ago."

"What was wrong?" Maun asked as the hair on the back of his neck rose.

"He said you made the bank look bad by apologizing to the evictee for serving papers on him. He thought you were not performing your duty. He said you even asked him, in front of the man and the family you were serving, if the bank couldn't give them more time. He feels you were involving yourself in something that was none of your business, and suggested you be disciplined for unprofessional behavior and put on notice that such behavior will not be tolerated."

Maun took a deep breath, took his hat off, and threw it on his desk.

"That man was lucky he got out of there without getting beat up, Councilman. He was brutal to that family. The guy's wife was crying on the front steps, his kids were hiding in the kitchen, probably hunting food. They looked like they were starving, for God's sake! Sure, I asked him if they couldn't give them another month to find a place to go. They hadn't been told they were going to be kicked out of their house *that day!* They just knew they had mortgage problems. Hell, I drove back out there with some groceries that night. Does he want to discipline me for that too?"

Maun was mad, and about to get more so.

"Sheriff, I know you've got your side of the story, but we can't ignore this. He complained in an open meeting," Teggart went on.

"He probably complained at the meeting because he knows it will appear in the paper and make me look bad. He could have privately talked to any Council member. You want my opinion, Councilman? The man's an asshole! And you can tell him that's my professional opinion. I don't give a damn if you fire me. The man's an asshole. I know I'm a little out of line here, but if you'd been there . . . ," he ended, shaking his head.

Councilman Teggart took a coffee cup from the stack beside the water container on the end table, filled it, and quietly set it down in front of the Sheriff.

"Look, Sheriff, no one wants to fire you. We like you, your work, and your professional behavior. Be that as it may, we still have to address complaints stated in a council meeting. Let's start over. We have this complaint to deal with. How can you help us?" Teggart ended his question with a smile that calmed Jason. Jason drank the water and set the cup gently down on the desk.

"This has been on my mind for weeks, Councilman. My wife and I hardly have a meal without this topic coming up. She's sick of hearing about it. Yesterday, she said I should quit bitching about it, and do something. So, I did. I looked at my contract, which says nothing about serving foreclosure papers. I would appreciate it if you would show me where it is written in the law, or who it is, that says serving foreclosure papers is part of the Sheriff's duties? I also inquired of a few other Sheriffs in Wisconsin, and every one of them told me, that was a U.S. Marshal's task. It was my error that I got sucked into serving those papers last month, because I should have known that was a marshal's job. Not knowing, I was trying to help and I was wrong in doing that. I herewith refuse to be involved in any more serving of papers. I'll tell the council myself if you want me to."

"I didn't know that myself, Sheriff, but I will quickly verify it for all concerned, including the bank. The bank came to us and asked for your help. I will find out what they know about marshals serving papers. In the mean time, just remember it was us, the council, that asked you to go out there with the bank. Don't worry too much about this, Sheriff. The reason I wanted to talk to you alone was so I could tell you, I think Anderson's man is an asshole too," he laughed, as he slapped Jason on the back.

Jason Maun let his appreciation of that remark be seen with a smile and a shake of his head. "Sorry I went off on you, Councilman. That serving was one of the most difficult things I've ever done. I was ashamed to be there. I still am. There has to be a better way."

"Ok, Jason, let me see what I can dig up. And, don't worry about the paper. I think you are right about the U.S. Marshall's duties. We were told by the bank that no marshalls were available and that's why they asked for help from the Council. No one in the County would agree with Anderson's man's evaluation . . . well, maybe Anderson," he grinned, then added, "If anything shows up in the paper I will personally be sure something else shows up that corrects it, and defends your position," as he walked out the door.

Thinking of his wife's last statement that morning, Maun thought, *well, I did something.*

Chapter 60

Andre hired three additional people to be cookers and laborers in the Robinson operation. They were all old friends, and desperate for work. Each signed on with less trepidation than Andre had exhibited when Hutton first talked to him. The first was John Raft, father of Mollie and Dan, Henri and Carolyn's friends. John and the family had lived with his brother since losing their farm. His brother was Cartier's nearest neighbor on the north side of the Cartier farm. Andre went over there and talked at length with John. He wanted to be sure he wasn't making a mistake.

"This can be a good opportunity for you, John, but it's demanding. There is considerable night work, and everything is done in secrecy. I'm managing the Robinson farm for the real estate agency, and they will rent you that house inexpensively, even let you do some farming by renting the land on a percentage."

"I want it, Andre," he said almost pleadingly. "I've got to do something. My brother has been good to us, letting us live here for this month, but it can't continue. We couldn't get along as kids and we aren't doing much better now. It's too hard on everybody. I want the job, and I'll rent the house if I can work off the rent. I'm willing to work the farm any way they want. I need this!"

"Can I be sure you won't be drinking, John? I heard you had a few bad nights after you lost the farm." Andre asked.

"I did. You can't believe what losing your life's work and home does to you, Andre. But, I've got a rope around it. I promise you no problems, and you won't believe how hard I'll work to get a new start. I've got to take care of my family, just like you, Andre," he implored. "Hire me. You won't see a drop of booze and won't believe how hard I will work."

"Ok, John. We'll talk tomorrow. I'll tell you how to explain it all to your family. For now, just tell them you may be able to get a job with the new chicken operation I'm managing." Andre finished with a handshake, and left the burden of responsibility in John Raft's mind with an intent and prolonged stare as he shook his committed hand.

Andre hired another man he'd known in school. Pete Johnson was single, and had been a mechanic most of his adult life, but wasn't getting enough business now to sustain him. He needed some part-time work. Andre knew Pete could be trusted, and was savvy enough to keep that work secret. Ralph found the third man and he and Andre both talked to him. Andre asked him some questions, then said, "You're foreman now, Ralph. Go ahead and hire him. I'll talk to all three of them with you about our rules of secrecy."

Now, three weeks later, the operation was in full swing, producing nearly 1000 gallons a week of twice-cooked moon. That meant 100 ten-gallon kegs a week had to be either transported to the cities, or stored for aging. They wanted to build up inventory in the chicken coops, both for aging, and to have readily available product for delivery in the winter when the stills would be shut down. The back-roads of the Barrens were not plowed in the winter. Consequently, trucking of sugar and other ingredients, in quantities large enough to accommodate 1000 gallon per week, was impossible. Because of that they would produce, ship and store all the moon they could before November.

Moving 100 ten-gallon kegs of illegal booze each week became more difficult once the chicken coop at the Robinson place became full. They had to invent ways to disguise or hide the kegs, even though they moved them only at night. Hutton's experience in Stearns County exposed him to some very clever stealth maneuvers by bootleggers who had enjoyed long-term success in evading feds. There seemed endless ways of disguising bootlegger's cars to carry hidden booze. Moving hundreds of ten-gallon kegs, however, was more challenging. Hutton picked Manny's brains, and asked him to do the same with those he knew in Stearns who were shipping large quantities of kegs. Their digging turned up kegs flown in airplanes to the Dakotas where they would then be driven south within large truckloads of grain. Kegs were shipped in every imaginable type of truck and cargo. Manny spoke of one piano company that would ship several pianos a week, completely boxed, to disguise that there was nothing but kegs of moonshine within the boxes. None of them could believe the variety of methods used to ship booze. It was Andre who came up with their most used method of shipping kegs from Robinson's to Andre's hen house basement. Andre and Ralph built a box about four feet wide and the length of the stake-bed platform on his Model A truck. They could get a single layer of 12 kegs within that box and still close the door. Around that box, they would then pile fifty-pound bags of chicken feed as high as the box, and then across its top, to make it appear to be a full truck of chicken feed. When they felt they might appear to be hauling too much chicken feed, or perhaps, too often, they would switch to hay bales around and over the box. Sometimes Andre would leave room near the tail gate end of the truck bed to accommodate six forty-eight-dozen egg cartons for delivery to stores selling Cartier eggs. It worked well, but even with those strategies, they seldom hauled kegs other than at night. Andre's mantra had become, *always err on the side of caution*.

Hauling sugar was a bigger problem than hauling booze. To maintain their production rate of 1000 gallons a week, they had to bring in thousands of pounds of sugar and hundreds of blocks of yeast, and both had to come from the Twin Cities. Corn seed for sprouts was easy, because it could be found locally from many farmers. As the business grew, Andre used the same livestock truckers he started with. He paid his truckers a fee to buy corn in bags from the farmers they were hauling cattle for. Farmers were shipping less livestock to the cities at this time, so occasionally; he had to pay extra to get a trucker to deadhead into the cities, but they would return full of the products Hutton bought that Andre needed. The cattle business was way down, but they still went in occasionally with a load of cows. They'd use the slaughter-house's hose to swab out the truck. When mopped dry, they were clean enough to carry sugar. There were two occasions when sugar bags covered with manure on their bottom side were delivered. Following a quick discussion in which Andre refused both deliveries, only clean deliveries were ever left in the old saw mill parking lot.

Containers were one of the hardest items to have delivered. Kegs came from St. Cloud coopers, who, because of the Stearns County demand, operated some of the best cooperages in the state. A full truckload of ten-gallon kegs was difficult to drive down the highway unnoticed. Consequently, the cooperage had one truck with a full canvas cover on which an advertisement was sewn, boldly saying "Ma's Pickles." If challenged by a Revenue Agent the trucker always had a bill of lading addressed to some pickle processor. St. Cloud was just two hours from the Robinson place, but the trucks were too big to come across on the St. Croix on a ferry. Consequently, Andre demanded all deliveries between midnight and 4:00 a.m. and was willing to pay extra for the service. It was Hutton who finally arranged with Manny, that all kegs delivered to the syndicate, whose content was bottled in the Twin Cities before being delivered to their speakeasies, be returned to Andre via a variety of unrecognizable delivery trucks whenever possible. Manny was a wizard.

Chapter 61

It was Sampson himself who picked up the evidence truck in Stillwater and delivered it to another old warehouse in Minneapolis, where it could be unloaded inside and out of sight. No one but Bob Sampson knew where evidence was stored. After unloading, he returned the truck to the place he'd rented it. The other truck was returned the day before by the driver. Sampson's plan was to continue to accrue evidence in that warehouse until he could secretly arrange to sell the contraband moon to some distribution outlet. He hadn't yet learned who was in charge of the Minneapolis syndicates, but was working on it. He wanted to carefully make this connection, but keep himself invisible and seemingly uninvolved in the transactions. He had learned in Chicago that being known to well by the syndicates could be unhealthy.

It took him all morning to unload the truck by himself, but he didn't mind. With each keg, croc, or bottle he envisioned *how he would eventually spend their value on women, other things he wanted, or his retirement.* He knew each new haul of evidence added to what he had already accrued in Chicago and what he intended to gain from Wisconsin's Barrens in the coming months. Now that he had had the opportunity to meet Lundquist, he was fairly certain he would be able to talk him into asking O'Hara to let him hang onto Sampson longer than the one-year period they initially agreed upon. Sampson knew O'Hara didn't want him back in Chicago. He felt Lundquist would be able to talk O'Hara into whatever Sampson convinced him was necessary to accomplish the Barren's task. Sampson was again *pleased with himself for the way he had, so far, manipulated this assignment.*

The only part of his new surroundings he didn't like was the lack of available women he was used to in Chicago. He had the Lucile he had met his first weekend in Minneapolis, but had already worn out his welcome with her. The last two times he had called her she managed to be *unavailable.* He needed to fix that.

Chapter 62

Andre pulled his pickup up to the chicken coop door about 1:00 a.m. He slid the pallets of chicken feed bags into the feed storage room of the upper level away from the wall. He swept off the floor, and lifted the floor-door covering the ramp. Beneath them the sloping ramp descended into the basement over the length of the door's opening, which allowed a gradual enough grade to wheel kegs up or down the ramp on a dolly without hitting your head on the floor's edge as you passed beneath it. The door's floor hinges were about six inches out from the wall, so when open, the doors just leaned against the wall. This was the tenth delivery by pickup he had made in the last three weeks. After tonight's delivery, they would have 240 ten-gallon kegs of moon stored in the chicken coop's hidden basement.

No one in the operation knew where these kegs were stored but Andre and Hutton. When he finished carting tonight's twenty kegs down the ramp he closed the floor-door and slid the pallets of chicken feed bags back over the door. The door was narrower than the pallets, so the pallet ends stuck out beyond the edges of the door itself. He then swept the dust, dirt, and chicken feed back over the floor around the pallets so it looked natural, leaving no evidence of the pallets having been moved.

So far, he had been lucky. With all of the time Carolyn, Henri, and Clair, and even some of their friends had spent in the coop playing with the peepers, not one had even a clue the basement even existed. That's the way Andre wanted to keep it as long as possible.

Using that space this way they were accomplishing two things. They were building inventory that would allow them to supply demand during the winter, and they were aging and flavoring their moonshine. Each keg stored below the chicken coop's floor had a charred interior and a measured amount of oak wood chips which, combined with the passing of time and weekly turning of the kegs, which was accomplished most often in the middle of the night, flavored the moon. According to Hutton, this was one of the claimed secrets to the dominance of Minnesota 13 in the quality contest. The more their basement storage aged, the more valuable it became. Andre and Hutton had not yet come up with a method of adding heat to the storage area.

Andre was using the Robinson chicken coop basement to also store sugar, yeast, and containers when needed. That method protected them against the possibility of a raid at Robinson's. Should that occur, they would only lose what they were cooking, and what was about to be used in the next mash mix. They would lose no finished moon, and only the ingredients and empty containers in the building at the time of the raid. Even if raided, they did not expect the chicken coop basement to be discovered. With no moon to be found, arrest was unlikely.

Using Hutton as his coach, Andre was running the Robinson stills with Ralph now the operations foreman. They, and their new help, had the operation running like a Swiss watch. They had only two months of maximized production left before they shut down for winter.

Chapter 63

Carolyn walked out of the grocery store in Cedarville, carrying an empty forty-eight dozen egg carton she had just emptied onto the egg shelves of the store. She walked back to Andre's pickup, placing the box into the back of the truck. Parked across the street, and sitting behind the wheel of the unmarked car, was Robert Sampson, Federal Revenue Agent from Chicago. He had been watching Carolyn since she pulled up to the store, alone. Carolyn had been driving for two years, and looked to Sampson to be, at least eighteen. He had been scrutinizing the community, trying to get an idea of whether or not there was any kind of moonshine activity in this little town. When Carolyn pulled up and began carrying boxes from the pickup, Sampson had completely lost his train of thought. She reminded him of another young girl he knew in Chicago.

Now, there is something I'd like to get tangled up with, he thought. He stared at her, remembering an incident outside of Chicago last year. After discovering her father's still and moonshine on his farm outside of Chicago, he also discovered his daughter. She was attractive, about nineteen years old and something he decided he wanted. Without ever confronting her father, he arranged to bump into her when she was in a nearby town. Sampson knew how to set things up. When she came out of the store he had watched her enter, she saw a man down on one knee, pushing his fingers into her front tire. As she got near the car, he looked up at her, then said, "Miss, is this your car? You have nearly a flat tire here." He had let some air out of the tire's valve stem as she shopped inside the store.

"Yes it is," she responded.

Sampson smiled, then said, "You won't get to wherever you're going with this tire. You need air."

"Where can I get that?" she asked. She had watched her father add air to the tires more than once, but had never inflated a tire herself.

Thinking, *I didn't know she'd be coming out that soon. I barely got the valve cap back on,* Sampson pointed at the gas station across the street. "You can get air right over there at that gas station. Why don't you let me help you? It will just take two minutes."

Acting as though she didn't have a clue of how to put air into the tire, she responded, "Thank you, I'd appreciate that."

"I'll walk across," Sampson smiled, "Just pull up to where I point, so the air hose will reach," he finished as he began to walk across the street.

He filled up her tire and they chatted for a minute. He told her he was in the vicinity looking for a place to rent. He was going to be doing some work for a farm insurance company in the region. Then, he asked her if she knew of any places that might be for rent. She didn't, but after a few more minutes of conversation, and hearing Sampson say his car was being worked on, she offered to drop him off at a real estate office nearby. Those fifteen minutes together was all it took for him to learn how to contact her, and he promised to do that after he got settled in. Within two weeks, Sampson had befriended this young lady enough to arrange to be alone with her on more than one occasion.

Though she initially resisted his advances, which she didn't altogether dislike, Sampson played his trump card leveraging her cooperation. He let her know who he really was, a revenue-fed, and that he knew of her father's moonshine activities. Then, he announced that the only way she could keep her dad from being arrested, jailed, and sentenced to prison was to be friendlier, with Sampson. She was not the brightest young woman, but not the dumbest either, and more than attractive enough to stimulate Sampson's lust. In the end, after Sampson eased her into a courtship before making demands she acquiesced and didn't entirely regret it. She tangled with Sampson for over a month. During that month, she kept him happy, her father from being raided and jailed and kept herself happy spending Sampson's money. She actually enjoyed their interludes, sometimes. That is, until Sampson began to get rough. Once started, he couldn't seem to enjoy their couplings unless he got a little rougher each time. She soon became accomplished at covering welts on her cheeks with makeup. When, at the end of that month, she heard about his assignment causing him to move to Minneapolis, she was greatly relieved." Now, knowing Sampson needed to declare his dominance more forcefully each time they were together, she was glad to see him go.

Watching Carolyn caused Sampson to think of *that month of control he had exercised so well. It's been a long dry spell. I need to work something out with someone up here.* He'd been so focused on Carolyn he'd not noticed the man walk up to the passenger side of his car until that man said, "Can I help you with something, you look like you are lost."

Sampson was totally caught off guard when he found himself looking into eyes beneath the brim of a hat with the word, SHERIFF, on it.

"Hello, Sheriff," he smiled. "I was trying to decide if I was going to go into that store to find something for lunch, or find a restaurant in town. I'm from out of town, so don't know my way around," he finished, wondering, *did he buy that?*

Jason Maun said, "I could tell you were trying to figure something out. There's a restaurant just a block down that way I'd recommend. What brings you to Cedarville?"

"A friend and I did some trout fishing here last spring. I'll be up here doing some insurance work for the next month, so I thought I'd try to get some more info today on where the big trout are."

Maun thought, *I wonder if this is one of the guys that made Bill suspicious,* then looked up when Carolyn shouted, "Hey Sheriff, need any eggs?," with the same big smile she always had for Jason.

"Well, thanks for the information. You've found someone prettier than me to talk to. I'll try your restaurant," Sampson finished.

Maun went across the street with a wide grin, gave Carolyn a hug, and said, "I can't take eggs from you and your dad every time you come to town, but I know somebody who could use a few."

"Dad said we always have a few extra eggs for the Sheriff," she said, "And they are always, no charge. I've still got six-dozen in the truck. They're yours," Carolyn smiled. "Who was that man?"

"He says he's a trout fisherman," Jason answered.

"He sure knows how to stare at girls," she finished.

He nodded slowly, as he turned to take another look at the guy pulling away down the street. "If you see him staring again, you let me know, Carolyn. These eggs are going to that same family I gave the last ones to. That man still hasn't found work and they're hurting. Thanks, Carolyn, and tell your dad too."

Jason took the eggs and walked on back towards his office, *noticing the guy's car was not parked by the restaurant.*

Chapter 64

Judge Adler was a Federal Judge living in Madison, Wisconsin. He carried a substantial workload year round and much of his time, since the passing of Prohibition, was used listening to prosecuting attorneys in Federal Revenue cases involving moonshine violations. Many times a month, Adler would judge cases against those found cooking moon, bootlegging moon, selling moon and in other ways trying to profit from its existence.

The intensity of his days in court would often result in the Judge coming home from a day's work wishing he had a tall, cool refreshment of some nature that would medicate his stress load. He had a cultivated taste for moonshine, which was quite contrary to his court-dictated role of stamping out the availability of the most important ingredient of his tall, cool, day-enders.

Because of his position with the court, Judge Adler had to be careful to keep his visible public responsibilities separate from his private tastes and behavior, not unlike so many others who occupied government jobs demanding perfection in their public behavior, but living their private lives as they wished. It was the typical, "do as I say, not as I do," role sometimes needed by public officials who wish a portion of their lives to be real.

For two years he had had an arrangement with a local auto dealership which enabled his cocktail hour to exist. Once a month, he would deliver his car to the garage for an oil change and would leave a twenty-dollar bill in the glove compartment. In the evening, when he returned home with fresh oil in the car's engine, the glove compartment would be empty, but in the car's trunk would be four quarts of quality moonshine. Nothing was ever said except, "Good Morning" between himself and the dealer, but every two years he bought his new car at the same place.

Part IV

A New Harvest Crop

Chapter 65

John Raft, Pete Sanderson, and Mike Sivard had all worked for Ralph and Andre for the last two weeks. They actually liked their work, and best of all, being paid. Doing cooking and labor they were all being paid $15 per day or night worked. Andre and Ralph had agreed to raise them to $20 after their first month. That's why they were happy. They were making big money. The average farm worker, or "hired man," averaged less than $300 per year after the crash of '29; the average non-farm worker averaged around $800 in a year, if, they could find a job. If the three new workers' current pay lasted all year they'd earn over $5000, but that would not be the case. Andre and Ralph had made it clear that they could not keep them busy during the winter when the stills were quiet, but would likely hire them back in April. Still, they were making more than anyone else they knew, and were grateful. The biggest bonus was that there were no records of these payments, and there would, consequently, be no taxes.

Andre wrestled with his conscience daily over what he was doing. Knowing every hour of work outside of that spent with farming and chickens, was illegal bothered him a lot. He rationalized it; he could do it, but couldn't stop the little voice within from reminding him he was breaking the law. When it would begin to get to him he would think *I have to learn to live with this*. With that thought he could get the required work of the day done, but the concerns would always pop up again.

When Clair asked him how they handled their taxes with this arrangement, he realized he had not even thought about that. They could only pay taxes on farming and chicken income without being discovered. Andre had always paid taxes; hell, he was proud to pay taxes which made him unique among many. He had always wanted to do his share no matter the task. Paying your share of taxes meant to him he was earning a living and doing his share as a citizen. After this fact dawned on him he wrestled with tax-thoughts all week. He was angry about the depression and the way the government seemed to be handling it, yet still wanted to do his share. He also felt if his taxes changed much that would also make the tax people suspicious of him.

After supper one night, he said to Clair, "I've got something I want you to think about. You already know how I feel about doing illegal work. But there's another issue. Taxes. We've always calculated and paid our taxes. Now, because of what we are doing we can't pay our normal taxes without our illegal income being discovered. I think we should continue to pay our normal taxes as we always have, adding our new earnings from the expanded chicken business. That should make no one suspicious. Now that we are getting financially back on our feet, Clair, I'd like us to give a little money to other out-of-work families that are hurting. I know of a few, as do you." Andre looked at Clair, then, added, "It will make me feel less guilty and it will sure help some others who haven't been as fortunate. I know we are taking great risk that they aren't, but I still think we should try and help. What do you think?

"They are good thoughts, Andre." I feel guilty all of the time, too. I don't know if it will help that, but it always helps me to help others if I can. No one can know about it, though, Andre. How do we handle that?"

"We are not talking about a lot of money, so I think we can give it through the mail. We have to be certain no one will ever know ever know it came from us. If any one finds out it's from us we'll be found out and I could end up in jail. Here's how we'll do it. When we agree on a donation, we will just put ten or twenty dollars into an envelope and mail it from a post office box in the Twin Cities."

The discussion went on for a while, its content, easing their anxiety and concern because of secrets they each held. It made them feel better. Having the discussion, even if they never did anything about it, eased their guilt.

Chapter 66

The work load for Andre and Ralph was increasing dramatically. Even though the bank had refused their spring planting loans, they still had their hay crops to harvest and store to feed their livestock through the winter. Haying took considerable time because they both harvested loose hay and stored it loose in their hay mows. Though balers were now in use, neither of them were yet into hay bales. Baling would have required one of them to either, buy, rent, or borrow a hay baler, which was costly. Because of the current economic situation, both had decided to stay with loose hay methods. Andre and Ralph had teamed up for years for the haying, each helping the other to cut, load, haul, and store their hay in their barn's lofts. Now, with the demands of the Robinson operation, since it wasn't possible for them to both be away from the cooking and storing of moon, at the same time, they were each back to haying on their own.

Andre actually had enough seed corn left over from the prior year to plant his corn crop, which required occasional cultivating throughout the growth time before harvest. Cartier's still had their beef and dairy cows, only a dozen beef, and four dairy, but they all took time to milk and to care for. They still had six pigs. Their livestock had remained about the same size as during the last three years, except for the chickens.

Even with the 300 peepers, the chickens were not taking much more time. Carolyn handled all of the eggs from those laying, and insisted on taking over all the duties of the new 300. It took her another two hours each day to feed and water the peepers, and to fuel the small chick heaters they lit at night for warmth when needed. Henri and Carolyn were able to keep up with Andre's absence now, but Andre knew it would become more of a problem when school started in September. Schools accommodated the agricultural calendar for farm families needing labor during harvest. Carolyn and Henri would both have some flexibility in September and October.

Calculating all that, Andre felt they'd be able to keep up, because the stills would shut down in November. The usual snow storms and unplowed roads would all but eliminate moon trafficking from the locations selected for their terrain's secrecy.

Chapter 67

Sampson and his men were scrutinizing their notes after a week of watching the bridges. They had each followed through on their duties, watching the flow of traffic day and night for a week. Two of them had hired helpers to get almost twenty-four hour periods covered each day. Eastman tried to do it alone, claiming he slept only about four hours a day.

Eastman was saying, "By the third day I began to recognize some cars regularly, but by the fifth day I realized they were likely commuters who worked somewhere between Taylors Falls and the Twin Cities."

Eggert added, "Yeh, I found the same thing, but I've noted about a dozen cars, all big, expensive-looking roadsters, that sound like they have big engines, crossing in both directions and mostly after dark. The other thing I noticed is that they only seem to gas up when they are heading east. Westbound, they never stop. The other thing I noticed is that most of the drivers wore suits."

When Sampson nodded at him, Brown added, "My experience was similar. There must be a ton of commuters, because I saw the same cars morning and night, but, it changes at night. There were several cars I'd like to stop and go through. Several came over the Stillwater bridge, that were always together, in other words, the same two cars with the same one always in front of the other and they never stopped either way. They looked suspicious. The one in back always seemed to look extra heavy, but there was no one in the back seat." And those two cars looked expensive. The drivers were in suits too, if that means anything."

"Ok," said Sampson, "You guys are starting to get the feel of picking out bootleggers. That's good. The next time we do it we will be a team of four, so we can stop cars in each direction if we want to. Bootleggers can be dangerous. More than once in Chicago, we were shot at with machine guns and pistols, and the cars those suits drive go like hell. If they choose to run away from you, they can. They have much bigger engines than what we drive. That's the advantage of setting up road traps at bridges. But, road traps are messy, because you stop so much traffic. Dangerous, too. You're more apt to get hit if shot at from close range. Another man and I once had our windshield shot out with machine gun fire, then we thought they'd run out of bullets because they stopped firing. We were still chasing them when both our front tires went flat. After we stopped, we discovered shingle nails all over the highway. They were dumping a keg of shingle nails out the back of their car onto the highway! I don't think you have that kind of bootleggers up here, but Chief Lundquist says there have been some real shootouts between Revenue Agents and bootleggers over in Stearns."

They went on through the morning reviewing and discussing what the week's traffic patterns had taught them. All agreed that the most suspicious cars crossed the Stillwater Bridge. The further north of the bridge, the less suspicious traffic there was. That discovery fortified their notion of Somerset being the epicenter of moon activities connected to the Twin Cities. Stillwater was also the only bridge where they spotted these two-car teams crossing the bridge at night. Sampson pointed out that, before they began stopping cars, he wanted to station the men secretively in the parking lots of some of the famous Wisconsin road houses throughout the nights watching for deliveries. "They're all selling it," Sampson said. "We have to figure out how they're getting it."

Chapter 68

"We've had several cars drive over the front end," the Barnes girl laughed, as she spoke to Hutton. "They just forget to put the brakes on. That's why we have those logging chains across the front now. That stops them, because they don't want to scratch the front ends of their cars on the chain."

Hutton laughed. He was driving a new Oldsmobile sedan from Manny's brother's Olds dealership in Minneapolis. "Well, I didn't want to scratch this one either," he said. "I crossed at Stillwater last week, and the guy there said I looked like a rum-runner, no, a bootlegger he said," laughing, "I just deliver cars between Chicago and the Twin Cities, but I don't want to be stopped by Federal agents, so I came back up here to cross."

The Barnes girl responded, "Yeh, I think you're safer up here. We've never seen an agent that we could identify. But I talked to the Marine ferry driver Sunday, and he said he was sure there was an agent watching them last week. He said they parked and sat in their car just off the ferry driveway, for one whole night and part of the next day. Then, they just drove off."

Hutton thought it was interesting to watch her drive the ferry. A cable about twenty-feet long was attached to the middle of the hull of the ferry. It ran up at a forty-five degree angle and attached to a big pulley wheel that rolled along the big cable crossing the river from shore to shore, about twenty-five feet above the water. As the ferry crossed, the short cable and pulley-wheel rolling along the big cable, kept the ferry from drifting downstream. He asked her why she ruddered the stern at an angle, making the bow of the ferry point upstream.

"That way, the river's downstream current helps push the ferry across the river. It's like sailing a boat. The current just straight, flat, against the side would make it harder to cross, but at this angle the current pushes us. Nobody gets it at first," she added, "But after a few trips it starts to make sense," she grinned.

Hutton had been in talking to Manny, his usual monthly update, and wanted to check out the Sunrise Ferry again. "I heard some guy rolled his car down into the river a few weeks ago. Was that here?" he asked.

"Yup, on the Wisconsin side," she grinned again. "He forgot to set the brake up on the hill there, when he came down to talk to me. The car damn near ran over us both. We pulled it out of the river the next morning with our team of horses. No damage to the car, and lucky not the ferry either. It was late at night so it didn't affect our traffic."

"What was he hauling in the middle of the night?" Hutton purposefully asked.

"I don't think he was hauling anything," she responded, with a straight face, "Just crossing I think."

That was exactly the answer Hutton wanted to hear. As he drove off the ferry, he dropped a dollar in her hand and then, another, as he smiled and said, "See you next trip."

Chapter 69

Hutton, Andre, Ralph and the other three workers were all sitting in the Robinson operation. Hutton had asked Andre to set up the meeting for first thing in the morning, He wanted to review some things all had to understand to remain part of the operation.

"It is absolutely essential that each of us follow these rules, men. It will take only one slip up to undo what we've accomplished. So let's look at them again. None of us ever take any moon home. We want no small containers ever leaving the premises in your vehicles. We never sell any moon to anyone. We have no moon to sell. If any of us ever want moonshine, we buy it from another operation. Ralph knows of other smaller stills that sell small quantities, and where you can pick it up. I would prefer that each of you buy a small amount of moon from one of them. That way, if you are ever arrested you can say, where you bought it. You can never even know about this place if questioned. Now, any questions about any of this?" Hutton finished.

"Everyone understands, Jim, we've been over it several times, and we all understand the need for cover. My wife and I almost took it to extremes last week. At the urging of her mother, my wife almost joined the Cedarville WCTU group. On top of that," Andre smiled, "I don't even drink."

"Ralph, where do you go now, to buy moon, in Cedarville?" Hutton asked.

"Frankly, I'm not real sure. I haven't bought any for some time. I do know of some other stills because I quietly deliver gas to some of them for Bill. Let me check it out this week and I'll give you a couple of places," he finished. "Bill told me he thought he'd seen a Revenue Agent in town in the last month. They claimed to be trout fishermen. He said at first he didn't believe them, then, the next time they came in for gas, they showed him a creel full of brook trout. Bill likes to talk, so everyone may have tightened up a bit on selling. I'll find out."

Hutton said, "Ok, fellas, I appreciate that you are paying attention to the rules. The feds will give us no second chances."

Ralph was grateful every time Hutton or Andre spoke to the other help without ever bringing up his driving into the St. Croix River at Sunrise. That was another secret he wanted kept.

Hutton went on, "I've got to go now, Andre. I'm buying another farm, just north up by Trade Lake. We should close on it next week. It's totally empty, no one living in the house, no livestock or critters, but it could be turned into something."

Chapter 70

Chief Lundquist looked seriously at Sampson. "Well, they know you're there now, Sampson. I saw the pictures in the Cedarville *Gazette*. They were better than the week before, when the *Gazette* ran an article on the WCTU. They announced in their article that you were coming," he shrugged. "How the hell did that happen? I thought you were keeping your presence over there secret."

"I don't know, Chief. The rumor mill says she heard about it from someone in Stearns County. I will talk to her when I get a chance. I'm sure I can talk her out of any more articles. Some of the WCTU ladies get pretty fired up about what they want, but don't have a clue about enforcement." Sampson finished.

"That was a good series of raids in Somerset, Sampson. It sounds like you plan on working that area for the rest of the month. That's a good plan. Somerset has been the center of moon activities. The Revenue Service made that one raid I told you about last year, just before the crash. That's the biggest raid ever made in Wisconsin. There were thirty-two Federal Revenue Agents involved. We borrowed men from every midwest region to pull it off. We literally surrounded Somerset, and made simultaneous raids throughout downtown. Two of the farms had 500 gallon stills. The Agents captured and destroyed 3000 gallons of mash and 175 gallons of moon. Five of ten men arrested during the raids were from the Twin Cities. We confirmed our suspicions that those stills were owned by the syndicate. They also picked up two brand new Cadillac Roadsters," he grinned, "another symptom of syndicate ownership. They raided every farm two or three miles south of Somerset, but they were all clean, which surprised us. They found two or three more stills north of town, which they tore up."

"That sounds like the kind of raids we used in Chicago," Sampson added. "Did it slow down the bootlegging to the cities?"

Lundquist frowned, "Well, a little. The St. Paul *Dispatch* gave them front-page headlines, something like, 'Somerset Moonshine Source Plugged,' which made it sound like we totally shut them down, but that's not the case. Most of those thirty-two Agents were borrowed from other territories. As soon as they were gone, many of the stills were back in business and then, we didn't have any agents over there to stop them."

"The way you've explained it to me, you haven't had any agents over there for the last six months. Is that correct?" Sampson asked.

"Yeh, that's right, which is why I sent you and your team. I think you and your men will get more done being there full-time, than thirty-two Revenue agents can in a day-long, or week-long, raid. That's how I justified plugging you into our budget this year, Sampson. Now you're off to a good start, but what I need is for you to continue making arrests and destroying stills and booze. If you can keep doing that I will have no problem sustaining the budget, and we will definitely slow down business for both the cookers and the bootleggers," he finished.

"I think we'll make it, Chief. We've been eyeballing for bootleggers. We watched the bridges for a week last month. We're going to stop cars both randomly, if they look suspicious, and in an organized routine manner as well. We have a list of suspect still locations and now we are beginning to work the supply routes that keep those stills operating. I'm going to begin working the local law enforcement for help soon." he ended.

"Don't count on much help from them," Lundquist shrugged, "We've had a hell of a time with the local Sheriff over in Stearns. I can't prove it, but I think that Sheriff tends to protect those farmers and has even tipped off some of the still operators about raids! When you start trying to work with them, you'll find out we aren't too popular as Revenue Agents," Lundquist complained.

"It's that way in Chicago, too, Chief. I kicked the shit out of two or three local law officers down there. After that, I got cooperation. How careful do I have to be? I like to get rough with them. That's how I got so much done around Chicago. They were all afraid of me. It makes one hell of a difference if they're scared of you," he smiled.

"It's as I told you the first day you arrived, Sampson. Play by the rules. Don't get too nasty, at least not publicly. We brought you up here to see how your methods worked. Do what you think you need to do, but make damn sure I can justify your actions if I am pressed."

Chapter 71

"We brought 10,000 pounds of sugar in last night," Ralph said to Andre. "They left the trucks at the saw mill. Our guys picked them up, we unloaded what we needed here and put the rest in the Robinson coop. We've got a pickup-load of yeast coming in tonight at the Sunrise Ferry, and Thursday night, there's two trucks full of kegs from St. Cloud coming in. I get more nervous about truck loads, because they can't come across on the ferry."

"Yes, me too, Ralph. Hutton's bridge-watch help seems to be working. The kegs are coming in from the north, up around Grantsburg. That way we avoid the southern bridges the feds watch more closely."

"Yeh, that helps," said Ralph.

"Hutton has a contact in the Twin Cities he can call for bridge-watch information. He says somebody over in Stearns County somehow works for the Fed's office in Minneapolis. Jim says they know which bridges are being worked and when and that their information is reliable. If it's true, that removes the risk of being caught crossing the river via bridges, but I still want to avoid them when we can," Andre finished.

"Some of the places I make gas deliveries for Bill are shipping small-scale booze across in cars all the time. It's incredible how they keep it hidden, Andre. Most of them won't tell me how they do it, but a couple of them are proud of how they hide it. One has it in car door tanks he made of inner tube rubber! Can you imagine that?" Ralph laughed. "He says he's been doing it for two years, with no problems. There's another guy that is hauling crocks in a car. He gets all his, and the neighbor's kids, to sit on top of a carpet over the crocks. Then, they laugh and celebrate a birthday party by having kids hanging out the windows as they cross the bridge. He says the feds have waved him through more than once."

Chapter 72

"Our production is up, we're producing consistently and we've got two basements nearly full of kegs," Hutton smiled. "Now, Andre, I'm going to show you how to use some things I learned the hard way over in Stearns."

"I've learned so much in the last six months," Andre responded, "But, I'm ready for more. Let's hear it."

"Ok," Hutton went on, "We want this inventory we've built up to deliver successfully and to maximize profits, which means get the highest price and create demand for more. First, let's talk about delivery. We've seen how dangerous this business can be when the feds concentrate their activities, as they have over in Stearns. We now know they are beginning to snoop around over here. They are setting up road-blocks and bridge surveillance between here and the Twin Cities, just as they have over in Stearns. Do you agree with that, Andre?"

"Yes, that's exactly what they've been doing. It seemed to start with the Somerset raids, but we know they're snooping around up here, too, and that worries me." Andre finished.

"Ok, so I want to go, south. I want us to take over some of the deliveries to Chicago, which are being restricted by the feds over in Stearns. There are almost clear paths of delivery between here and Chicago through Wisconsin and my sources say Chicago wants more moon than they are currently getting from Stearns." Hutton stopped to measure Andre's reaction.

"That never entered my mind, Jim. Will it work?" Andre asked.

"Not only will it work, Andre, but it will increase our profits substantially. Minnesota 13 is the moonshine most in demand in that market. We are going to begin shipping south next month!" Hutton grinned his enthusiasm. "Here's an interesting fact, Andre. For some strange reason, a dollar's worth of moonshine is worth two dollars if it has a good label. People see a label, and automatically think it's better booze, even if it's the same stuff that's unlabeled. Most people don't have a clue what moonshine tastes like, and no idea what good moonshine should taste like. Here's another interesting fact. People think it's better if it's older. Some change the taste slightly, using measured amounts of wood chips, heat, corn, and charred barrels. Then, because of what they then call, *aged taste*, say it's older; no, they say it's 'aged.' People automatically believe it's better when they think it's 'aged' and are willing to pay more for it, even though they have no way of knowing if it is really older at all. It's incredibly dumb, if you think it through, but that's how it is. Some moonshiners will argue to the death that everything about aging is true, some say it's bullshit, but the fact is the more it is claimed that aging works the more people will pay for *aged moon*." Hutton smiled, took a breath, and continued, "Now, you and I have to do two things to get more money for our product. Some phony aging, and then, some phony labeling."

"We've discussed the aging," Andre went on. "Adding oak chips to the containers, twice-weekly rotation of the kegs and adding heat, at least according to your taste buds seems to be working. We haven't got the heat process down yet, but are still working on it. So, what about the labeling? What do we call it?"

Hutton's face bloomed into one of the biggest smiles Andre had seen on it. "Minnesota 13!" he boomed, with an almost insidious laugh.

"How in hell do we do that, Jim?" Andre exclaimed. That's the Stearns County label."

"Now you know why I've insisted we buy all our kegs from the same cooperage that supplies most of Stearns County stills, Andre. Our kegs look like their kegs. Here's another surprise for you," he continued as he began opening a cardboard box. Jim lifted a metal piece that resembled a brake shoe with a handle on the back side of it. Grasping the handle, he held it against the round end of a keg, which its curvature fit perfectly. Then, he held the inside of the curve up in front of Andre. There, written backwards in raised letters, was "Minnesota 13." "Andre, this is the same label stamp used by the Stearns County boys to label their kegs. We are about to get busy with their stamp in our chicken coops!" he laughed.

Andre was astounded by the brazenness of Hutton's suggestion. He was still basically a farmer. For six months he'd been learning how to lie, break the law, and keep it all secret, things he had never before done in his life. He sensed he was about to also become a thief by stealing a label from Stearns County. "Jim, how do we get away with using their label?" he asked.

"What the hell are they going to do, Andre? Call the cops?" Hutton smiled. "There's nothing they can do, Andre, and the likelihood of them ever finding out we are using it is very small. We have to be careful about that. And here's another benefit. If one of our shipments is ever caught by the feds, they are going to think it came from Stearns County, not Stephens. Add to that, the fact that we are going to get at least the same price for our moon as Stearns gets for Minnesota 13, and this label maker becomes even more attractive," he finished, with satisfaction. I've even brought four kegs of Minnesota 13 from Stearns, so you can get the labeling exactly as they do. I'll show you how I want the, 'Aged 3 Years' label added."

He reached into the box and brought out a smaller metal plate of the same curvature, again with a handle on the back side. Holding it up to Andre, he asked, "What does this one say?"

Andre had to look at it twice, because of the smaller type on it. "3 Years Aged," he responded, and couldn't help smiling. He shook his head at the duplicities which seemed now to be the normal environment of illegal persuasions. *How am I ever, going to explain all this to the kids?*

"I started dreaming all this up over a year ago, when the feds started closing in on Stearns, Andre. My syndicate contacts in the Twin Cities have connections in Chicago. They don't really give a damn where their Minnesota 13 comes from. They just want, as much as they need, and when, they want it. We are going to help make that happen. We are already working out agreements, shipping routes and methods. Before we're finished, Andre, the Stearns County boys are going to be learning from us," he laughed. "Now let's talk about what you and Ralph and the crew need to do. We'll keep making smaller shipments of five gallon crocks to the Twin Cities via the Sunrise route, Andre, but those will all be out of the Trade Lake farm. Remember, you and I are the only ones in our crew that know of Trade Lake."

Chapter 73

"According to your uncle, Carolyn, you can expect approximately six eggs per week per chicken in the spring and summer; then it will taper off to three or four through the winter. As you pointed out, that is almost exactly what our chickens have been producing for the last couple of years. With 300 additional chickens here and another 300 at the Robinson place, we are looking at roughly 300 dozen eggs per week in prime laying season and about 200 dozen in winter." Andre said.

"That's going to take a lot more of my time, Dad." Carolyn worried. "How are we going to keep up?"

"Well, with you to advise him, Ralph is going to take care of the Robinson Coop. He will do the cleaning and packaging there and then I'll bring the eggs here. We'll combine our eggs with those I bring home and then deliver, with one trip, to all our stores using the bigger truck. That's about as efficient a way as I can see right now, Carolyn, and that will keep you from getting buried in eggs," he grinned. "School comes first, young lady, then chickens."

"That sounds like it will work, Dad."

"I think I will have all chicken feed bags delivered to the Robinson place. Then, I'll bring home what we need here," thinking to himself, *that will give me the opportunity of hiding moon within the load when I need to.* "I've also talked to Nyquist at the grocery store. He has a man that we can hire to process chickens for resale. We have to capture and contain the hens we want to sell as meat, then, he comes here, kills, feathers, and prepares them for store delivery. That way, you and I don't have to do any of the processing. After we learn more about the chicken business we'll know better how to handle that part, but your uncle says we'll want to purge slow layers and sell them as meat, so we can add more new layers. He says it's a profitable part of the chicken and egg business."

"You may have to help me with that, Dad. I fall in love with peepers and become pretty good friends with the chickens. I still eat chicken, but sending them to the butcher shop . . . I don't know."

Chapter 74

Hutton and Andre agreed about Ralph continuing to work two or three nights a week for Bill at the gas station. Bill gave Ralph responsibility for bulk deliveries of gas. Ralph would fill the tank truck at the station, drive to the farms and fill their stationary bulk tanks. Farmers who ordered larger bulk deliveries could get a cheaper price and Bill could still profit from the larger volume orders. Ralph didn't really want to keep driving the gas truck because he could make more working those hours for Hutton at the Robinson place, but both Hutton and Andre encouraged him to do it. There would be less cooking in the winter, so Ralph would still have some winter-income. In addition, Ralph continued to learn locations where other stills were in operation in Stephens County, because of the gas requested by some of those farmers he delivered too.

"Ralph, after you fill that bulk tank, will you pull over to the barn door over there," Johnson pointed. "I've got about ten five-gallon cans I want you to fill." That's how it often went.

Bill told him to go ahead and fill those requests while he was there, but to then forget about them. "Add those gallons to the bill, Ralph, but don't list them separately. Just add them to the bulk-tank amounts and bill for one number of total gallons. I've heard the feds sometimes come in and check the books of bulk gas deliveries, and I don't want to have anything to tip them off to farmers who ask us to fill a bunch of gas cans in addition to their bulk tank. Also Ralph, you have to remember to forget about those deliveries. If a fed ever asks you, you make one delivery per farm to their bulk-tank. What they do with the gas after that is up to them. Even if they have two bulk-tanks, just write the invoice for the total gallons delivered."

"Yeh, I understand, Bill. The feds ought to leave those people alone. That's the only money some of them can make now," Ralph lamented.

"That's true," Bill added. "Well, it looks like, between the chicken business you are doing with Andre, and the hours you are getting from me, you are making it through now. I'm glad to see that."

"Yeh, Bill, I appreciate the hours you give me. Have you really seen feds around that you think might be watching your gas deliveries?" Ralph asked. "I didn't know they even did that sort of thing."

Bill frowned, then added, "It hasn't happened to me, but I've heard from some stations down by Somerset it has happened to them. Roy Jones said they made a list of small deliveries from his books, then raided a whole batch of farms just south of Somerset. Roy said he thought it was just sort of an experiment by the feds, because they didn't find a thing to do with moon on those farms and haven't done it since. But, you never know. I want to be ready if they come here. How many farms on our delivery books do you think are involved with moon, Ralph?"

Ralph was surprised by the question, but responded right off, "At least a dozen, because of comments they've made to me when I bring gas, but I have no idea how big their operations might be. I think most of them just sell locally in small containers. You know, the kind they line the fence posts with at the Saturday night dances," he grinned. I've never really even seen a still on any of the farms I deliver, but I can just tell by the way the farmers ask me to fill those extra gas cans that there's something going on."

"But, we've got a few big ones too, Ralph. Like Hutton up at the old Robinson place and that one over east that everyone is afraid to go near. They paid their bill last month with a check from a Chicago bank." Bill ended.

"Well, the Robinson place has to do with the big chicken business, and there's little doubt about those Chicago boys over there. They make me jumpy, the way they watch me when I deliver. I dump and get out of there as quick as I can." Ralph finished.

"Well, it's all good business for us; Ralph, just be careful. If you ever get stopped by a fed, tell him you just fill the orders I tell you to and have him talk to me. I'll handle it and keep you in the clear." he finished.

"Ok, Bill. You know we seem to be getting more people coming in here, with gas cans to fill up, too." Ralph added.

"Just fill them up, and don't ask what they're doing with it, Ralph. We just sell gas."

Chapter 75

"We've gotten Somerset's attention now," said Sampson. "Now we're going to start moving north. I want the three of you to check out the region between Somerset and Osceola along the St. Croix River. According to Lundquist there's never been a raid in that area. Eggert saw several cars he would have stopped on the Osceola Bridge, so there is likely traffic there. I don't expect to find many stills in that region because Osceola and Taylors Falls are rumored to be dry. There is a concentration of Swedish Lutherans and Methodists up there, and Osceola, according to those I've spoken with, has lots of Methodists and Baptists, with ties to the WCTU. That makes those regions an unlikely place for operating stills. Those WCTU ladies have a big impact. I've seen them set up a meeting at the front door of a saloon in Chicago and shut the saloon down. When they teamed up with the Anti-Saloon League they caused a lot of saloons to close."

The three Agents nodded their agreement; then Sampson went on.

"The Osceola Bridge is where we're going to find some action. Bootleggers have to be using that bridge. Eggert, I want you to set up a twenty-four hour watch for random car checks. The three of you will work the bridge in shifts for that period. While you are doing that, I am bringing in four more Agents from Minneapolis who will quietly work the Stillwater and Taylors Falls bridges. I think the word will get out that we are stopping cars in Osceola, which will drive bootleggers to the other two bridges. They watch the bridges the same way we do. We won't make any stops on the bridges at Stillwater and Taylors Falls, but will follow and stop suspicious cars heading towards the Twin Cities, a mile or so beyond the bridges. This will be an interesting experiment." Sampson finished.

Agent Brown asked, "Are we going to keep working north then?"

Sampson responded, "Yes, each week, unless we find a lot to raid, we will keep moving north. While you three are working this region I will continue to look around Stephens County. I want to be sure Lundquist is happy with our actions over here, so big or small, I want to shut down stills, nab bootleggers and interrupt moon coming into the Twin Cities. Remember, we also want to stop sugar and containers like kegs and crocs from coming into this region. That stuff's coming from somewhere and we have to watch for it. Nobody can make moon without supplies, so the more we can do to interrupt deliveries and make arrests, the more we slow down moonshine. I want Lundquist to see action over here. One last thing - don't forget to keep raiding anything that looks suspicious around Somerset in your spare time. During my years in Chicago, we found that often, within a week of shutting down a still, even if we wrecked it, they'd be back in business quickly. That's because the courts are so reluctant to send them to prison. So, in addition to moving north we've got to keep the pressure on around Somerset." he finished. "According to what Lundquist told me, somebody around Somerset must be making and repairing stills. We need to find that out too."

Eggert added, "There was a Catholic Priest convention or something last week in Minneapolis. I saw at least a dozen Priests drive across the Osceola Bridge last week. They were all headed for the cities. I was going to stop one and ask him, but I thought it would look pretty stupid, stopping a Priest."

"Next time, stop one. That's the only way you find out," finished Sampson. "Even I could wear a collar to get across a bridge."

Chapter 76

Sheriff Maun was walking over to Bill's station to pick up his county car. Bill had repaired a tire for him. As he approached the station down the block, he saw a car parked across the street that looked familiar. The driver looked familiar as well. It was the same man he'd seen watching Carolyn last month. Maun crossed the street and quietly walked up to the open window of the car.

He surprised Agent Sampson with, "What is it you keep looking for in our town? Last time you said it was about trout fishing."

"Oh, hello, Sheriff. I guess it's time we were formally introduced," he said as he pulled out his wallet. He opened it and showed Maun his metal shield and Revenue Agent's license. "I'm Chief Agent Robert Sampson, of the Revenue Department, in charge of Revenue activities regarding moonshine in western Wisconsin." he smiled.

Sheriff Maun answered, "I knew you weren't a trout fisherman the last time I watched you eyeballing that young lady. I would never have guessed you to be with law enforcement either," he said sternly. "Most law enforcement I've worked with usually display their credentials to each other right off, rather than some hogwash story about trout fishing. Why are you here this time?"

Sampson was caught off guard with Maun's attitude towards him, and the last thing he wanted to hear about from a County Sheriff was how he was "eyeballing some young lady." He also knew, as a Federal Agent, he needed to be in charge of the relationship between himself and the local sheriff. "You sound irritated, Sheriff. First, the trout thing. I didn't want anyone in the County to know any feds were around. Second, it wasn't the girl I was watching, it was what she was unloading from that egg truck. Third, you'll notice that the first thing I did this time was show you my badge and license. I'm sorry if I irritated you. Let's start over. I've got a job to do, and I'm going to do it my way, but I hope to have your help as well. Why don't we have lunch? I'll buy. I'll bring you up to speed on why I am here and perhaps we can work out some ways to be useful to each other."

Maun wasn't at all sure he even wanted to know this man. He knew he didn't trust him, believed he was still lying to him, at least about watching Carolyn, and didn't really want to be seen locally having lunch with a fed. He did, however, want to know what feds were doing or planning to do in his County. Maun decided to do it, his way.

"I'm in the middle of something I can't change right now, Agent Sampson, but we can meet in my office later today if that works," he offered.

Sampson didn't like being turned down, but wanted to enact some damage repair between them. "Ok, what time, and where's your office?" he responded.

"Let's make it 2:00 p.m. and I'm in the lower floor of that red brick building right down the street," he pointed.

"Ok, see you then," Sampson smiled, thinking *this was not a good start.*

Chapter 77

Sampson walked into Sheriff Maun's office at 2:00 p.m. Maun was sitting behind his desk talking on the phone. Sampson, in his take charge manner, without a signal from Maun, grabbed a chair, spun it around and sat down in front of him.

Maun was talking to a councilman. *Sampson is pushy, feels superior, and I don't like him already*, thought Jason. "Ok, Councilman, thanks for letting me know," he ended the conversation.

"Well, Mr. Sampson, what's on your mind," he asked.

"Well, as you've no doubt heard by now, Sheriff, we've begun some new action over here on the east side of the St. Croix River. We made a few arrests in Somerset last week, and we're starting to move north. The Revenue Department's assigned task is to get rid of the moonshine business in this area of Wisconsin, so that's what we are doing. I wanted to bring you up to speed and see if you could help us out." Sampson finished.

"That's a little different story than the first time we met and also from the stories you've been telling others in town. Did you give up trout fishing?" Maun asked, a little sarcastically.

Sampson smiled. "We always do a little undercover research before announcing our presence in a new territory. I shouldn't have to explain that to a Sheriff."

Maun disliked Sampson's attitude right off and decided not to put up with it. "Oh, you didn't have to bring me up to speed about being here. I read about it in a WCTU news release last week in the *Gazette*. Those women said you'd be working over here this week, so everyone knew you were coming," he finished, still with a straight face thinking *it was kind of stupid to announce your coming here in the paper wasn't it?*

"Yeah, that one surprised us too, but no harm done. We were already making arrests in Somerset when that came out." Sampson smiled. "They meant no harm. The WCTU always supports our work, so we knew they'd be glad to see us," Sampson went on. "This week our squad is working the bridges and the area between Somerset and Osceola. We plan to be up this way in the next two or three weeks, which is why I wanted to talk to you."

"You should have come right in to my office, rather than staking out the town. I might have saved you some work." Maun said. "If I hadn't introduced myself to you today, how long would your surveillance have continued, without you acknowledging local law enforcement?"

"I just explained that to you, Sheriff. You've gotten all the explanation you'll be getting from me. We are a federal agency, and often work throughout the country without alerting local law enforcement unless we need their help. But it's your help we should be discussing now. I need information from you on moonshine activities in Stephens County. I won't need help in enforcement, or raids, but info on *who's* making moonshine, and *where,* would be helpful. We are familiar with some activities we discovered while trout fishing, but I'm sure you know of more." he finished.

"I can't help you much with that, Agent Sampson," Maun answered. I've paid little attention to moonshine, because we have little of it over here. I help them keep it out of the Saturday night town hall dances, but nothing beyond that. I'm told you were assigned up here from Chicago. You'll find the people up here a lot different from those who've been shooting at you in Chicago. Up here, anyone cooking moon is trying to scrape up enough money to keep from losing their farm, or to feed their kids. We've got no Al Capones, just good folks, mostly farmers who are trying to survive the depression." Jason ended.

"How did you know I was assigned from Chicago?" Sampson asked.

"Well, we're not as high-powered as the feds but we have our small town sources of information, Agent Sampson. I don't remember where I heard it, though." the Sheriff nodded, *with satisfaction. Take that, trout fisherman from Chicago,* Jason thought.

"Well, I guess the people may be different, but the law is still the same and must be enforced equally in all regions of the country, Sheriff. We are going to be working Stephens County for the next month, and I'd appreciate any information you might send my way to save us work. We will find them either way, with or without your help"

Sensing he had to be careful, Jason Maun thought, *I'll try to help him in a way that doesn't hurt the locals, but I'm not sure, yet, how to go about that.* "Well, now that I know you are here, let me keep my eyes and ears open, Agent Sampson; perhaps I can help you, but don't ask me to make arrests, or participate in raids. That's up to the feds," he finished. "My sense has always been that moonshine activities have always been centered around Somerset. They are close to the Twin Cities for deliveries and the terrain and soil are not very good for farming down there. That's why moonshine has developed there, and the farming more up here. I do understand bootleggers tend to use the bridges at Stillwater, Osceola, and sometimes Taylors Falls and that the cars travel west when full, and east when empty, but most of the bridge action is down south I think."

They talked for another fifteen minutes, agreed to try to be helpful to each other, though each obviously disliked the other, and couldn't hide it. They finally parted with a cool handshake.

Sampson thought, *I'll get little help from him, but he isn't capable of much anyway.*

Maun thought, *this man is dangerous, and he's going to cause trouble here in Stephens. I hope I can minimize it. He's still lying . . . he was checking out Carolyn . . . not looking for moonshine.*

Chapter 78

On Friday, about 2:30 p.m., Andre walked into Sheriff Maun's office carrying a box. "Afternoon, Jason," he said, as he placed the box on the floor. "Here's twelve dozen eggs the last store didn't need. Spread them around as you see fit."

"Thanks, Andre. I know just where they need to go. We need more like you to work with, rather than the last guy who walked in here," he grimaced.

"You got problems, Jase?"

"I think so. The feds are here and I think that's going to cause some grief. They've assigned an agent from Chicago to work the east side of the St. Croix, including Stephens County. He thinks we're hiding Capone or somebody up here in the Barrens. They made a bunch of raids down in Somerset last week and now they're working their way north. He thinks he can come in here and give me orders. Naturally, I don't like that, but I've probably got to figure out how to dance with this guy, to protect my county. I'm not looking forward to it, Andre."

"Well, what in particular is he after?" Andre asked.

"He's mostly looking for stills if I heard him correctly. He says feds don't usually waste their time on speakeasies and saloons. They go after stills, try to wreck them, shut them down, destroy any moonshine they find and also chase down bootleggers. There were some pictures in the *Gazette* this week of his squad chopping up kegs of moon down in Somerset. He says they're working the bridges this week for bootleggers, but he had a lot of questions about stills around the Barrens. I couldn't tell him much, because I've always made it a point to not know where stills were. The ones I'm aware of are using it to make house and farm mortgage payments. This guy doesn't give a shit, though, Andre."

"Makes me glad I'm in the chicken business, Jase," Andre smiled. "He won't want chicken shit on his shoes."

"He can cause some real grief for some locals, though, Andre. I know Ralph is working with you on chickens, but I also know he delivers gas to a lot of people at night. You might tell him to mention that *Uncle Ben's in town*, and might be visiting," Maun said with an eyeball to eyeball message within. "The Somerset cops told me that's the expression they use to let everyone know when the feds are around. Most of the farmers I know, with stills, couldn't afford such a visit and only make enough to drink anyway. Well, I can't say much more, I'm a sheriff you know. Thanks for the eggs, Andre. Tell Carolyn, too," he finished thinking *he perhaps should tell Andre about Agent Sampson, eyeballing Carolyn, as she unloaded eggs at the store. He decided against it, after reminding himself,*

I think I'm right, but I'm not sure. I will keep an eye on her, though.

"Jason, our family has talked this over. For the next few weeks you should plan on having about twelve dozen eggs a week to spread around. You can decide what to do with them. It's something we want to do and we appreciate your help doing. If at any time you find you have too many, just give them to the church. They might be aware of some we don't know about. And, if you occasionally feel the need for more, let me know." he finished.

"Thanks again, Andre. I know just where they'll go."

Chapter 79

Agent Brown approached the driver's side window of the stopped car, flashing his badge at the man behind the wheel of the big Oldsmobile roadster. He, Eggert, and Eastman were working the west end of the Osceola Bridge. They had about three more cars stopped behind this Olds. It was about 10:00 p.m., so traffic was slow. Their practice was to slow all westbound cars on the east end of the bridge, warn them they would be stopped on the west end, and to be prepared to pull over to the side of the road if told to do so. That way, if any car picked up speed on the way across the bridge, they knew they were going to make a run for it. When there was a lot of traffic, they'd watch them cross, witness their behavior, and as they arrived at the check point on the other end, would quickly look in through the car's windows. If they saw nothing suspicious, they'd wave them through. If suspect, they were waved over to the side of the road by another agent. When there wasn't much traffic, they'd check each car more carefully. Eastman had waved from across the bridge, pointing to the Olds, so Eggert and Brown knew that car was suspect. When it reached the checkpoint, Eastman waved it to the side where Brown stood waiting.

Seeing Brown's badge waved in front of him, the driver said, "What's up, officer?" with a strained and nervous expression on his face.

"We're Federal Revenue agents, and are checking for cars carrying illegal substances." Brown stated. "Apply the emergency brake, and shut off your engine. Then, step out of the car and walk around to the other side. I want to see your driver's license, and ask you a few questions." The man complied, looking more nervous now than when on the other side of the car, "I'm just delivering this car to the Twin Cities. I do this on a fee basis. It's how I earn a living. I normally deliver cars from Milwaukee to the Twin Cities, but this one is from Madison, officer. I have no idea what's in it. I just picked it up about five hours ago, and have been driving ever since."

While the driver and Brown were talking, Eastman was already rummaging through the back seat beneath what appeared to be folded blankets. In less time than it took Brown and the driver to get to the other side of the car, Eastman held up a one gallon can, then another. Brown told the man to get back into the car, in the front passenger seat. He handcuffed him to the door handle and said, "You are under arrest for suspicion of bootlegging. I want you to sit here in the car until I come back to talk to you. We're going to finish these car checks first. That will take only a few minutes."

"You can't arrest me, officer, it's not my car! I'm just paid to deliver the car. I didn't know what was in it," he pleaded.

"Well, you're wrong about that. I just did arrest you. Now, sit here quietly until I get back to you," Brown finished firmly.

The squad continued to check cars for the next hour. By the time they were done there were two more cars on the side of the road behind the Oldsmobile. The Olds had 100 gallons of moon in it. The driver spent the night in jail, and was charged with possession the next morning. He would go through intense questioning. The Revenue Agents wanted to know the source of that booze. The Chevrolet had two five-gallon crocks in it, which the driver had purchased north of Somerset for personal use. They confiscated the crocks and let him go without arrest, after he told them he had bought it from a friend, who had bought four crocs and split with him. The third car, a Model A, Ford, had four fifty-pound bags of cane sugar in the back seat. The driver claimed they were for his wife who used it in her fruit canning. They let him go.

Chapter 80

Clair and Carolyn were talking of chickens, school and how busy they all were. Carolyn was kind of working her way up to a mother-daughter conversation of deeper concern. They toured the new coop, as Carolyn tried to hide her pride while showing how the peepers had become, healthy cluckers, beginning to look like real chickens. "Next month they'll start laying, mom, and the money will start rolling in from all those new stores we promised good service," Carolyn grinned. "Mrs. Raymond said I should be careful not to get so chicken busy that I didn't have time to keep up my school work, but she also said I'm a strong student and doesn't think I'll have a problem."

Clair agreed, "You'll do fine. Are your friends having a good junior year?"

"I am having a problem this year and I don't know how to handle it." Carolyn frowned. "His name is Dan Anderson."

"How is he a problem?" Clair asked as she noted color flooding Carolyn's cheeks as her brows pulled down.

"He's a year older, and he won't leave me alone. When we play softball, or any outdoor activities, he keeps inventing reasons to get close, then, squeezes me instead of tagging me, and last week he pinched my butt! I yelled at him straight out to leave me alone." The anger and frustration in her face said it all. "Nothing works, mom. I'd feel like a little kid to tattle on him to Mrs. Raymond, but he is being a jerk and I hate being around him."

Clair nodded her head and asked why his name didn't' sound familiar. For years, she had known all of the kids as well as their families in both Henri and Carolyn's classes.

"He's from south Minneapolis, just moved out here, and says he's living with his uncle on a farm the other side of Cedarville; I don't know if his parents are living there, too, or what," Carolyn explained. "He is *the new kid* at school and I think he has made a few friends. I just don't want him following me around," her pretty face tensed again, "or pinching me! What should I do, Mom? He just laughs and kind of swaggers off to join his friends. I don't know them very well, but I don't think I like them much either."

"Have your girl friends seen or noticed this unwanted attention?" Clair asked.

"Yes, and they know I'm not making it up. They think he is kind of strange, too."

"How about your other classmates, the boys, are they aware that he is picking on you and you don't like it?"

"Not really. I don't know if they've noticed anything or not. They are totally into whatever game they're playing and he tends to hang out with just a few guys in that class. A lot of them are a year older and I don't know them all that well. When some of them stare at me it's embarrassing."

"Even some old men look at women that way, Carolyn. Women kind of get used to that and openly ignore such rude behavior, but not pinching. Well, you've made a good decision by telling someone; the last thing you want to do is keep it a secret when your efforts haven't worked. Taking freedoms like he is doing is a kind of bullying he shouldn't get away with. Let me think on this and I'll talk it over with your dad, if you don't mind. He loves you and wouldn't want you to put up with bad behavior from anyone. You don't deserve this kind of attention, so for now stay with your group of friends as much as you can. We'll help you work it out."

"Ok, Mom. I was going to tell Henri, but this guy is older and pretty big, and I'm afraid Henri might just punch him."

Chapter 81

Agents Eggert and Brown had received a tip about a possible moon-cooker's farm north of Somerset and south of Osceola, about midway in between. The tip came from a bootlegger they had arrested on the Osceola bridge who was carrying twenty crocks of moonshine to the Twin Cities. After worrying him for a week after his arrest, with talk of prison-time, the bootlegger agreed to identify a source in exchange for just a $200 fine and probation. He actually never went to court, the judge was never told of his violation, and there never was any official probation process or paperwork. After receiving the tip, Brown and Eggert split the $200 for expenses, and told the bootlegger to keep quiet and keep his nose clean. They said, if arrested again, he would do time.

It was late afternoon when Eggert and Brown stealthily approached a barn just north of Somerset. The farmer was milking cows with his two teen-age sons when Eggert and Brown opened the barn door. The milk cows were in stanchions eating while milking was in process. They walked down the center aisle between the two rows of cows. The father saw them coming, and immediately said to his boys, "Get me that hay I told you about, right now, boys."

The two boys stood up from their milking stools, walked down to the far end of the barn and began forking the hay that had been dropped from the loft above into a pile near the end wall. The farmer then said, "What can I do for you?" to the two men in dark suits.

"We are federal revenue agents, here to arrest you for cooking moonshine," Brown said. "Where is your still?"

"We are milking cows, not cooking moonshine," the farmer smiled.

"Where is your still?" said Brown, again.

"What still?" said the farmer.

As Brown and the farmer talked, Eggert watched the two boys forking hay. One of them seemed to be moving it with his foot, as well as the pitchfork, as though to cover something up with it. He walked down past the farmer to where the boys were working. The bootlegger had told them it was a small still and that he picked up crocks from that downstairs area of the barn. Eggert stopped the boy's forking hay, then, kicked hay away from what the boy appeared to be covering up. He found a defined joint between the concrete floor and wood flooring. "Fork the rest of this hay off this wooden flooring," he demanded of the boys.

The boys looked at their father as though asking what they should do. The father nodded affirmatively, knowing they were caught. It took only seconds to remove what the boys had so hastily started throwing to cover up. "Now, lift up those planks," said Eggert.

As the boys lifted the planks, crocks of moonshine began to appear. Lifting the last plank, Eggert counted ten, totaling fifty gallons.

"Where's your still?" Brown asked the farmer.

"In the milk room at the end," pointing to the end of the barn. "I'm a very small cooker, just enough to keep food on the table. Will this mean jail?"

"I doubt it, but a fine for sure," said Eggert.

The boys looked scared as their father talked. Eggert had them load the ten crocks into their car outside, while Brown talked to the farmer. Both Brown and Eggert felt odd about their successful raid and arrest. This guy was so small that they actually worried whether or not they were removing sustenance from the family. If they hadn't been tipped off by the young bootlegger they'd never have even found this place.

"You're going to have to go before the judge tomorrow, just you, not the boys," said Brown.

"I knew I shouldn't get involved with moonshine, but we needed money for food. I don't earn a dam thing anymore on this farm. I'm done with it now," the farmer finished, imploringly eyeballing Brown.

Eggert and Brown left with the evidence in their car, taking the farmer at his word to show up in court the next day, and instructing him that they would pick up the still that Brown inspected in the milk room, the next day.

As they drove down the road, discussing what they would tell Sampson about the raid, the farmer was talking to his boys in the barn.

"You did perfect, boys! I told you we wouldn't know when they were coming. You did it all just the way we rehearsed it. It couldn't have been better. Those two never even suspected the 200 gallons we've got in the hayloft, or the big still out in the machine shed." He laughed, "When that one saw you kicking that hay around the edge, Bill, his ears dam near lit up! He knew he had us."

"Ok, let's get those forty crocks down from the loft. We're going to move them tonight. The feds just might decide to snoop around tomorrow when they come back for that old still in the milk room. I got that thing for nothing last year, but it sure saved us a lot of money today. After they leave here tomorrow, we'll start setting up the big still in the machine shed again. We should be able to cook some big batches for a while without being visited again."

Chapter 82

"Jim, the reason I asked you to meet with us this morning is a conversation I had with Sheriff Maun yesterday," said Andre.

Andre and Ralph were talking to Hutton at the Robinson place. Andre had asked Hutton to meet with them as quickly as possible. They all arrived at about 8:00 a.m. and Andre quickly brought Hutton up to speed on what he'd learned from the Sheriff the day before.

"You did right by letting me know right away, Andre. I knew about the Somerset raids, and some people I know in the Cities brought me up to speed on the fact that the feds are also watching the bridges. They lost a bootlegging car to the feds last week, crossing the bridge in Taylors Falls. I didn't know they were going to work Stephens County, though," Hutton finished. Then, as though he'd been planning it for weeks, Hutton abruptly said, "Ok, here's what we're going to do. We've got a lot of inventory built up in both chicken coop's storage."

Ralph's eyes opened wide, as a wave of discovery swept his face because of Hutton's mistake. Of course! There's a full basement beneath Andre's coop, too!

Realizing from Ralph's expression, what had just occurred, Jim looked at Ralph and said, "Sorry, Ralph. We didn't tell you earlier, because the less everyone in our operation knows, the better off we all are. Now you know, so you have more to worry about keeping quiet about. Be certain you do, though."

"Ok, back to our inventory. With our process we can easily claim what's in those two basements to be three years old. We are going to totally shut down the Robinson stills. Finish up whatever mash is ready in the next five days. Friday is the last day of cooking. Get all moon stored, dated, and tagged as usual. When you finish, everything we have is in ten-gallon kegs, and stored for aging."

"Ok, then what?" Ralph asked, feeling more important with his new knowledge, after Jim's mistake.

"Then, we're going to make this operation disappear. The following week, at night, we're going to move all of these stills up to Trade Lake. That place is a lot harder to find than this one, and up there I can make these stills disappear. Andre, you and I will handle that move after you guys get the truck loaded. Three stills per load, means four trips. After the move, you guys clean this place up totally. Not a hint of sugar, yeast, old mash, containers, nothing that would even hint that moon had ever been within its walls. That will take the two of you two or three days to accomplish. Also, Andre, remember our talk about dumping the old mash. Ralph, I told Andre of when one of our stills got busted over in Stearns because a farmer dumped his entire mash residue into a small pond. After a big dump, his cattle got loaded. They were so drunk they couldn't walk. They were just lying around the pond. It was funny, until the word got out in the County, with everybody talking about drunken cows. Then, the feds heard about it. It wasn't funny then! Make sure there are no tell-tale signs of a mash dump." Then Hutton started laughing. Andre and Ralph couldn't figure out why.

"You aren't even going to believe the next thing I want you to do," he laughed, grinning at the expressions on their faces. I want you to put a wall-partition about a third of the way down from this end of the building. We're going to fill up that part of the building with chickens!" he laughed. "I talked this over with Mann...," he stopped abruptly, "with one of my friends over in Stearns. He said the best thing to do when the feds get thick, is to arrange to get raided," he grinned. "We are going to make the moon disappear and give them chickens!"

"That's a good idea, Jim. It will remove any suspicions, lend credit to our chicken business, and legitimize everything we are doing." Andre said.

"Are we going to buy more peepers?" Ralph asked.

"No, just take about 50 out of the big coop right here. They're three months old now. Big chickens will make it look more like a hatchery. We'll just convert this third of the building, with box nests and chicken stuff, into a coop. Our story will be that we have 300 in the big coop, and as we hatch more chicks we are filling this place, too. In fact, what we'll do later in the spring, is put the other two-thirds of the building back into cooking. These moves should prevent suspicions of our operations. It's a lot of work, but what the hell, you're making money! While the feds are worrying about moon flowing from Stephens County into the Twin Cities, we'll be shipping this winter, in the opposite direction, south, to Chicago."

Andre and Ralph were actually relieved at Hutton's plan of shutdown. Since talking to Maun, both had visions of Feds swooping down on them while cooking. They'd both read the article in the *Gazette* and had seen the pictures of feds chopping kegs with fire axes in Somerset. Andre's imagination envisioned a headline *of, Local Chicken Rancher Guilty of Moon.*

"Good plan, Jim," said Andre, with Ralph nodding affirmatively. "Remember, though, I still haven't come up with a good way to get heat into those basements to help the moon age."

Chapter 83

All four cars were parked behind the Catholic Church in Cedarville at 9:00 a.m. on Thursday morning. The three agents were sitting in Sampson's car, having a discussion planned by Sampson.

"These people over here are different than the ones in Stearns," Agent Eggert said. "Over there, Revenue Agents offer them the opportunity to avoid jail-time and to keep quiet about the informants if they give them info on other stills. The agent I worked with said they were ratting each other out frequently to avoid jail. But, over here nobody seems to know of other stills. I'm inclined to believe them. I don't think they know about others," he finished.

Agent Brown added, "Me too. I agree. Those we've found from Osceola north, seem to be too small to be making it more than just for themselves to drink. The only exception so far has been the few bootleggers but they don't seem to be coming from around here. That last one Tuesday night was from Madison."

Sampson spoke up aggressively, "Don't go soft on these people, men. We just haven't worked the territory enough yet. I want us to keep our arrest rate up, even if they are small stills. Lundquist needs to see action, or he can't justify our existence over here. If you guys want to keep getting paid, we've got to produce. I want Eggert to go back down and work Somerset. Those first arrests will be in court this week, and I want one of you in the court room. We need a little pressure on the judge so he doesn't let them off too easily. Brown and I are going to continue sniffing around Stephens. We are going to check out the gas stations for fuel deliveries, and also find out where the Wisconsin road houses are getting their booze. They're all selling it. And, don't forget to work the bridges at least two nights a week." he finished.

Chapter 84

"Well, your Honor, I had so many debts, and no income, I had to do something to feed my family. I'm sorry I ever got into moon, but I didn't know what else to do," Henry Risard said, apologetically, to the Judge. Henry had a small still that enabled him to deliver a few gallons a week to three saloons he'd done business with for the last year. It just barely sustained his wife and kids, but it did that. "I've got no money, and I still have debts to pay, your Honor. What am I supposed to do? Let the family starve?" he pleaded.

"So many have similar problems in this depression, Henry, but there is also the law. I have no liking for the problems caused by Prohibition, and think its laws are doing more harm than good, but I am charged with enforcing the laws of this County, State and Country. I must charge you with the felony you've committed, but I will suspend jail-time and forgive the fine. Doing more would only make you and your family worse off. Don't let me see you here again." the judge finished firmly.

Agent Eggert stomped out of the courtroom thinking, *so this is how it's going to be, laws, but no enforcement of arrests. How do they expect us to stamp out booze?*

Before Henry Risard was let off the hook in the morning, the court had confronted the traveling salesman, Roger Naab, whose Somerset basement had been raided. Agents found fifty ten-gallon kegs of moonshine sitting on his basement floor. This was a considerably larger offense than that of Mr. Risard. Naab was given the opportunity to turn State's evidence as to the source of his fifty kegs, but he refused. Couldn't, is the more proper term. He agreed he had taken delivery of the kegs, but insisted he did not know where they came from. Naab said he had spoken to a man in a bar in the Twin Cities about buying ten kegs of moon. Naab paid him half of the money in cash, and agreed to give the other half in cash to the truck driver when he made the delivery, which was to be unscheduled and unannounced, by beating on Naab's door in the middle of the night. He said it was a gamble on his part. He had never seen either the man in the cities, or the truck driver before. Either could have disappeared with his money, but didn't. Naab stated he'd been promised Minnesota 13, but what showed up wasn't even labeled. When he complained of bait and switch tactics, the truck driver apologized and dropped the price from $5 a gallon to $4, which Naab accepted after tasting the moon of one keg.

"I didn't know they were bringing this much, your honor. I said I would take ten kegs as an experiment, to see if I could sell it on the road in small quantities to some of my customers. When the truck driver showed up with fifty kegs, and gave me a price I couldn't refuse, I took it. Hell, even my wife was mad at me for filling up the basement and smelling up the house. I was going to bottle it into quarts and give it as gifts to some of my best lumber customers. I could have done that for five years with fifty kegs! So far, I've given away about two kegs and haven't sold any! Then, customers I gave quarts to, started asking me if they could buy some more. They wanted to give it as gifts to their friends. I regret it now, your Honor, but nearly everyone in town was somehow making money with moon except me. If you arrest everyone who buys or sells a little moon here the town will be empty," he pleaded.

The prosecuting attorney didn't buy his story, but Naab's case was difficult for the judge. Naab didn't make the moon, he had no stills, wasn't cooking, wasn't really a bootlegger either. He had a full-time job as a salesman and was just giving it as gifts to some of his steady customers, and planning to eventually pick up a little money on the side selling it as quarts and in small quantities, which he hadn't even done yet, in fact claimed he hadn't sold a drop.

Naab had a good story, and whether the judge believed it or not, there was no proof he had done anything wrong other than buy moon in the first place. Admittedly, it was a large amount, but buying that amount was also a surprise to Naab. Any charge beyond buying would be difficult to prove. Naab's was the first moon case he had seen so cluttered with things gray instead of black and white, and the last place he wanted to find himself was having to arrest everyone who bought moonshine. Not being sure how to handle Naab's case, the judge fined him $200, placed him on probation for one year and released him upon payment of the fine.

As Agent Eggert listened to Naab's story unfold, he felt his raid and subsequent charges leaking into the ground like the two kegs he had axed on the Naab's front lawn. *I thought it would be easier than this. Why arrest if you can't convict?* After Risard's case, he listened to Naab's. Then, feeling even more undermined, he stomped out of the court room to call Sampson. This court room experience made him remember what his trainer in Stearns County had said. "What's frustrating is that only a small percentage of the arrests we make ever result in enforcement of substantial fines, jail-time, or prison. It makes you feel, as an agent, like you've been given an impossible task."

Chapter 85

Sampson's squad continued to nail bootleggers on the bridges and to raid stills above Somerset as far up as Taylors Falls, but they were all small operations in terms of gallons confiscated. He was surprised to find they were getting more moonshine from bootlegger's cars than stills. This was disappointing. To make money he needed more confiscated evidence. He was beginning to think *he had overestimated the potential of the Barrens of Wisconsin.* He guessed the reason they had so little moon *was they delivered it to Wisconsin road houses and saloons almost as fast as they could make it.* The bootleggers, when caught, usually had a full load, which normally produced about 100 gallons of moon. That evidence was easy for Sampson to hide as soon as the agents separated the drivers from the cars.

Sampson had trained his men to arrest the driver, take him to the County jail, and deliver the car to either himself or his drop- off lot in Hudson. Then, he would personally take the car to his Twin Cities building, drop off the moon and deliver the car to the Revenue Impound-lot in the Twin Cities. His reports always included photos of evidence being destroyed. Sampson made sure he retained the arrest reports of his squad's members as well as destruction photos. Once they turned their reports over to him, his men never saw them again unless Sampson had questions about their reporting.

One intriguing thing about arresting bootleggers was none of them would ever reveal their sources. All made similar claims. They were hired to drive and deliver cars, didn't know what was in them, didn't care, because they'd already been paid for delivering the car. They knew nothing of prohibition, moonshine, stills, and all claimed they didn't drink. They weren't bootleggers they all said; just, hired drivers who delivered cars. These facts left them subject to arrest, but difficult to charge and even more difficult to prosecute. They were another dilemma delivered to judges by the feds, Prohibition and the Volstead Act. Most were also from out-of-state, which complicated prosecution because of State lines.

Sampson and his squad were getting frustrated with lack of enforcement and the limited amount of moon they were confiscating. Lundquist was initially satisfied with their Somerset raids, but for the last two weeks thought their results looked anemic in comparison to the numbers he was seeing in Stearns. Sampson had to do something to keep the chief satisfied. He did not want to be sent back to Chicago without successfully establishing himself as a winner in the Twin Cities

Revenue Department and without his retirement secure.

He was sure the moonshine that was always headed west crossing the bridges was coming from Wisconsin. Though the cars usually had Illinois license plates, he did not believe the booze was coming from Chicago. The plates were a ploy to help hide the real source. His Illinois experience told him it made no sense to ship from Chicago, north. Capone and his associates always brought booze down from the north. Though he had not yet been able to locate any larger stills, or determine where the confiscated cars with phony license plates were coming from he still strongly suspected they were from somewhere in the Barrens, or further east, into Wisconsin. He didn't have enough men to put all that territory under surveillance. He really didn't have enough to even cover his immediate territory. This was a dilemma, but he knew he would get no more Agents. Lundquist had no more budget and he wasn't sure how long he could hang on to what he had without better results.

He decided to take a closer look at Stephens County and the Barrens.

Chapter 86

When Bill arrived at his gas station at 7:00 a.m., Agents Sampson and Brown were waiting in his parking area. As he unlocked the station door, they exited the car and walked towards him.

"Good morning, Bill. We need to formally introduce ourselves to you. You've known us as customers for some time and as trout fishermen, but we are actually more official than that. I'm Agent Sampson, this is Agent Brown. We are both Federal Revenue Agents enforcing federal laws of Prohibition," Sampson finished, without a smile.

"I always knew you weren't trout fishermen," Bill responded. "But you have been good gas customers," he smiled.

"We need some information, Bill. I hope you will accommodate us. Under law, we can officially demand it, but it's simple enough that I hope you will just work with us. We know you have that bulk truck we see running around the County, and we'd like to see a list of your bulk customers," Sampson added. "We want to see their addresses, the amounts they buy, and who pays the bills. If you just show us your bulk books, agent Brown and I will make our own notes this morning and be out of here by noon. This will not cause you problems with your customers, Bill. You can just tell them federal revenue agents demanded to see your bulk delivery books, which you were obligated by law to give us," Sampson went on, "We can work right in your office there, and no one will even know we are here."

"Why are you singling me out?" Bill asked. "My bulk customers are farmers I've delivered to for years."

"It takes gasoline to cook moonshine, Bill. I'm sure you're aware of that." Sampson responded.

"Well, hell, we just put the bulk gasoline into their farm tanks and they use it for their tractors and gas-powered engines," Bill replied.

"Moonshine operations often require gas-fueled pumps, gas-fired cookers and things like that, Bill. There's no need to debate our request. If you want, we can close you down for the day and go through your books without you. Let's make it your choice. Do you want to help us, or should we do it on our own?" Sampson demanded.

"Hell, I've nothing to hide. Come on in. Just don't get me in trouble with my customers. I'm barely making a living now, with this god-damned depression. If you guys get me in trouble with the few customers I've got left, you could put me out of business!" Bill cursed. "I'll give you what you've asked for, but don't cause me more problems by telling my customers where you got the information."

Sampson and Brown combed his delivery records, invoices, accounts receivable, and payment records. They were surprised at how small his business really was. Sampson was used to Chicago sizes. Brown wasn't used to anything. They made two lists, one of large volume users and one of seemingly too-small volume users to make sense as *bulk deliveries*. The big ones could easily be moonshiners, in addition to farming, the way it was around Chicago. The little ones could be farmers not farming, but using smaller amounts of bulk gas to cook moon. It was a crap shoot, but Sampson was determined to take that *closer look* he always thought about. They were finished by 11:00 a.m., thanked Bill and left. Bill's last comment to them was, "Don't cause me problems!"

That afternoon, the word went out in a variety of ways to Bill's customers, that *Uncle Ben was in town*, and might visit them. It was also suggested that word of, *Uncle Ben's presence*, be spread around.

Chapter 87

"We've all had similar problems enforcing laws of the Prohibition Act," said Judge Ramsey. "It makes total sense that we share our problems, analysis and solutions for court processing of the enormous number of citizen-criminals being manufactured by this law."

He was speaking at the annual gathering of the Wisconsin County Judge Association held each year in Madison. This event gave county judges the opportunity to rub elbows with their cohorts, to compare problems, share solutions, and try to anticipate additional problems on the horizon. It was a three-day event, limited to invitation-only attendees, and only to credentialed, licensed, elected and appointed judges. Screening of participants created an environment in which the judges could be honest, ask dumb questions, and not worry about their comments being seen in the weekly editions of their county newspapers. This was an environment seriously needed when dealing with the dilemmas associate with prosecuting the laws of Prohibition.

Prohibition had been in place for nearly ten years. The longer it lasted the more many judges became convinced, or at least suspected it to be, *inappropriate law*. While at first there was considerable enthusiasm for dry law, as the years passed, consensus or unanimity dwindled. Initially, there had been strong advocate groups to help sway political votes to pass Prohibition, like the WCTU, the Anti Saloon League and the organized host of Protestant churches. Once passed, however, the challenge of Prohibition laws became *enforcement*. There was never adequate money, attention, or manpower dedicated to enforcement and upholding of the law's demands. In fact, as the magnitude of the task became apparent to those tasked with enforcement, it became obvious that those evangelizing a dry world had never even considered the magnitude of costs enforcement would require. Dry marchers envisioned voluntary compliance to Prohibition. How wrong they were.

The Volstead Act had created an impossible task, making Prohibition sort of a *fictitious law of the land*. Each year of the law's existence, enforcement became increasingly anemic compared to the rapid growth of illegal booze and crime. The Revenue Department was forced to operate in an environment, dictated by politicians above their pay grade, whose decisions had little to do with practicality or what the Revenue Department could actually accomplish. It was a mess that grew, as did efforts to repeal Prohibition, on the streets of America. It was meetings like this one in Madison, which allowed reason to surface, reason, which dry evangelizer's wanted muted. Dry arguments forced principle to subjugate practicality, ignoring the practicality required to enforce Prohibition law. For laws to work, citizens must believe in them, see merit in the law's parameters and be willing to behave within them. Unfortunately, this had never been the case since Prohibition was passed.

Judge Ramsey went on with his speech to the group: "While our opinions still run the gamut, from the hanging judge of Stearns County who wants to jail them all, to the growing number of judges advocating repeal, growing dissent is causing major dilemmas for those of us tasked with enforcement, prosecution, and sentencing. Sentencing today is far more difficult than it was in the 1920s. How can we be expected to sentence erred citizens to one or two years in prison, when we fully expect the law to be repealed before they complete their sentences? If, as law demands, we remain neutral to either wet or dry persuasions, how can we be expected to damage lives of citizens erring to the extent of felony by what is now perceived as inappropriate and almost fictitious law, to such a harsh sentence? Judges are normally asked to enforce laws demanded by sound thought and the ideal of protecting the populace from unfairness and abuse while maintaining their rights under the constitution. Judges currently have the task of passing sentences judged by the majority of us to be unsuitable to the degree of crime involved with Prohibition violation. Most of you are aware the majority of us sentence impoverished farmers caught with a still to a year-and-a day sentence, to make them eligible for parole in just six months. That is because most of us feel the law too harsh and inappropriate to the degree of crime involved. And, we are not the only citizens feeling guilty about it. Those of you who follow statistical trends, know that since 1929, votes throughout Wisconsin have dramatically shifted in support of repeal and the imbalance favoring repeal continues to grow. Is it any wonder many of us sleep less pleasantly? No wonder we question our own decisions? And, no wonder, with all of the questions we ask each other here, that we cannot come up with practical answers to the dilemmas forced upon us by hollow, unsuitable law, which many of us feel should not have been added to the Constitution in the first place. We are told by politicians - most of whom I suspect drink booze - that ours is not to reason why . . . we are to simply *enforce the law*. Simple, it is not. Well, enough from me. My goal with these words is to encourage you all to admit the complexity of the dilemma we face and to share both your problems and your solutions with all who are present. Our goal is to find ways to help each other through the seemingly impenetrable jungle of Prohibition law. We have three days to work on this. I wish you all success in this endeavor."

Three days of meetings followed in which judges suggested, probed, debated, and rationalized their way through that Prohibition jungle ignored by the majority of America's citizens, trying to find solutions to simplify enforcement, and with suitable penalties. Interestingly, poll after poll in 1930, that included numbers of those *illegally drinking,* demonstrated Prohibition was actually motivating more people to drink booze than had before Prohibition became law.

During the evenings, more than one group of judges sat around tables discussing the day's debates and drinking moonshine with their favorite mix. One of the judges from Madison had called a bootlegger he had done business with for years, to arrange a few jar deliveries to his hotel that evening. After exchanging cash for jars, with the judge behind the hotel, the bootlegger returned to his Madison apartment. Once inside, he removed the Priest's white collar he wore as disguise when driving booze. "Until next time," he said, as he placed it onto a shelf in his closet.

Chapter 88

Hutton, Andre, and Ralph were looking at chickens. They were back in the woods, at the original still operation, on the old Robinson acres. Where they now stood, just two days before, had been a line of ten stills running the length of the building on the lower floor. Now they could lean against the new wall Ralph and his men had erected. As Hutton had suggested, this wall now separated the chicken area from what used to be still area. All around them were noisy, four-month old chickens laying claim to their new nest coveys, now stacked five-high on the upper floor where mash barrels formerly rested. It made the inside of the building look half as wide as it actually was, but suited the egg business. On the other side of the nesting wall, the other half of the floor was stacked with bags of chicken feed and other essentials chickens need. Everything was real, looked authentic, and had been completely transformed in just three days. They had even heartily swept floor dust into the air to let it again settle on the building's new contents to add authenticity.

"You guys did a hell of a job," Hutton declared. "We made some fast transformations over in Stearns, but I think you broke a record on this one."

"Well," said Ralph, who now made it his practice not to speak up in meetings unless he truly had something important to say, "Those were your orders, Jim."

Andre added, "That's true, Ralph, but you did do a great job."

"Ok," Hutton added, "Now let me get into what I've got in mind next. Over in Stearns we learned how to create and strategically use a diversion when we needed it. A couple of times we set up a raid on ourselves to erase any suspicions the feds might have had. I want us to do the same thing here. Ralph told us about the feds screening Bill's bulk delivery records to pinpoint possible stills. We can use that to remove suspicion and do it quickly by placing ourselves at the top of the fed's list.

"How do we go about it, Jim?" Andre asked.

"You are both going to enjoy this," Jim grinned.

Chapter 89

It was 7:00 a.m. Sheriff Maun and Sampson were drinking coffee in Maun's office.

"When Bill told me you had checked his bulk delivery records, I realized you were screening for possible still-operations," Maun said. "I thought maybe I could help you, at least enough that you couldn't tell the powers that be that I didn't help you at all," he smiled. "I can think of about three places I would check out if I were in your shoes, Agent Sampson, and in this order, meaning the order I think you're most likely to find something. One might be the old Robinson farm. That place has changed hands, and the new owners have set up a new chicken business on the acreage. A friend of mine manages the chickens, and he wouldn't have anything to do with moonshine activities, but he might not know what's going on around the rest of the place. They also have lots of truckloads of eggs, chicken feed, and other supplies moving about which I suppose might be used for some kind of disguised distribution. I know Cartier wouldn't involve himself with moon - hell, his wife's mother is a member of the WCTU - but you might learn something looking at the rest of the place," Maun finished.

"Cartier showed up as a big bulk account at the gas station, Sheriff. I will check them out." Sampson nodded.

"Second, I'd check out the place east of Lake Schellor. It has been rumored for some time that it is owned and operated by Chicago owners. County folk tend to stay away from the place. I received a complaint from some hunters last fall who said they'd been harassed by somebody over there who chased them from the property. I figured they'd just been hunting the property without asking permission, but the hunters claimed they hadn't done that. Did that place show up on your bulk delivery list?"

"I don't know, because I don't know their names, but we'll check it out as we work the list," Sampson responded.

"Then, the third one is probably too small to interest you, but I think there could be moon there. I think they might just provide a small amount to a few road houses. I don't have an address, but I can show you on this map," Maun ended.

"I appreciate your help, Sheriff. What changed your mind? I thought you were going to put up a brick wall." Sampson asked.

"Just what I told you. Frankly, I think you'd be quick to turn me in to the council, or County, as uncooperative. Now, that is no longer the case. I am also counting on the courtesy usually extended between law enforcement officers of confidentiality of your source of information. That protects me, and allows you to take credit for whatever you find. Agreed?" Maun asked.

"Agreed," Sampson answered, as he headed for the door. "We'll check these out tomorrow."

Well, that went as planned, Jason thought. Ralph had talked to Jason the day before, suggesting this idea. It would allow Bill to appear to have helped the feds. It would let Sheriff Maun appear to cooperate and it would clear Andre and put his chicken business near the top of their *cleared* investigation list. Ralph said Andre agreed and said he didn't care since he had nothing to hide. Ralph added that, Andre thought it would help Jason, too. Since everyone thought it a good idea, Jason had agreed, and called Sampson suggesting coffee that morning.

Chapter 90

It was 5:00 a.m. and looked to Andre there was to be a bright, sunny day ahead. Because he had to deliver eggs with Carolyn today, he had gotten up at 3:00 a.m. to go through the twice-weekly routine of rotating kegs in the basement of the coop to expedite the aging process. The kegs were stored horizontally on the floor, with bricks between them, to prevent them rolling. It was a simple process. He would straddle the keg's length with his feet, lift the keg from the floor just enough to allow him to turn it one-half turn, which reversed, what had been the bottom, to the top. He also mildly shook each keg as he turned it, causing the oak chips, residue, and anything settled on the bottom to remix with the moonshine within. This was all part of the flavoring process, claimed to be *the results of aging* by the sellers. He laughed as he rotated the last keg, thinking, *I wonder how old drinkers will think this stuff is?* Then, he remembered the "3 years aged" stamp he had burned into the ends of each keg, and chuckled again. Andre was frustrated, because he had still not been able to figure out a way to heat the basement that satisfied him. He had tried fuel oil burners, but fueling them was cumbersome and doing so while still maintaining secrecy was worse. Secretly exhausting smoke and fumes from the flame of the burner in the basement was a challenging task if you thought of *being inspected by revenue agents.*

Wanting to finish before any of the family got up, he walked back up the ramp to the upper floor of the coop, *wondering why none of the chickens ever tried to come down,* when the floor-doors were open. As he grasped the first door to lower it to the floor, Carolyn burst through the outside door with, "Hi Dad, I wanted to surprise . . .," which became a gasp as she saw the doors to the basement, *which she didn't know existed,* standing upright and open. Andre thought, *looks like it's time for some explaining.*

"I didn't even know this was here, Dad. What's down there?"

"Well, I think this is a good time to talk about that, Carolyn. Walk down the ramp with me and I'll show you." Andre smiled.

Halfway down the ramp, Carolyn saw well over 200 kegs lying on the floor. She knew immediately what it was. She had seen enough pictures in the papers, just last week in fact, which showed a revenue agent chopping a keg with a big axe. "I wasn't supposed to know about this, was I?" she asked, *with a look of uncertainty* at her Dad.

"It wasn't that you weren't supposed to know, Carolyn. It was that we wanted to protect you from knowing. Your mother and I told both you and Henri that we would only tell you what we felt was important that you know. Each time you know something more about the work we are doing you have something else to keep secret. It's safer to not know," he explained. "The more you know the more dangerous it becomes that a careless mistake can untie the knots holding our secrets together. You must never forget that."

"Well, I can keep secrets, Dad, you know that."

"I have every confidence in you, Carolyn. I'm going to explain about this basement to you now, but I want to be quick about it, before your mother or Henri show up. You now know more than either of them about this storage beneath the coop."

Andre explained the details of the inventory, what he'd been doing with it twice weekly and of how it would be removed and delivered, piece-meal, throughout the winter season. He also explained that she too, now had additional secrets to keep from her mother and Henri. He showed her how to close the doors, pivot the nest shelves and pallets back into place above them, and sweep the wood shavings and chicken manure all around what had been moved, to make it again appear, immovable. Though he totally trusted and loved Carolyn as a father loves a daughter, he knew this morning they had both climbed another rung of the ladder of risk.

"Well, that's about it then, Carolyn," Andre finished as they stepped out of the coop.

"No, it isn't Dad," she stared.

"What do you mean?" he asked.

"There's one of these storage places beneath the coop on the Robinson place isn't there?" she smiled.

"Not that you know about, daughter," he smiled back.

As they walked up to the house to join breakfast, Carolyn felt more important, as though she was a bigger cog on the wheel of conspiracy that had absorbed this whole family in the last few months. She didn't think she should, but was enjoying the feeling of importance.

Chapter 91

One of the interesting things about Jim Hutton was that everyone in Stephens County who knew him, knew only what Jim Hutton allowed them to know. None really knew him in detail. Those familiar with him in real estate, knew only that he was an active real estate agent. The few who knew him through moonshine activities, knew he was in the moon business and real estate. Some of his moon acquaintances new he also had some background in Stearns County, but only the things he allowed them to know. The feds now working the County, also knew of him as being somehow in the real estate business. None, however, even those who thought they knew him, were aware of how much he was more involved in everything.

He had bought more places in Stephens County than anyone knew. Though he told Andre he was closing on property near Trade Lake, Andre didn't know that he'd actually closed on it six months earlier, and that the property was producing more moonshine now than the Robinson place, or that weekly shipments from Trade Lake had been ongoing for months. No one but Hutton and Andre knew those shipments were going north to Superior to avoid the barrier of feds surrounding the Twin Cities. Another example of Hutton's stealth was that Bill, who thought he was Hutton's only supplier of bulk-delivery gasoline, had no idea that Hutton was bringing in bulk loads of gas to Trade Lake from another source at an even better price than Bill gave him at the Robinson place. None, other than Manny, knew Jim was still active in Stearns County. Andre knew that Hutton had been active in Stearns, but was unaware if he still was.

Andre and Ralph thought the Robinson stills were now in cold storage in Trade Lake and inactive since they shut down the Robinson operation. Actually, those stills were currently producing record amounts of moon in Trade Lake. They'd cooled just three days while being moved there before being pressed back into action with five-day old mash the day after they arrived. Hutton's Trade Lake crew was mostly from Stearns County and had all spent nearly three years in the moon business before crossing the St. Croix River at Hutton's direction. To sum it up, those who knew Hutton, knew exactly as much as Hutton wanted known. There was one common trait all these people had with Jim Hutton. They all liked him.

The one person who knew more about Hutton than anyone else was Manny Goldfin. He knew, trusted, and liked him too.

Chapter 92

It was 10:00 a.m. on a Tuesday morning, when two black Ford sedans pulled into the Robinson property. One stopped by the house, the other by the new chicken coop. Two men exited the car by the house and knocked on the door. The other two approached the door of the chicken coop as Andre stepped out from the coop's door. Agent Eggert flashed his badge and ID at Andre saying, "We are Federal Revenue Agents and have a few questions for you. What is your name?"

"Andre Cartier," Andre responded, holding out his right hand. "I'm pleased to meet you. What can I do for you?"

"We understand you are in the moonshine business on this property," Eggert stared, watching Andre's eyes and facial expression, for his response. "We are going to look around this property, unless you'd like to tell us where everything involved with moonshine is?"

"Well, since that's news to me," he smiled, "I can't be of much help to you. You are welcome to look around all you want and I'll help you in any way I can," Andre added. "We are in the chicken business, not moonshine."

Agent Brown was beside Eggert. He said, "Lets walk through your chicken coop; you can give us a tour."

"Be glad to," Andre responded, then added, "follow me," as he held the door to the newly constructed coop open for them. "This is a fairly new hatchery and egg-producing coop. It's about six months old. These hens are just beginning to produce. I'm the hired manager of this operation," Andre went on as they walked through the chickens on the floor and past the nests. Andre occasionally reached in beneath a setting hen and pulled out an egg to show them. Then he carefully replaced it beneath the hen. "Another month and we'll almost be in full production. Chickens lay slower in the winter. It's a seasonal thing, but it will pick up in the spring," he went on, saying it just as he'd first heard it from Carolyn's uncle. "We've 300 hens in here now. This floor will mess up your shoes a little. I was just spreading a new layer of wood shavings and saw-dust when you arrived," he apologized.

Eggert and Brown both looked down at their black shoes.

Sampson and Eisner found no one home at the house. The place looked empty, unlived in. As they looked at the old red barn and smaller unpainted machine shed beside it, it appeared that all activity on the place was around the chicken coop where Eggert and Brown were. As they saw them coming out of the coop with another man, Sampson and Eisner walked over to join them.

Brown said to Sampson, "This is Andre Cartier, the manager of the chicken operation here. We walked through; it's genuine," he added.

Sampson looked at Andre, saying, "It's been suggested to us that someone was cooking moonshine at this place. Do you know anything about that?"

"I'm afraid not," Andre answered. "I can tell you all about the chicken business, though," he smiled.

"Its moon we're looking for," Sampson said firmly. "Where's that?"

"You'll have to ask whoever sent you out here, Mr. uh, what was your name?" Andre asked.

"Sampson," he responded as he flashed his credentials to Andre.

"Who lives in the house?" Sampson asked.

"No one," Andre answered. "The farm was lost to foreclosure last year. Then someone from the Twin Cities bought it. They wanted to invest a little, bring it back to life with the chicken business, and hired me to manage it. I was already in the chicken business on my own place. No one has lived here since I've been here. I did hear that another farmer who just lost his place because he couldn't make his mortgage payments may move in there. That's good, because as production grows I'll need more help," Andre finished.

"Eggert, why don't you and Brown continue looking around while I talk to this man," Sampson said. After they moved off, he asked Andre some more questions, the last of which was, "Why do you suppose anyone would think you were in the moon business out here?"

"I have no idea, Mr. Sampson. So many farmers are losing properties, and there's so much trouble trying to farm these days. I suppose someone knew this place had been foreclosed and was abandoned . . . I don't know," he finished, shaking his head. "I'm dam lucky to still be making it myself. If I didn't have the chicken business I couldn't keep my own place. I don't know what in hell the government of this country thinks is going to keep farming alive. They don't really seem to give a damn either," he said with anger.

They met Brown and Eggert in the middle of the yard. Both were shaking their heads indicating there was nothing to be found, which Sampson quickly interpreted. Then, Brown said to Andre, "Where does that drive into that patch of woods go?"

"We needed more room for chickens, so we are gradually moving into an older building that was there. Want to see it?" Andre asked.

"Yes," Sampson responded. Sampson thought, *everything appears legitimate here, and this guy isn't the least bit concerned about four Revenue Agents visiting him. I think we got a bum tip from Sheriff Maun.*

"It's quicker if we just walk out there," Andre pointed and waved them to follow him. "It just takes a few minutes."

As they entered the building, they found Ralph spreading wood shavings onto the floor. All five of them walked through the first third of the building up to the new wall. It was just more chickens and more chicken shit on their black shoes.

Andre introduced Sampson to Ralph, "This is Ralph Johnson. He works with me here seasonally."

Sampson said, "Aren't you the guy that works at Bill's station and drives his bulk truck?"

"That's me. I work a number of different jobs, now that I can't afford to farm my Dad's acreage. I thought you guys were trout fishermen." Ralph answered.

"We were when you filled up our gas tanks at Bill's. Let me ask you a question." Sampson said. "Do you deliver gas to that place over east of town, the one they say is owned by people from Chicago? We think they might be mooning."

"Yeh, I do. They use quite a bit of gas, but that's all I know about them," he quickly added. "I don't think those people like visitors. I get out of there as quick as I fill them up. If you go over there don't tell them I sent you. I want no trouble with those guys."

Sensing that Sampson was done asking questions, Brown asked Andre, "What's in the rest of the building?"

"This way," Andre waved. "I'll show you." They stepped out of the chicken area and through the next outside door into the empty part of the building. They were on the upper, higher floor of the building now. "On your left there, you can see we keep chicken feed, wood shavings, and the other stuff we need for the hens. Down there on your right we'll continue to expand into as we have more chickens."

Sampson asked, "Why the difference in the level of these two floors?" as he stroked his index finger down a chicken feed bag to see how thick the dust was on it.

"I'm actually not sure, but I think at one time it was going to be used with milk cows. I think they were going to put in milking stanchions down there, and keep everything that needed to be dry on this upper level. That's how we are using it and it really does keep stuff dry. I think the water pipes in here were piped in for the water needs of a milking operation. Their well may have run dry, because they're not hooked up to anything now. We have to haul water for the chickens," Andre finished.

"Ok," Sampson said. "Are there any more buildings on the property?"

"No. This is it," Andre answered.

"Anything else any of you want to see?" Sampson said eyeballing his agents.

All shook their heads no, then, Eisner asked of Sampson, "Is there any reason to look inside the house?"

"What do you think, Mr. Cartier?" Sampson asked without a smile.

"I went through the house once, when the owner was thinking of renting the property. He'd like to have some farmer live there and rent the fields for a percentage of the crops. He says that the more active he can keep the place the better it will be kept up. I don't know anything about moonshine, so I wouldn't know what to look for in the first place, but I didn't see anything that would make me think it's other than a normal house. Want to see it? I think I know where a key is stashed." Andre finished with a smile.

"No." Sampson said. "We've wasted enough of your time. Thank you for your help. Do you know of anything anywhere in the County that would make you suspicious of moonshine, Mr. Cartier?"

"I truly don't. I've never been a drinker. In fact, my wife's mother is a member of the WCTU," Andre answered.

"You said you have another chicken place of your own, is that right?" Sampson asked.

"Yes. Cartier Chicken and Egg Service is the name. We've sold eggs and chickens to local grocery stores for some time." Andre replied.

"I saw a young lady carrying egg crates from the Cedarville Grocery to a pickup a few weeks ago," Sampson said. "Is that your operation then?"

"Probably my daughter," Andre smiled.

"Well, she sure gave your local sheriff a big hug." Sampson said.

"Yup. That was my daughter."

As the two black Fords drove out the Robinson driveway, Andre said to Ralph, "I'm glad that's over, but I think it went ok."

Ralph answered, "Yeh, I think it went just about the way Hutton thought it would. They better not mention my name to those Chicago guys, though!"

Chapter 93

"We set up a scenario of information that coaxed those revenue agents into raiding our Robinson operation, Manny," said Hutton. "It went well. My guys handled it perfectly. The feds left, unsuspicious, and headed for that Chicago operation yesterday. None of us have heard a word so far, but I expect to today. I have heard it's a big operation, but have never been able to confirm it. We'll soon know, though. If that turns out the way we expect, it will not only take some heat off us, but also remove some future competition," Hutton grinned. "I think that new agent from Chicago thought he was going to find a lot of action in the Barrens, but now realizes it's not that big. They have found a number of stills in the last few weeks, but they were all small. I know they've gotten a number of tips from the game warden in the Barrens, but we can tell they're sort of scrambling around more now, without any kind of a plan. I hope I'm right about that."

"I do too, Jim, "Manny said. "I've got orders for us from Chicago anytime we want them. I've got one associate down there that will take 1000 gallons a week, cash in advance, and he wants that to start by next month. Can we do it? This is a big, steady customer, with lots of money, Jim."

"I think we can. Trade Lake is producing 500 gallons a day now, when things run smoothly. I think we could get them up to 1000 if we felt safe enough from the feds. I considered shutting them down when I shut down Robinson, but decided to gamble and didn't do it. That's why we set up those phony tips for the agents. I've stashed everything up near the Trade Lake farm, but it's well hidden. We've got to really watch these guys carefully, though. I can't shut down Trade Lake as fast as we did the Robinson place."

"The guy we planted in Lundquist's office keeps us well posted on info, but I get the idea that Lundquist doesn't really know what this Chicago agent is doing over in Stephens. Stay alert!" Manny finished.

"Yes, we will, Manny, and I'll let you know as soon as I hear about the raid on the Chicago operation."

"How are things going up in Superior?" Manny asked.

"They're bringing in Canadian booze up there. It's mostly Scotch and Canadian whiskey in bottles, some kegs on the boats, but the supply is intermittent in comparison to ours. Some of the Chicago boys try to bring it from Fort William and Port Arthur down Lake Superior by boat to Duluth, and they're also running it in hopped-up cars down the back roads through Grand Marais. The Revenue Department has a Coast Guard cutter now, called the "Cook", which is chasing down some of the boats, and some of the cars are being caught at the border by revenue agents working the roads between Canada and Duluth. Our feedback from Superior is that our supply is more stable and they feel it's safer to work with us, so I think our business will improve throughout the coming months."

"That is one crazy place, Manny, but it's a gold mine for us because of the city of Superior's politics. Up there the law focuses on speakeasies and saloons instead of bootleggers and stills. The city makes so much money on daily fines; they don't want moonshine to go away. They've got a red-light district there that Superior is famous for, so they want booze to flow. One of my cousins runs a saloon right on the edge of that district. He says he gets raided once a week. The next morning he goes into Superior Police-Court, enters a line with others who were raided and all wait for the morning court session. The judge asks each of them if they plead guilty or not guilty, has them raise their hands for God's sake! My cousin says, guilty," every time. The judge fines those who raised their hands to guilty, $200, They pay it right there to a collection officer, then go right back to their saloons and keep selling beer, booze, and moon! He says there are often ten to twenty people in the lineup and they're all on a first-name basis," he laughed. "The new ones, who haven't been arrested before, and who don't plead guilty, get fined $500! The city is making so much money with daily arrests for moonshine activities, they don't want anything to change, Manny, and neither do we! My cousin says Superior, Wisconsin, generated half of the Revenue Agent's production of fine-revenue in the entire state of Wisconsin last year. The best part of all of it, is that now with our production up in the Barren's stills, instead of wrestling with the feds surrounding Minneapolis and St. Paul, we are shipping north to Superior and south to Chicago out of Wisconsin. Doing that, we're minimizing risk of seeing feds and maximizing our price and sales. We couldn't have it much better!" Hutton finished, enthusiastically. "On top of that, we're delivering aged Minnesota 13 starting next month, at $50 per keg."

"That's good, Jim. You've set things up well. Just don't get too comfortable. It just takes one mistake to upset the best of plans." Manny ended.

Chapter 94

"It was about 2:00 a.m.," Agent Eggert said to Sampson. "The local cop came down to the bridge to see who was sitting on the side of the road. He was surprised to see it was me," he grinned. "Then, across came this big four-door Packard from the Wisconsin side. It looked as though its rear bumper was damn near dragging. I knew he was carrying a load, so I asked the cop to help me. There was no other traffic that time of the night, so I told him to just follow me. I'd block the west bound lane at the end of the bridge, and he'd block the eastbound side right beside me. We did it so fast, the driver of the Packard didn't realize what we were doing. He slammed on his brakes and before he could back up, I jumped out of the car and aimed my pistol at him. He caved in quickly. The town cop put him in jail. His car had fifty one-gallon cans of moon in it! That's the biggest car load I've seen."

"So, where's the car now?" Sampson asked.

"I parked it up behind the Lutheran Church. I didn't think anybody would bother it there and the town cop is keeping an eye on it. I had to get some quick shut-eye to meet you now for this new raid. I told him I'd pick it up later today. It's all locked up." Eggert finished, adding, "Here's the keys if you want to take it down to Hudson."

Sampson took the keys and said, "I'll get pictures back to you for your report when we destroy the cans. Good work," Sampson added. "Now let's get on over to take a look at that Chicago hangout. I hope we accomplish more than we did yesterday at the chicken ranch, though."

They stopped in Cedarville to notify Sheriff Maun where they were going. "The chicken ranch was a waste of time, Sheriff," Sampson complained.

"I told you I thought it would be, Agent Sampson. That Chicago farm is a little more suspicious though. I wouldn't be surprised if you found what you were looking for there." Jason said.

"Well, you're invited to come with us, Sheriff." Sampson invited.

"No, I've got a court appointment this morning, but let me know what you find," Maun said, thinking *the last thing I need is to have the people of Stephens County thinking I'm raiding stills.*

Chapter 95

Brown and Eastman were working the Taylors Falls Bridge. It was Wednesday evening, and as usual traffic slowed down at night. Though they had stopped a few cars for a close-up peek into the windows, they'd found nothing for their efforts. It was midnight when a big Oldsmobile sedan came across from the east side of the bridge. Brown and Eastman had just been getting ready to call it a night, so were both surprised when the car showed up. They were both on the Minnesota side when they flagged the car to a stop on the west end of the bridge. Brown was on the driver side of the car, Eastman the other. Because of their rookie status when Sampson picked them, neither of them had ever really had experience flagging down or arresting cars from traffic lanes; however, since they started working bridges two weeks before, it had gone well for them. They weren't expecting any trouble.

As the window came down on the driver's side of the Olds, the driver waved and said, "What's up?"

"We are Revenue Officers, and we want to take a look inside your car. Pull over to the right on the edge of the road right there," Brown pointed, as Eastman waved them on to where he wanted them to park. The driver began to slowly move over to the right, off the asphalt onto the gravel edge and stopped, with Eastman directly in front of the car's front bumper.

Just then, another car, of the same kind and color, came across the bridge again from the east heading towards Minneapolis. The coincidence of seeing two Oldsmobiles the same color and this close together triggered a response in Brown's mind - *These two are traveling together. We've got something here!* He hollered at Eastman, "I'm going to stop this one too, right behind the other."

Brown stepped back onto the road, waving the second car over to the side. Eastman stepped back onto the road, too, pointing to the other car and waving him in, right behind the first one. Just as he stepped out of the way, the first car put the hammer down in first gear and with roaring exhaust from its big engine and gravel and dust from its spinning rear tires, caused a burnt-rubber squeal when its tires hit asphalt! Brown and Eastman were caught off guard by the first car's breakaway and that surprise caused them both to watch a second too long. That second gave the second car's driver the opportunity to do the same as the first. He, too, burned rubber onto the highway and both cars' big engines had them quickly up the hill and out of sight from the Minnesota side of the Taylors Falls bridge. The sound of their exhausts went on for a full two minutes, as Brown and Eastman stood beside the highway in disbelief. "Shit!" Brown shouted, "We blew that one! Those were pros! There's no point in even giving chase. Neither of us drives anything that will catch those Oldsmobiles."

"Now I remember Agent Johnson over in Stearns saying, "stop them on the side of the road, take the keys from the ignition, and handcuff them to the steering wheel," Eastman grinned. "And both those cars were full of moon. Dammit! I didn't even get a plate number did you?"

"They were both Illinois, but I didn't get the numbers either. It doesn't matter. Those plates will be changed from Illinois to Minnesota within the next ten minutes," Brown grumbled.

Fortunately, there were no other cars around and no one else saw this happen. Brown looked at Eastman, then, said, "I'll make you a deal. I won't tell Sampson about this one if you don't."

"Agreed," smiled Eastman.

Part IV

Consequences

Chapter 96

Sampson and his men did a lot of planning before this raid. He thought it would be a big operation. After their first look at the suspected farm, Sampson ordered three nights of surveillance. He, Brown, and Eggert had taken turns at surveillance of the Chicago farm's activities for the last three nights. They found a place they could park about 100 feet into a patch of woods they accessed via a narrow tire-track path that couldn't be seen from the road. Their car protected them from rain and mosquitoes, and let them snooze a little as well, without being detected by traffic on the road in daylight or darkness because of the thickly wooded brush. The brush also made it easy to pee, or worse, in the woods without being seen. The surveillance was enlightening. Six different trucks had come from the west towards the Twin Cities and driven in on the driveway of the suspect farm. All seemed heavily loaded by their slow movement and labored engine sounds. Each had been covered with canvas, so they were unable to detect what they hauled. Each truck left, later the same night, sounding empty. Sampson assumed the incoming trucks were likely filled with 100-pound bags of sugar, yeast, kegs, and whatever else a large moon operation needed. He instructed all agents to only observe, and to not be seen by anyone. He wanted no one to know *Uncle Ben was around.* That exposure's name had cost him several successful raids back in Chicago.

It was Thursday. They had not seen a heavy load of anything leaving the place for the last two days, which made Sampson feel their timing for the raid was good. Seeing no loaded trucks leaving the premises meant there should be a substantial amount of moon on site. He was almost certain this was a moonshine operation. In addition to the telltale signs of night-hauling, none of the locals wanted anything to do with the place they referred to as "the place those Chicago boys run." Seeing those loaded night-haul trucks confirmed his suspicions.

Sampson decided to wait until about 10:00 a.m. to implement the raid. During their three nights of surveillance, they had watched about ten different cars, some, with two people in them, arriving about 10:00 p.m., leaving again about 6:00 a.m. About 7:30 a.m. two or three more cars would pull into the place with only one individual in them. Sampson guessed from these observations that they were cooking at night with 10 to 15 people and preparing mash and filling containers during the day with a smaller crew. While he would like to catch and arrest all involved he wasn't about to take on a fifteen-man crew with just himself and three rookies. He decided to move on them about 10:00 a.m. thinking, *they'd be into the projects of a normal workday, not expecting a raid, and be too busy to attempt to escape.*

His last words to his agents were, "Assuming, we find moon activities on the premises, here's the plan. We take charge immediately. Remember, we are all armed; we use our weapons if the situation demands and once on the premises, we take charge! Shut everyone down from movement to a stationary spot. Eastman, you remain outside until I call you in. Block the driveway with your car and remain by it to make sure there is no movement in or out of the driveway after we trigger the action. If there are escape attempts you are in charge of anything outside the buildings. Brown, Eggert, and I will split up on buildings as I direct, after I see what we're up against. The three of us will get everyone assembled in one place; have them lie face down on the floor, no movements, no talking. Take charge!" Sampson added, firmly, "If any one gives you any bullshit fire a round into the ceiling to get their attention! Intimidate the hell out of them! There are only four of us, so we can't lose control. No one leaves the premises in a vehicle or on foot. No one! Shoot if you have to. That's an order! Brown, what's the plan we've discussed?"

"Surprise them, take charge, herd them together in one place, and immobilize them. Then, one at a time, empty their pockets, handcuff them to something stationary, or together in a line. We've all got four sets of cuffs, grab all car-keys and their wallet I.D." Brown concluded.

"Good," Sampson added. "Once they're secured I will call the shots. If this really is a Chicago operation there could be some experienced people in there running it. Local help won't be dangerous, but the bosses might be. Watch out for weapons; they're not afraid to use them. I've been shot at and I've shot back. Be ready," he demanded. "We are pulling in with all four of our cars, one behind the other, to make the raid look bigger. When the cars stop, get out of your car fast, then, draw your weapons and keep them visible. Take charge!"

The men followed Sampson's example of pulling their weapons, checking their action, and making ready for whatever it was that was scaring hell out of each of them right now.

"Ok," Sampson said at 9:45 a.m. "Let's go." I asked Sheriff Maun to pull in the driveway at 10:15 a.m. That will make it appear we have reinforcements and if we get in trouble he will find out. If everything is secure by his arrival time, he will simply observe or respond to my requests. He has no responsibility in this raid."

All four entered their cars, and followed Sampson the remaining mile to the raid site. The driveway into the property went in through a wooded area, which prevented seeing any of the old farm's buildings from the road. About three hundred feet from the road, the driveway turned ninety degrees to the right, and in another 100 feet spilled traffic into an open farmyard. In that yard was a big barn, another smaller barn, an old chicken coop, and a machine shed. Across the open farmyard from the work buildings sat an older farmhouse with farm fields behind it. There were seven cars and three trucks parked beside the big barn. Two of the three trucks were covered with white canvas covers with the name "Anderson Pickles" in bold, green-lettered, banner logos on each side of the trucks. Two men appeared to be loading kegs from the barn door into the open back end of the third truck. They were the only people visible in the farmyard. The two men set down the kegs they were carrying, and stared at the fleet of black Fords as they came to a stop in the yard.

Chapter 97

The Cartiers were enjoying the last week before school started. Carolyn and Henri would go back to their daily school routines, now as a senior and a sophomore, the coming Monday. Andre and Clair had planned Thursday and Friday to organize chores and work in a manner that accommodated the school schedule. They enjoyed a great breakfast together, talked their way through the chore assignments, and were just finishing a hike through the chicken coop where Carolyn was showing them how hens were beginning to lay. Andre had built a new packaging table in the same end of the coop where the hidden floor-doors were beneath the feed pallets. It would make it easy to clean eggs, package in dozens and fill the bigger delivery boxes for store distribution. Hens were still laying in the original coop too. Carolyn had suggested bringing eggs from the old coop into the new one for packaging. With the anticipated increase in volume of eggs they had to streamline processing. All agreed they were ready to take over the egg business in Stephens County, and eventually, even a larger area.

"Ok, so we're all in agreement on our work, chores, and school, so we should be set for the winter," Andre said. "Have you anything to add, Clair?"

"Well, actually there is something that Henri and I have wanted to talk with you two about," Clair said, with a grin on her face.

"All right, you have the coop floor," Andre bowed with a return smile.

"Just when, exactly, were the two of you going to tell Henri and me what is beneath this floor we are standing on?"

Andre and Carolyn looked at each other in surprise; then Carolyn responded, "Well, I was told to keep it a secret."

Andre put his hands out to his sides, palms up, shrugged his shoulders and said, "She was told that by me, Clair. Carolyn, accidentally discovered the basement, so I told her to keep it secret. I just figured the fewer who knew of it the less likely the secret was to escape. I wanted you and Henri to have one less thing to worry about."

"Henri and I have known about it since before you put the floor on it," Clair smiled. "We knew you were trying to keep it a secret, so we kept quiet. Henri is the one who told me about it."

"Some secret!" crowed Henri. "We couldn't believe you two thought we didn't know. You forget, Dad," he laughed. You and Carolyn aren't the only ones that get up early in the morning. I watched them pour the floor! You weren't even here," he grinned. "Mom and I just wanted to see how long you would go on without telling us."

"But, that's not it," said Clair. "What we don't know, either of us, is what's down there?"

"That's right, Dad, and I'm sick of being kept in the dark around here," Henri said with a straight face. "You and Carolyn have no right to keep things secret from Mom and me. If I'm supposed to do all your chore-work while you're gone I deserve to know what's going on!" Henri spoke those words as an adult, with satisfaction, declaring his right for equality in stature with his sister. Both Andre and Carolyn were surprised to hear it. To Henri, it felt good to say it.

"OK, Henri. I'm sorry, Clair. Tonight," said Andre. "I never open up the floor doors unless it's very early, or very late, when there's no possibility of anyone showing up at the wrong time. We'll meet you here at 10:00 p.m. tonight, and give you the full tour and explanation. The lighting is not great. There's only two light bulbs down there, but you can still see. I was tired of keeping that secret anyway," he smiled, along with Carolyn's.

That night they all took the tour.

Chapter 98

Sampson leaped from his car, pistol drawn, and walked to the two men standing by the truck. He, quietly, said," Federal Revenue Agents. You are under arrest. How many are inside?"

"Eight or ten," one of the men responded nervously.

"Walk directly over to the man beside that car, now!" he pointed. "Not a sound!" Sampson said, again quietly, not wanting to alert those inside the building to their presence. He waved a signal to Eastman, pointing at the two men walking toward him, indicating he was to handle and secure them.

Sampson signaled Eggert and Brown by pointing to the big barn, with three fingers, beckoning both to follow him. When all three were at the door he grasped the door handle and said, "Take charge men!"

The three of them burst through the door, guns in hand! All three were surprised by what they saw. No one seemed to be waiting for them as they had anticipated, or even, to be surprised by their presence. Everyone inside was busy with tasks at hand. There was a clean concrete floor the length of the barn, on which sat five large stills. Behind each still and across to the other barn wall sat what looked like unending barrels of mash. Three or four men were working the stills and four were stirring mash in the barrels. One, who was wearing a long shop coat, open in front showing no shirt beneath it, was walking towards them with a clip-board in his hand. All but the one walking towards Sampson slowed, but didn't stop what they were doing. They stared at the three men wearing black trench coats who had just come in the door waving pistols. It must have been ninety-five degrees inside. Most of the men wore just undershirts, or none at all, and were sweating profusely. All of the stills were cooking and the stale air of the entire barn contained an alcohol fog.

"Good morning, gentlemen," said the man carrying the clipboard. "What can I do for you?" he asked, as he raised his hands in the air, as if surrendering.

"U.S. Federal Revenue Agents! Everybody freeze! You are all under arrest," Sampson shouted. "Call all of your men down here right now," Sampson ordered, loud enough that all could hear, while pointing at the floor against the wall. Then, he added, "Is anybody going to do anything stupid?" staring directly at the man who appeared to be in charge.

"Not a chance, Mr. Sampson," he smiled. "These are all local farmers and workers," he finished, laying his clipboard on the floor, as he sat down on the concrete where Sampson had pointed.

With a surprised and curious look on his face, Sampson asked, "How did you know my name?"

"You raided my Uncle's farm in Janesville a little over a year ago," he said. "I was there, but got off without going to jail. My uncle's still in Leavenworth. He got a year and a day from the judge, because that was his third arrest. How would I forget you?"

Looking scared, their eyes screaming for a way out of the barn, the rest of the men now sat on the floor beside the clip-board man, as Brown and Eggert directed them. Sampson aimed words at the man he now called "clip-board," "Anyone else on the farm outside of those in this building?"

"Two truck drivers should be outside. I think the third one is sitting in the outhouse across the yard. He'll do anything to avoid work."

"All right, listen up!" Sampson half-shouted for effect. "We are U.S. Federal Revenue Agents enforcing Prohibition law. You are all under arrest for violation. Sit right where you are until directed by me, or one of my agents, to do something. Not a move, do not stand up, do not put your hands in your pockets. Just sit. Do not talk until told to do so," he finished by waving his gun at them.

"You will be called over to that table, one at a time, by one of these agents. They will direct you from there."

Sampson turned the processing over to Brown and Eggert, then stepped outside and told Eastman to bring the truck drivers into the barn, as he walked towards the outhouse across the yard. Before he reached it, the outhouse door opened and a man stepped out ,buckling his belt. The expression on his face changed to fear as he saw Sampson, with a gun in his hand, wave him towards the barn. One trucker recognized Sampson's dark suit immediately and knew this day would not have a happy ending for an Illinois trucker who had planned on being home in Janesville for supper by evening.

Sampson sat the third trucker on the floor, said a few words to Brown, set three of his four sets of handcuffs on the table and took Clipboard and his fourth set of cuffs through the barn door to get outside the building. Sampson quickly patted him down which was easy, because the man wore no shirt beneath his shop coat, because of the heat. It looked like he wore the coat to have a pocket for pencils and glasses. "Your uncle's name was Sieverson wasn't it?" Sampson asked, finishing the pat-down.

"Yes, Samuel Sieverson. He was arrested three different times by Revenue Agents. You were the last, but in court he unfortunately got the same judge that fined him the first two times. After the third arrest by you, the judge said something like, 'Three times and out Sieverson. This time, it's Leavenworth as a repeat-offender,' and off my uncle went. The judge did him a favor with the year and a day sentence that made him eligible for parole in only six months, but for some reason he didn't get pardoned. He's still there. That was kind of a friendly judge. He only made me pay a $200 fine and suggested I find another line of work. That's why I came up here. I suppose, now, I'm going to visit my uncle?" he questioned, with an almost pleading expression on his face.

Sampson looked through Clip-board's wallet and discovered him to be Charles R. Woodruff, of Janesville, Illinois, and twenty-eight years of age. He was unmarried, no kids, and had been sent up to run this operation by a friend of his uncle's, who worked with the Chicago people, the land's owner's. "People" was the term Charles Woodruff used, because he knew almost nothing about the syndicates or who made things happen in Chicago. He just took the money and did what he was told. He admitted to Sampson that he had been doing very well financially since coming up to Stephens County a year ago.

As Sampson was talking to Woodward, Sheriff Maun pulled into the driveway and parked behind Eastman's car, which was blocking the road, and walked over to Sampson. It was 10:45a.m.

"What did you find?" Maun asked Sampson.

"Walk inside and take a look, Sheriff. It might motivate you to know a little more about what's going on in your County. Maybe you can give my men some help in processing the ten prisoners inside. I want them all locked up in local jails until their court appearance. Please ask Agent Brown to come out here for a moment. Maybe you can stand in for him while he's out here, help us keep things in order," he nodded to Maun with an appreciative look on his face. "I want to interview this man a little more right now."

Sampson had Brown retrieve the three truck drivers from the barn and bring them outside to him. Brown kept an eye on the others, while demanding there to be no talking, between them. Sampson took one at a time to his car where he interviewed each, making notes as he talked. When finished, Brown took them back inside to finish processing for jail. Sampson left the premises with James "clip-board" Woodruff in his car. He left it up to his agents and whatever degree of cooperative aid they could solicit from Sheriff Maun, to secure the other prisoners' transport to jail. He assigned Brown and Eastman to return from the jail runs and stay on the premises for the next forty-eight hours. He wanted the premises under tight security for two reasons; first, to capture and interview, perhaps arrest, anyone else that showed up at the farm; second, to keep the inventory on the premises secure until he could arrange for his trucks to pick it up. Then, they would deliver what wasn't destroyed for photos, to the evidence-holding facility in Hudson. He would personally supervise destruction of the stills and evidence and also be involved with the photos, the next day. This was a big raid and Sampson intended to make hay while the sun was shining. He had plans for the inventory, and would personally supervise all the handling.

He kept Clip-board and the three truck drivers at the farm most of the afternoon. He immediately separated them so they had no opportunity to concoct a story. It also gave Sampson an opportunity to intimidate each with threats of prison time. He wanted to know, specifically who they worked for, who paid them, and how and where, they were to deliver those truckloads of booze. He also wanted to be sure no one had an opportunity to phone news of the raid to anyone in Chicago. By evening, Clip-board was still handcuffed to a radiator in the farm house, with Sampson interviewing him. His agents, who returned after dropping prisoners at two different jails in Stephens county, had done a thorough inventory of all evidence on the farm. Between the loaded trucks and what was still in the barn, they counted over 1000 gallons of moon in ten-gallon kegs. Thinking themselves successful in the raid, they then discovered another 300 gallons in the building formerly used as a corn crib.

Thirteen-hundred gallons of evidence, Sampson thought. *Lundquist is going to like this. So is Sampson.*

Chapter 99

Sheriff Maun was thinking of the men arrested the day before. He knew three of them. Two were local farmers just looking for ways to make a few bucks they weren't earning farming. The other was a fellow who never really had a steady job, but had worked as a handyman on farms during harvests along with any other work he could find. Cooking had been the most profitable job any of the three had in the last two years. Each of them was bringing home twenty dollars a night, tax-free. That was big money since the Crash. The others he didn't personally know, but judged their circumstances to be nearly identical to the rest. The raid and arrests had changed Maun's life overnight.

He'd received at least ten phone calls before the normal morning coffee break. Four had been from wives and family members of those arrested. The Catholic priest, Father Baptiste, called urging him to do what he could to temper grounds for arrest and their subsequent fines, expecting no jail time for any of them. "These are good salt-of-the-earth people, Sheriff, trying to keep the wolves from the door and food on the table."

Three council-men had stopped in to see him, having received calls themselves from family members of those jailed. "This is going to bring some real heat, Sheriff. How do we deal with these Federal Revenue Agents? What level of authority do they have over you?" Each wanted him to have answers, and answers they wanted to hear. Family members wanted to hear it would be nothing more than a small fine and a slap on the hands before sending them home. Council-members wanted the same and to also know what would satisfy the Federal Revenue Agents, who would now likely go away and leave Stephens County alone.

What none of the callers realized was that Sheriff Maun didn't know any more than they did. He just wore the hat that said "Sheriff." Wanting to come up with answers he could at least pass on to callers he tried unsuccessfully to reach Agent Sampson all morning. He was able to reach Judge Rasperson, who indicated court appearances for all of the arrested wouldn't occur for a week when a Federal Judge would be available locally, and yes, he realized that would cause them all to spend a week in jail. They should have realized this hazard before getting into the business of moonshine in the first place, he added. At least that gave Maun one message he could use to ease the anxiety of callers. *Yes, Judge Rasperson says they'll all be in court within a week, and yes, I realize that means a few days and nights in jail, but they should have realized moonshine has prob-*

lems as well as profits. He liked his modification of the judge's words. They sounded more like a Sheriff talking. He still wished, however, the phone calls would stop.

"Sheriff Maun," the city cop said, "Pastor Ecklund of the first Baptist Church is here to see you with Mrs. Girard of the WCTU. I told them you were tied up with all the arrest business, but they insist on seeing you now. Also, Jim Niesen with the *Gazette* called. I didn't tell him you were here, but he said he was coming over, too."

"It looks like today's the day I earn my hat," Maun said. "Fortunately, I was able to get away from the raid with a carload of prisoners before they started taking pictures out there yesterday." *I sure as hell hope I'm not in any of them.*

Chapter 100

The next day, Sampson had Eggert and Eastman go into the County Seat and finish filling out arrest records for the next day's court appearances. He was surprised to see what a big deal the results of this raid were to authorities of Stephens County. He spoke to the judge, who himself had questions enough for the need to track Sampson down. There had been raids by the feds before, but never this big and never so many at once. These arrests were going to ruffle some feathers in Stephens County.

While Eggert and Eastman spent the day in Cedarville, doing paperwork on those arrested, Sampson and Brown coordinated the clean-up of the premises. Sampson's trucks arrived from Hudson at 9:00 a.m. Each truck driver, per Sampson's instructions, had brought along two helpers to load the trucks. By 11:00 a.m., 1200 gallons of evidence had left the premises headed for Hudson. The remaining 100 gallons had been set up in keg-rows to make it look like more.

Then, with all of Sampson's truck drivers, and either Sampson or Brown also in the picture, the agents handed the camera back and forth as they took multiple photos of moonshine spraying and splashing into the air from the pressure of the axe's splitting the staves of the kegs. Moon splashed onto the faces and clothing of those closest to the strikes and it made for great press release photos, which Sampson would have in the hands of the *Gazette* and a couple of other papers by afternoon. He would also send some to Lundquist couriered by one of his men the next day. The puddles beneath the burst kegs looked to be in the hundreds of gallons and Sampson had his help stack fifty more empty kegs from inside the barn behind those they were taking pictures of, to make it appear the largest cache of moonshine- destruction to ever hit the local papers. He wanted no one thinking of *undestroyed* evidence. Sampson staged another set of photos that afternoon, with Eastman and Eggert and axes in hand, destroying the ten stills inside the barn. The clean concrete floor made excellent background for broken off worms, bent copper tubing, and copper kettles with gaping axe-slashes in them. They were dramatic photos that would make people fear Revenue Agents wherever the pictures were seen, and also leave each observer feeling everything on this moon operation was destroyed.

With the same thoughts in mind yesterday Sampson delivered pictures to Eggert, of what looked like over 100 axe-burst-cans sitting in a puddle of moon. They were to go with Brown's report on the bootlegger arrest on the Taylors Fall's bridge the week before. No one would ever know those cans were empty when Sampson destroyed them with a fire axe.

This was the kind of action that would make Lundquist happy.

Chapter 101

The hullabaloo over the arrests continued to mushroom throughout the week. The *Gazette* came out with large, front page pictures of axe-wielding Revenue Agents standing in puddles of moon, surrounded by smashed kegs. The headline was, "SOURCE DRIED UP", followed by a story of the raid, the destruction by agents, and courtroom consequences. The three trucks were confiscated and impounded and each trucker was fined $300 and released on probation which forbade them reentry into Wisconsin for the next year. Each of the local workers was fined $200 and released with a warning that should they be found again in the moonshine business they would be subject to the year-and-a-day sentence category of Prohibition repeat-offenders. The man Sampson called Clip-board was not tried by the local judge and simply disappeared after the raid. The rumor among those jailed was that he had been taken back to Chicago, where he had the opportunity to work with the feds in lieu of jail time. There was no information beyond the rumor and the *Gazette's* article didn't mention him.

After talking to Chief O'Hara, his former boss in the Chicago Revenue Office, Sampson had sent the hand-cuffed clip-board-man back to Chicago, driven by agent Eastman. The Chicago feds would learn all the arrested man knew about the Chicago operation that financed the Wisconsin farm Sampson raided. What the Chicago office did with him when they were finished, Sampson didn't know or care. Before sending the prisoner to Chicago with Eastman, Sampson had done his own interrogation, resulting in a sizable welt on the side of Clip-board's head and cheek, but also with Sampson knowing who it was, that ordered those three truckloads of moon they were about to ship before the raid. *He might need that info to move his own inventory.* In addition, he had made himself look good to O'Hara and the Chicago crew of agents, by sending them his prisoner. They now owed him.

There was a letter-to-the-editor from Mrs. Girard, Chairwoman of the local WCTU, lauding the action of local law enforcement for what she referred to as "their role" in the raid on the evils of alcohol in Stephens County. She said she had personally passed on her congratulations to Sheriff Jason Maun before bringing this letter to the *Gazette*. In short, it was exactly the attention sheriff Maun, did not want.

The Drys shared favorable attitudes toward the *Gazette* story; the Wets wondered if it would affect local availability; and the families of the local workers wondered where they would get the $200 to pay the fine, as well as what they were now going to now do to earn a living.

Sampson and his federal revenue agents walked with more authority in their strides, felt pleased with, themselves, and were ready for the next raid. They had learned that successful raids felt better than weeks of fruitless searching.

Sampson thought, *I have accrued over 1500 gallons of moon in my warehouse. At $20 per gallon, that's $30,000! A man can retire on that alone. I've got to move those kegs quickly, so there's no possibility of discovery. No evidence!*

Sheriff Maun thought, *"My role!"* Hell, *all I did was haul three locals to jail. I wish Mrs. Girard would keep her mouth closed. I had no idea those three local guys were working out there. Maybe Sampson is right. I should keep a better eye on what's going on in Stephens County.*

Chapter 102

It was September. Carolyn and Henri had been back in school for two weeks. Carolyn and Molly Raft were eating lunch together on the edge of the school yard. The Raft family had moved into the farm house on the Robinson place, at the invitation of Andre, after Molly's dad had started working for Andre on the new chicken business there.

"My dad is really happy working with your chickens, Carolyn. He said he never thought he'd be raising chickens, but he is so glad to be working again, at all. He's getting along with my uncle better since we moved from there and isn't drinking any more. My mother says she thinks the worst is behind us, and that's what my brother and I hope, too."

"That's great, Molly," Carolyn laughed.

"Yesterday, we got the greatest surprise. My mother opened a letter from Minneapolis and out fell a check for $100 made out to my mother and dad! She said she couldn't believe it at first, thought it was a mistake. Then she found a note in the envelope that said (From friends who want to help see you through some tough times.) When she showed it to my dad he cried. We didn't think anyone even liked us anymore, except you, Carolyn."

"How great is that?" Carolyn smiled. "My mother told me she'd heard of something like that, a friend of hers, who helped people through tough times. Before we got into the chicken business, I heard my dad say that he was hoping someone would come along that could lend a helping hand. I guess we were almost in the same trouble your family found itself. Maybe sometime, down the way, you, or your family, will be able to help someone else out."

"I hope so," Molly added. "Oh, oh, here comes that Dan Anderson. Is he still after you?"

"He quit bothering me two weeks ago. I think Henri and Dan had a talk, or something." Carolyn said quietly to Molly, with a raised eyebrow.

"Yeh, some of the boys can't keep their hands to themselves," Molly said, knowingly.

"Hello, Carolyn," Dan said, "Hi, Molly. What are you two doing off here by yourselves?"

"We were just wondering why you were coming over here," Molly responded, almost accusatorily.

"Just saying hello," Dan said. "Carolyn's brother told me the way we used to talk to the girls at my old school made you mad. I thought I was being friendly.

Did I ever make you mad, Molly?"

"No, but you didn't grab me, either," Molly answered, embarrassing Carolyn, whose face reddened.

"Sorry, I didn't mean nothing by it," Dan said, sort of apologetically, "Some of the girls at my old school thought it was funny."

"Dan," Carolyn said. "Thanks for coming over. Henri says you're ok."

Dan smiled, waved friendly, and walked on.

"Thanks, Molly," Carolyn smiled. "I talked to my dad the other day. Remember when the peepers were first coming, I said that maybe some time later you might be able to do some work with the chickens? I asked my dad, and he said he couldn't pay much, but if you wanted to work with your dad, as I do with mine, over in the Robinson coop, we could talk about it. It won't be for a while yet, until they start laying, but are you still interested?

Molly grinned, then, said, "I really am! I'd love to do that."

"Let me talk to my dad again. It's messy. You'd mostly be gathering eggs, cleaning them, and packaging in dozens like I do. My dad and I take care of all the deliveries to stores, so we'd pick them up from the Robinson place. I'll talk to him tonight, Molly, but even if he says yes, I'm not sure yet how soon it will be."

Chapter 103

It was two weeks after the Chicago raid before Sampson got back together with his agents. He had assigned them all to work the Somerset region again, but just with surveillance and exploration, no raids. He just wanted to keep his men busy, which allowed him some time to accomplish other things.

He had found out from his old Chicago boss, O'Hara, who it was they thought was expecting those loads in Chicago, which confirmed what Sampson had learned from Charles Woodward, himself. O'Hara and his agents coaxed that same information from Woodward, during their interrogation, but discovered nothing more to cause them to take action, nor did they intend any in the near future. Revenue Agents often learned more by waiting and watching, than by staging impulsive raids.

Knowing they intended no immediate action motivated Sampson to make contact with a middle-man he'd once worked with in Chicago. That man was known to work both sides of the aisle between Wets and the Drys and the law and syndicates. He was a man, each side knew they could work with when necessary, and confidentially. Through him Sampson arranged a sale of 1300 gallons of evidence, which started out at $10 per gallon from the middleman, but finished at $16 per gallon from Sampson. The syndicate contact agreed to pay the higher price due to the recent disappearance of three of their trucks up in Wisconsin. The sale and delivery was accomplished as he planned, with no one knowing he was in any way involved. The transaction was done in cash, with pick up, transport, and delivery handled by different people who never saw each other. Sampson had learned, while working with the feds of Chicago, how to work behind multi-layered screens of smoke and mirrors to wind up unknown, but beneath a pile of cash.

He was $20,800 tax-free dollars richer, rid of the contraband his men thought had been destroyed or stored as evidence, and had landed what could become a ready sales outlet for future evidence. Having pocketed that amount of money, his plan was to now have his agents destroy 100% of the moon they confiscated in the next few weeks. That would help dissolve any suspicions on their part regarding the inventory of moonshine from that particular farm raid.

Still in Chicago and feeling flush due to his success in out-smarting everyone, Sampson tried to find his old for-hire girlfriend, but couldn't. When she heard he was looking for her, she spread the word she didn't want to be found. Consequently, he again located the young lady whose father had been kept from jail through her cooperative relationship with Sampson. At first reluctant when he made contact, she was soon coaxed, by renewed threats of exposing her father to again meet Sampson. They spent two afternoons and a night together which left him feeling, *young* was better, her feeling, *less,* would have been best. The longer he was around her, he increasingly lost control of what he considered passion, but what actually had much more to do with dominance and control. A growing opinion in his mind was, to control a woman was one thing, but to control and dominate *a young and inexperienced woman*, provided him a more warped and satisfying pleasure.

Driving north from Chicago, Sampson felt good, just as he had when he first drove up to meet with Lundquist months before. He had accomplished what he he'd planned when first sent to Minnesota by O'Hara, and he was really just getting started. He would now meet with Lundquist to give a final report on the Chicago raid, what he accomplished for the feds by delivering the *Clip-board* man, and by making his own quick visit to Chicago to advise them on details of the raid. He was looking forward to explaining how his next six-months would fit into Lundquist's plans and budget. He hadn't felt this good in a long time. As he drove, he fantasized about the last two afternoons and the previous night, thinking, *I need to find a couple of young girls up here.*

Chapter 104

"The feds appear to have backed off on this region a little since their raid on that Chicago place, Andre," Hutton explained. "My Twin Cities contact says Somerset is complaining about the attention they are getting. No raids, but they say feds are snooping around all over the place."

"That's great, as far as I'm concerned," Andre smiled. "I want nothing to do with headlines and photos with my name on them in our local *Gazette*!"

"There's been no attention whatsoever to the north, so we are cooking full-blast at Trade Lake and delivering *three-year-old* moon. Unless the feds show up again we're going to keep it up. That way we can save what we've stored at your place for delivery this winter. Your driveway and the road from there to the main highways south will be easier in the winter than the roads up by Trade Lake, where they don't plow worth a dam," Hutton finished.

"I can use a break anyway, Jim. We're producing eggs like crazy now, so I've got to organize processing and delivery routes for both the Robinson coop and mine to accommodate those new stores we lined up. I'm going to let my daughter do some of the deliveries from my place. She's driving well and doesn't mind the pickup at all. The Robinson hens are two months behind us in their laying rate, so we've got a little time. I'm keeping Raft busy with the chickens, because both Ralph and I have to get on with the haying at our places to be ready for winter. I'm trying to set up one large egg customer in the cities by next spring. A lot of local farmers still have a few chickens, but the Twin Cities is what will make our egg business grow," Andre finished.

"That's fine. Those two make a little less money when we aren't cooking, but you will still get your percentage on our winter deliveries, Andre. In the spring, if the feds ease off, we are going to jump right back into cooking at the Robinson place. You can spend part of the winter planning that out. I'd also like you to get the chicken business at both sites operationally efficient without you in the labor force by spring. We are going to need you full-time next summer. I'd also like to quietly bring in as much inventory of sugar, yeast, and containers over the winter, gasoline too, because, that way, on the gasoline station books it looks like we order about the same each month rather than bringing in a big order in the spring as though we're going to start cooking again. Accruing smaller amounts of that stuff all winter will give us less risk of exposure next spring."

"I'm still concerned about snooping feds," Andre said. "Ralph has told me of another dozen stills he knows of because of his gasoline deliveries. They are all small, but that still attracts feds. There are two between the Robinson place and the Sunrise ferry. They don't even use the ferry. They take it across at night in their own boat, then, deliver it to four different saloons on the Minnesota side. Ralph says there's another still just below Taylors Falls in Scandia. They take small amounts down the river to Osceola in their fishing boat," Andre laughed, "Ralph says it's in small jars in their minnow buckets. They dock on the Wisconsin shore and carry their minnow buckets and fishing poles right down Main Street into PY's Bar and a couple other places. Ralph said one of them carrying a bucket full of moon waved at a fed driving through Osceola last week!"

"Don't worry about the little guys, Andre. We want them to keep the feds busy, so they don't find us. Which reminds me," Hutton added. "When you're delivering eggs, or hauling chicken feed bags on your bigger truck, if you ever see the feds stopping cars, be sure to get in line. You want to be stopped, inspected, and found clean. That removes suspicion from Cartier Eggs," he finished.

"Good idea, Jim. We'll do it."

Chapter 105

Most of September was like old times for Andre and Ralph. The Robinson place remained inactive but for chickens, awaiting Hutton's all clear from snooping feds. Ralph and Andre concentrated on haying their own fields. First, they cut and wind-rowed, then, dried the rows in the fields, before loading the hay onto tarps on their wagons. Both Andre and Ralph used horses to pull the wagons. The two of them had shared labor and equipment for years, each helping the other on their farms. Each now had tractors so were consequently using the horses less all the time. But, haying gave the horses a chance to remember how to work, and for the drivers of the teams to remind them what was expected of them. Both Ralph and Andre missed working the horses as they had growing up on their farms. They weren't as efficient as a tractor but were usually friendlier. The whole family got involved in haying, and loved having the horses hitched up and hauling. Henri and Carolyn were always slipping them an apple, often enough in fact, that the horses grew to expect fresh fruit after each load to the barn. Everyone had hay-mow memories of great fun, especially when the mows were stuffed with that *one more load* attitude farmers so often had. Since hay would be their only crop this fall, Andre and Ralph's farms were less than the full-time job they had been. Henri could easily take care of the few beef cattle and the horses. That left time for more Andre involvement with moonshine.

The Cartier chickens increased their laying enough to enable Andre and Carolyn to open another grocery store on their delivery route. They had lined up more stores, for a total of five this winter, and hoped to be delivering to them by Christmas. By December, they expected to be bringing home eggs from the Robinson place as well. Throughout September, Andre and Carolyn delivered eggs together, but since Henri was still too young to get a driver's license, the plan was for Carolyn to begin using the pickup truck on Saturdays to deliver on her own by the end of October. That would free up Andre, who planned on being busier with Hutton once his farm was prepared for winter.

Andre had agreed to let Molly work the Robinson chickens with her dad starting in October. She and her dad had full responsibility for that coop, under Ralph's watch, and Andre and Carolyn would retrieve the prepared eggs from them for delivery. Andre hauled all supplies needed by either the Robinson coop or his own. They had a good plan and Andre remembered reading in some book that, *Good planning is half the job done.*

Clair was the strength behind the scenes in all this activity. She was the hub to which the kids' spokes were attached around home. Andre's too. Though she seldom took credit, she always showed up as a key ingredient in most anything any of them did. She was the reason it all seemed to work. It was Clair who smoothed over the rough days, who showed them how to make lemonade when dealt a lemon. Andre, too, knew Clair to often be the cement between his blocks when he grew discouraged or needed a reason to celebrate. It was Clair, the kids went to when they didn't know for sure how to approach dad about something. It was Clair who, rather than direct them all to church, made it seem to each of them the right thing to do on their own. It was Clair's beautiful laughter and creativity that lit up their home, when it was most needed.

Cartiers remained true to their family agreement. No one spoke of moonshine. The kids, even Clair, never asked where Andre was when he wasn't home. They automatically pretended it had something to do with Robinson Eggs, Cartier Eggs, or to do with the farm. No one ever mentioned what was below the chicken coop floor, or took notice of the sounds of trucks arriving in the middle of the night with no headlights on, or when they would hear Andre leave the house, then return after they heard the truck head down the driveway again. Each morning, he, she, or they, would remember that all of them were participants in a dangerous game.

Chapter 106

Lundquist was looking at pictures on the front page of the Gazette spread out on his desk. He pointed at the picture of axe-holed stills and the broken pieces of worms on the floor. "I sometimes wonder if we should destroy these stills even more thoroughly, Sampson. How much do you think it would cost these people to have them repaired?"

"Well, we could make them worse off than what you're pointing at there, Chief. I was in more of a hurry to get the man we called, *Clip-board* and those truck drivers processed, so we could pass on info to Chicago, than I was about the stills. Actually, the stills were worse off than these pictures indicate, but if you want more damage we can arrange it," Sampson answered. I'd like to make them worse, cuz I think somebody is quickly repairing them around Somerset."

"That much moon must have been a mess!" the Chief expressed.

"It was," Sampson answered. "The puddles were ankle-deep all over the yard, and we got some great pictures, and we got them in three different newspapers in Stephens County." Not wanting to pursue that topic of conversation further, Sampson inserted, "I want to run this strategy by you, Chief, to see what you think."

"Let's hear it."

"We first focused on Somerset because that's obviously the hub for moonshine in western Wisconsin. Then, we worked the bridges for a couple of weeks, to check out the flow of bootleggers. As we worked our way north we found a few small still operations, but not as many as we expected. When we expanded our search around Stephens County we found this big Chicago bunch, but I really don't expect to find anything else that big over there. One thing we consistently noticed was the bootleggers with cars full of moon were always headed west. Empty, they headed east. That moonshine is coming into the Twin Cities from somewhere east of the St. Croix River. For the next month we are going to take a look further east, as well as refocus on Somerset again. I think some stills were quick to get back into business. The judges just don't scare them with stiff sentences. They tend to let them off easy. Your guys here in Stearns say the same thing. Well, anyway, that's our current plan. What do you think?" Sampson finished.

"It's a good plan. Keep the pressure on, especially around Somerset. That keeps it from growing. I don't want it to blossom as it has in Stearns," Lundquist waved. "You're slowing it down, which is what I wanted when I sent you over there, so go ahead with it. Keep me posted, and congratulations on that big one. That was good work. Cooking moon tends to slow down in the winter up here, Sampson. Minnesota and Wisconsin have a lot of snow, unplowed roads, and trees with no leaves, which makes it easier to find stills in the winter. That's why so many operations shut down till spring. You'll find it the same over in Wisconsin. I may call you and your men back over to Stearns in January. We are going to run a three-month surveillance along the Minnesota and Dakota borders with Canada. I could use another five men in that net, and your expertise from Chicago might help. I'll let you know by December."

That came as a big surprise to Sampson, but he had no choice. It would be less boring than spending the entire winter on the snow-covered roads of the Barrens, so he quickly replied, "No problem, Chief. Let me know. I just want to know I'll be back in Wisconsin in the spring. I'm not finished over there."

"Yes, you'll be back over there by the end of March, for sure," Lundquist nodded. "Well, that's it for today.. I've got to be at meeting in five minutes. Keep up the good work."

Sampson failed to inform Lundquist that the Chicago raid had resulted from a tip by the local Sheriff of Stephens County. *Take credit where credit is due* he thought. *Sheriff Maun would never have given me that information if I hadn't pushed him. I wonder what else he hasn't told me?*

After meeting with Lundquist, Sampson stayed the night in his apartment in Minneapolis. His Chicago visit had again ignited his interest in younger women, so he did some bar-hopping down on Washington and Hennepin Avenues. He turned down three different for-cash opportunities before finding a woman young enough to interest him for the night. She cost more but he currently had more to spend.

Chapter 107

Hutton's planning and caution had resulted in remarkably good luck so far for himself and those working with him. He hoped attention to detail would extend their run of luck. Stephens County moonshine business had been cleverly and successfully hidden behind a diversion of chickens and feathers.

He carefully supervised the selection of those they all worked with, making sure those hired needed the moon business and did not want to be caught. Andre, Ralph, and others they hired, and also the crew Hutton had put together up at Trade Lake, were first selected, then, interviewed and hired. No one had turned them down. Hutton and Andre had been careful, secretive and as strategic as they could. Even those on the payroll knew little of Hutton other than that he was in the real estate business. No one, including his employees, even knew where he lived. He never referred to his small efficiency apartment in Forest Lake, Minnesota, half-way between the Twin Cities and Stephens County, which made it convenient to be where he often needed to be. Hutton remained convinced the locals and feds knew nothing other than chickens and farming were going on at either the Robinson place or the Cartier farm.

Andre had listened to Hutton's suggestion of having both his pickup and larger truck's doors professionally painted with their logo. "Cartier Egg and Poultry" was printed in bold red letters on a white stripe on each of the doors. It felt good to all of the Cartier's that the logo stood for something legal. *"We can all be proud of those doors!"* Andre thought out loud.

Carolyn added "Now we get to drive them all over the County delivering eggs. Don't they look great, mom? "

I get to drive them too, right, dad?" Henri countered.

"Yes, you do, as soon as we can get you licensed; then, we'll use both trucks as we always have, but when people see those painted doors it will help us sell more eggs."

Cartier's were just leaving home for the Robinson place. Tomorrow was Saturday and Carolyn was to deliver eggs to several stores. She delivered Saturdays and Andre did midweek delivery when she was in school. They would retrieve eggs at the Robinson coop today, prepared for delivery by Molly and her dad, then combine them with those Carolyn had prepared. Andre and Carolyn drove the pickup and Clair and Henri followed in the family sedan, with Henri driving. This was the first time Clair and Henri visited the Robinson place. Carolyn had been there several times with her dad, helping Ralph get the chicken routine under way. Though she'd been at the Robinson coop several times, Carolyn was still unaware of the moon operation on the Robinson land. She knew her father had something to do with it, but didn't know how much, or even where it was. Clair did know that it was somewhere on the Robinson premises, but not where. Henri didn't have a clue.

Carolyn, however, did know the new chicken coop was identical to the new Cartier coop, and though she said nothing about it, there was little doubt in her mind about it having a hidden basement.

That was exactly how Andre wanted to keep it.

Chapter 108

"The word I've received from our Chicago contact has been positive all winter, Jim," Manny said. "They are happy with the price and the quality of the Minnesota 13 we've delivered. Their one complaint was that they want more than we've been able to supply."

"We can gear up our production by at least 30 percent, Manny, that is, if the feds don't become more intense than they've been so far. But I'm nervous about that. Agent Sampson and his boys have been over in the Dakotas, but the word is they are coming back to Wisconsin this spring. While they've tended to concentrate down around Somerset, they made that Chicago raid east of Cedarville last fall, so we have to plan as though they'll be back tomorrow. We've brought in supplies all winter, so we won't have a lot of inbound trucking for at least a month. That means only half the trucks of last year during the first half of the season, but then we have to start bringing stuff in again. Half the trucks, is half the exposure, so that helps, but I'm always edgy."

"Stay nervous, Jim. Our man who works for Lundquist keeps feeding Sampson tips around Somerset, but sooner or later they'll be back up your way. That Chicago bust made them heroes with Lundquist," Manny added. "He seems to like Sampson, but one of my contacts in Illinois says Sampson was not at all liked in the Chicago office. I'm going to ask some questions about him . . . see what I can learn."

"Ok, Manny. We'll do our best to gear up production. Anything you can do to keep the feds away, helps."

Chapter 109

By the end of November Stephens County had all but settled into the routine of winter. To Andre and Ralph, anything to do with the business of moonshine seemed to have gone into hibernation. The action they were aware of seemed to be all north of Trade Lake. Hutton told Andre to concentrate on the chicken business, and to make as much noise about it as he could so people wouldn't be suspicious of how he was making money when everyone else seemed to be hurting.

Andre and Ralph had finished haying, stocked up on grain and feed for winter, and Ralph expected no moon action until spring. Ralph was still doing bulk deliveries for Bill, so everyone who knew him was aware and envious that he had two part-time jobs, one with Bill and one helping Cartier Egg and Poultry at the Robinson place. Some also envied Ralph because on top of two jobs he still had his farm to provide what they raised as sustenance.

Andre's freshly, painted trucks, occasionally with a cute young lady driving one of them, were seen throughout the County, especially on Saturdays. Andre was following Hutton's suggestion of staying visible. It had paid off, since another store had been attracted when the owner saw the Cartier Egg and Poultry pickup on the road. He flagged the driver down and on the side of the road, made an agreement with the young lady driver for a sample egg delivery the following week. Carolyn could hardly wait to get home to tell her parents and Henri.

Clair was breathing more deeply now, thankful they had avoided foreclosure, that Carolyn and Henri were thriving in school and that Andre worked more time at home now that he was not so busy at the Robinson place. She continued to cheer each of them on and invested her time supportively in their ventures. She wasn't so quick to bark orders as she had been. Henri's resentment of his dad spending more time with Carolyn softened, too. Through Andre's efforts with Hutton, plus the new chickens, they had created enough income to keep the foreclosure wolves from the door, but had not built up enough surplus money to be casual with it. Clair and Andre wanted to build up a savings to ward off the next crises as well. What she did have to work with was the food they raised on the farm in excess of what they needed themselves. Between those known at church, and others by Sheriff Maun, she was aware of a dozen families who were truly barely scraping by.

Clair discreetly provided what she felt could be called surplus, in eggs and fresh chickens, and added potatoes, turnips, and carrots from their root cellar. Each week she anonymously delivered what she could to the Catholic Church.

She provided a list of those twelve families to the church and they took charge of distribution. She and Andre wanted no thanks from proud people in desperate need. It also provided Andre and Clair an opportunity for their kids to learn how those fortunate could quietly help those less fortunate. Carolyn was dropping off ten dozen eggs a week with Sheriff Maun. Helping others helped the Cartier family dilute some degree of guilt about their moon money source.

January, February, and March passed uneventfully. Other than an occasional planning meeting with Hutton, Andre's only involvement with moon was the occasional midnight shipment from the chicken coop cellar using midnight trucks. Andre made sure that activity involved only himself. He needed to be able to claim his family ignorant and innocent of any involvement. Though the chickens slowed their laying in winter, the egg business continued to flourish.

Chapter 110

After the Chicago raid, and much to Hutton's and Andre's satisfaction, the feds seemed to focus their efforts back down around Somerset through the winter. There were a half-dozen more stills destroyed in Stephens County, but they were small, and by mid-November the feds seemed to have disappeared. Hutton kept the stills up in Trade Lake going all winter. They were in a heavily wooded area, nearly a mile from the nearest dirt road, making them almost inaccessible. Even the telltale aromas escaped notice by the nearest neighbors, and the long cooking shed was well enough hidden to escape discovery by the feds. Hutton had been wise to man the Trade Lake operation only with former cohorts from the Stearns County stills, none from Stephens County, which he felt helped keep Trade Lake undiscovered. Keeping that location running throughout the winter enabled Hutton to ship moon north to Superior and to fill the occasional order or request from Manny. Those Twin Cities shipments were easier in the winter. They just drove across the ice near the Sunrise Ferry landing. The biggest detection danger they faced was someone following one of the supply trucks or its tracks across snow on the frozen river.

Hutton and his Stearns County crew had taken elaborate precautions to avoid detection of incoming sugar, yeast, and containers via their methodology of supply. The driveway into the old Trade Lake farm was nearly a half-mile long. It connected to a meandering dirt road through the hills of the Barrens for seven miles before it reached the highway running north and south along the St. Croix River.

The driveway between the road and the wooded area, was visible from the road, but about 100 head of beef cattle used each side of it for pasture in spring, summer, and fall. During the winter they fed from stacked hay, feed and water distributed along the driveway daily by a man who looked like a working farmer. The aroma of a hundred-head's droppings masked the smell of cooking, and the prevailing winds blew that aroma away from the road the majority of the time. From the perspective of any passerby it was a working beef ranch. The sign at the road-end of the driveway, "Beef of Barrens," aided the deception.

Anyone driving in, passed through a quarter-mile of cattle on each side of the driveway, then entered the forested acres for about 300 feet, then the opening which contained the farmhouse, a large barn, and a machine shed. Beyond those buildings the open land continued another 100 feet to the base of a steep hill which was again forested. A line of old faming equipment was parked along that edge and because of where an old threshing machine, a mower and a bailer were parked, one could not see the two-tracked road that continued on around the hill and through the woods to the long, low-roofed, shed that seemed to have no purpose on the farm. That was its purpose.

Chapter 111

Sampson and his agents had worked the Dakota border for the last three months. They all took a week off after returning to Minneapolis April 15, then, spent two days getting ready to return to duty in Wisconsin. It had been mostly bootlegger duty in the Dakotas. The bootleggers there worked from sedans with big hopped-up engines, trucks in disguise, whose logo freight covers led any observer to believe they had nothing to do with moonshine or the Canadian booze they were hauling. The agents even found two small airports, whose resident planes were used to transport booze from the Canadian Border to Chicago. It had been three months of intense surveillance, but few raids. On the few raids they did attempt, lack of evidence barred some arrests and the few arrests they made were dismissed in court due to lack of evidence. The lack of confiscated evidence was frustrating and it seemed to Sampson and his agents the word was out *that, Uncle Ben was in town.* Often, they felt the judges were on the side of those arrested.

They also found these bootleggers to be pros, like the ones Sampson used to chase in the Chicago region. They were not hungry farmers like those in Stephens County. These drivers, both men and women, knew how to drive and evade the feds and the snares they set. More than once Sampson saw bootleggers in the saloons along the main highway with the familiar bulge of a weapon behind the vests under their expensive-looking top coats. They stopped in to eat when returning from Chicago, their cars empty of moonshine, but never stopped when headed south full of booze. Agents determined from successful arrests, that there seemed to be more Canadian booze than local moonshine being hauled in that region. Sampson's men also discovered these bootleggers were willing to be chased, and when chased, were willing to use those guns they carried. There was one incident where the targeted car shot at Eastman three times when the bootleggers guessed he was going to block the road before they could get past him. The shots caused Eastman to brake and when he did the big Cadillac sedan shot past him and quickly pulled away from his Ford. The cars issued to revenue agents couldn't keep up with any of those big Dakota roadsters.

Eggert and Brown stopped a truck load of pickle barrels one day. Thinking they had struck gold, they began to unload the truck, only to find the barrels empty. While they were making the driver unload some barrels to determine if those on the inside rows were also empty, three big Oldsmobile sedans, with throaty exhausts, sped past them on the side of the road they were parked beside. Later, they felt certain the truck-full of barrels had been a diversion, allowing the cars to slip past their road block, but they had nothing to hold the truck driver for. There was no evidence. He had an invoice declaring the barrels purchased by the pickle company he was headed for in Chicago.

The week before they came back to Minneapolis, they destroyed two small stills on a farm near a small town airport. They learned the reason they found no moon was the cooker had shipped his weekly production out by small airplane to Chicago the day before. They smashed the stills, slashed his bags of sugar and yeast, and had a big bonfire of thirty ten-gallon empty-kegs on his property. They jailed the cooker, but had no confidence he would be sent off for a stiff sentence, or even fined.

Sampson's agents were glad to get back to the Twin Cities. The Dakota winter was not fun. The only one, who seemed to enjoy it was Sampson, who found a couple of young women fond of taking his money at a highway bar he frequented. Sampson resisted getting rough with the girls because of three or four muscled young men, either pimps, or those assigned the task of looking after those girls. The girls claimed it took only a word from them and mayhem would befall anyone taking more than the agreed-upon, paid-for, sex they offered. Sampson's men never questioned him directly about his actions, but none seemed to approve of his behavior, or of how he talked about the women the next day. Having been agents for less than a year, each seemed a bit less tainted, and almost unaware of the rough sex life Sampson had learned early and grown fond of in Chicago, even existed.

Chapter 112

It was March, and Andre and Hutton were gearing up to put the Robinson place back into operation. Through their quiet and small but steady deliveries throughout the winter, they had accrued enough sugar, yeast, corn, and containers to keep them running full production for a couple of months. As moon shipments from the coop cellars of both locations made empty space, they filled it with those deliveries to keep the inventory as secret as possible. Hutton sent three big double-cook stills down from the Trade Lake operation, which would enable doubling production at Robinson's. Andre had everyone lined up to start work April 15. It had been a light-snow winter, so they figured by then the mud-holes in the driveways would be dry and roads passable where needed. Ralph and Raft would be back sprouting corn and stirring mash a week ahead of the other cookers who were to check in the following week.

"We haven't heard of a single incident with the feds all winter, Andre," Hutton said. "The only place was Somerset, and that was before Christmas. My Twin Cities contact says they focused on Stearns County for stills, and the Dakota border trying to slow transportation of booze coming across from Canada aimed at Chicago."

"Maybe they're going to leave us alone this summer," Andre smiled at Jim. "I wouldn't mind that at all."

"We can never count on that, Andre. I learned the hard way over in Stearns the first year I got involved. I was just learning the business. We hadn't heard from the feds for over a month, so two of us decided what you just said. "Maybe they're going to leave us alone." We eased our alertness because of that and the next day almost got nailed. We were lucky. We didn't see them coming, but our watch a half-mile away sent our code-ring, three-shorts and a long-long. That tipped us off.

We just walked out the back door, got into the car and drove out the back drive. It was a small operation, but the moon was still cooking when the feds walked in the front door. Somebody tipped them on us, which wasn't uncommon over there. Fortunately, we had delivered the fifty gallons of moon the day before, but it still cost us the still and the location. Another bit of good luck was that we left nothing on the premises that could ID us. That's why I'm so picky about what we allow anyone to bring on the premises here. But for luck, I could easily have gotten a year and a day, or more, out of that one. That's why, Andre, we always think the feds are in the neighborhood and are ready to react. When it happens, it happens fast, just like the raid on those Chicago guys last October."

"Got it, Jim." Andre nodded. "I'm going to check with Maun tomorrow to see if he's heard anything. He and that agent, Sampson, don't seem to like each other much. Jason said, Sampson took all the credit for discovering that Chicago bunch, even though Jason gave him the information and you and I know where Maun got it. Jason said the WCTU has been trying to make a hero of him ever since the raid and he does not want anything to make it look as though he had anything to do with it. The WCTU just won't leave him alone," he grinned, then added, "Our accounting is in good shape. I've paid Ralph and Raft from the Cartier Egg checking account for work they did last winter, and will continue the same way through the summer. We'll continue to pay in cash for the cooking as we've been doing."

"Ok, Andre. I'll try to keep tabs on the feds through my Twin Cities contact, so I can warn you ahead of any visits they plan. Let's get that production up. Chicago is screaming for more Minnesota 13. Working the double shifts you have planned should make it happen. I may not have mentioned this before, Andre, but I'm really glad I bumped into you at the gas station with Ralph. You've done a hell of a job farming moonshine."

Chapter 113

Carolyn drove the pickup up beside the rear door of the grocery store in Balsam Lake. This was her third delivery to this newest store on her weekly route. She had discovered last week she could easily enlist aid when delivering. Inside, she announced her presence to the butcher, who agreed on her last visit to have someone help her unload the almost-too-heavy-for-her-alone, 48-dozen sized boxes she delivered. "Hi Jorge," she smiled. "I've got some eggs for you."

"Ok, Miss Cartier," Jorge grinned. "Hey, Brown!" he shouted at the teen-age boy who was pouring a small bag of fresh potatoes into a display bin. "I've got the best looking job you're going to find around here all day," pointing at Carolyn laughing. "Come and give her a hand."

"Behave yourself, Jorge," Carolyn laughed, waving at Brown as the teenager, named Jake, walked toward her.

"Hi, Carolyn. Two weeks in a row I get to help with eggs," he smiled. "How are you doing?"

He helped her unload the two boxes, and loaded four more empties onto the pickup bed. "Thanks again, for the help, Jake!" she added, as she dropped off the invoice with Jorge. Back in the pickup, she drove to the Cedarville store, her last delivery of the day before returning home.

After dropping eggs there, while driving out of Cedarville towards home, she saw a black Ford sedan close behind her. As she watched in her rear-view mirror it pulled out as though to pass her. When adjacent to her, she saw a man holding up some kind of a badge, waving it as though to encourage her to pull over to the side of the road. She was just a couple of blocks out of town, so pulled over to the side of the road before the driveway of a nearby house. The black car pulled in just ahead of her. Agent Sampson exited the car and walked back to her window.

"Good afternoon, young lady. I'm Revenue Agent, Sampson. This is a routine check of a delivery vehicle. Would you shut off your engine and step out of the car please."

It was then Carolyn remembered seeing this man once before in Cedarville. It was the day she saw Sheriff Maun talking to him by the gas station. She had no idea why she was being stopped, but felt no trepidation. She was parked right by a house on the edge of town. She even knew Mrs. Hanson who lived there.

"What is it you want?" she asked Sampson.

"We inspect delivery vehicles frequently to determine if they are carrying any kind of illegal alcohol. Are you?" he asked.

"Am I what?" she asked, with a curious expression on her face. She hadn't smiled yet, her normal first reaction when greeting someone.

"Are you delivering any kind of moonshine in your truck full of eggs?" he asked with a stern face.

She had never been asked such a question, and the word, "moonshine," hit a nerve. *Why is this happening?* Realizing she had hesitated with her response in the interests of secrecy, and remembering *she had a role to play,* she decided it was time for a little charm. "Yup, the truck is plumb full!" she smiled.

That brought a grin to Sampson's face. He had seen that smile when she talked to Sheriff Maun and wanted to see it again. *He wanted to see more of her than that* he thought. "Well, let's take a look in some of those boxes to see if we can find it," he responded, but still with a stern face after erasing his grin at her response.

That brief grin on Sampson's face told Carolyn she was not in trouble, and the lack of fear she exhibited with her "plumb full" remark restored her confidence. "Why in the world would you think moonshine would be found in empty egg cartons?" she said.

"You'd be surprised what we find, Miss . . . what is your last name? Are you a Cartier like it says on the truck?" still stern-faced.

"Yes, I am." Carolyn nodded, straight-faced herself.

Stopping her had nothing to do with moonshine, but Sampson did have three reasons for stopping this Cartier Egg & Poultry truck. He knew Carolyn was driving it. He wanted to experience talking to her, and if possible to intimidate her. But, her hesitant response to his first question, "are you delivering any moonshine?" triggered the well-honed blip-recognition many law officers continue to develop throughout their careers. He hadn't expected that, but made no issue of it. He simply filed it away in the place officers keep such blips until needed again. "I think I met your father a while back at the chicken ranch. He called it the Robinson place. Does he drive that bigger truck that has Cartier on the door?"

"Yes," she answered. "I deliver eggs on, Saturdays. He does it during the week."

"Does he carry any moonshine on that big truck?" Sampson asked, staring directly at her to see if she hesitated again.

"Sure, that truck holds more than this one," Carolyn smirked. "Does it say moonshine on the door?" she asked Sampson, facetiously. "We carry eggs!"

Sampson opened a couple of the boxes in the back of the pickup, then recognizing them empty he said, "There are no eggs in here now."

"That's because I dropped them off with the moonshine I delivered to all those grocery stores," she grinned again.

"Ok, Miss Cartier. I know you think you're being cute. I'm convinced there's no moonshine here, but I'm going to keep my eye on you," Sampson said with a look Carolyn wasn't so sure about. "I'm coming out for a tour of the Cartier Egg & Poultry ranch one of these days. Will you show me around the place so I can make sure you aren't in the moonshine business?"

"With my dad, or my brother, I will," she said with a straight face.

"All right, Miss Cartier, now that we have an appointment, you can be on your way. Thanks for the invitation," he winked as he walked back to his car.

Carolyn felt strange about the encounter. *That revenue officer knew there was no possibility of moonshine in this pickup* she thought. *Does he know something about Dad? I wonder what I've stirred up. There is something weird about him.*

All the way home, she continued to focus on how she could be suspect in any way. She felt *something strange about the entire encounter.*

Chapter 114

"I think the worst thing that could happen to us, just happened," Andre said to Hutton. "Carolyn said he was suddenly behind her on the road out of Cedarville. He stopped her right at Mrs. Hanson's driveway on the edge of town. Why in hell would he stop a pickup, delivering eggs?" Andre asked.

"Experience, both good and bad, has taught me not to think just of my first impression. With perspective, is the right way to observe a situation, Andre. The only thing we can be sure of is that he had a reason. At least, we know he and his agents are back. I think his stopping Carolyn likely has little to do with moonshine," Hutton finished.

"What does that mean?" Andre asked, almost angrily, at the thought of *anyone messing with his daughter.*

"I think the possibility of Sampson being interested in your daughter is more likely than him being suspicious of her smuggling moonshine in a pickup," Hutton said quietly.

Hutton felt Andre's anxiety. Unknown to Andre, or anyone else in Stephens County, he had two daughters of his own, one who had nearly been violated in a similar sort of situation. It was an event he didn't like to recall. He'd been divorced for ten years now, but still remembered the incident and how it impacted he and his wife, like it was yesterday. Someone followed his eighteen-year-old daughter home from her College in St. Paul, repeatedly and unbeknownst to her, or her parents. Then one night, he attacked her as she walked within a block of the school. Aided by two students, who heard her scream, she fought off her attacker,. The offender was arrested, convicted, and jailed. Hutton's daughter moved on, unscathed physically, but neither she nor her father and mother were ever to forget. The incident later played a role in Hutton's relationship with her mother, which eventually, helped their marriage end in divorce. That memory became a trigger like those blips stored in the minds of law enforcement officers. It was triggered again today by a fed stopping a pickup with, "Cartier Egg and Poultry" painted on the door and driven by an attractive young woman, who was alone.

"What do you mean?" asked Andre, knowing full well, what Hutton meant.

"We both know he didn't expect to find moonshine in that pickup, Andre," Hutton stared. "Let's not jump to conclusions. Just keep an eye on things and pay close attention to the fact that Sampson and his agents are back. He did nothing illegal or beyond his authority and law enforcement assignment. I'm wondering if he's suspicious of Cartier Egg for other reasons. That's something we need to know, but just knowing him and his agents are back, gives us the opportunity to be more careful, keep a closer eye on Sampson, and create a few diversions. What else can we do to keep him busy south of here?"

"Why would he be suspicious? I gave him a tour of this place and he found nothing but chickens and eggs."

"His job is to be suspicious, Andre."

Chapter 115

Sampson lifted the phone in his Minneapolis apartment. "Bob, it's Ambrotz in Chicago."

Surprised, Sampson said, "What's up?" Sampson knew he would only be getting a call from Ambrotz if there was a problem.

"I need some advice. Things have been pretty routine down here, since you left, as I told you last month but things are stirring up all of a sudden."

"How so?" questioned Sampson.

"All of a sudden O'Hara and some of the office agents are beginning to tighten up on evidence handling. Nobody has asked me any questions, but all the agents are talking about last week's incident up in Janesville."

"Tell me about it." Sampson urged, impatiently.

"You remember Agent Aldrich? He worked with Sorenson and Jones on that team we used to bump up against once in awhile. He raided what he thought was a small still, but it turned out to be a 500-gallon-a-day operation. Anyway, he had only one other agent with him, so after shutting it down and herding the cookers together, he called for more revenue agents to help him. O'Hara sent six men up to the site. After they got there, Aldrich let them process the arrests, while he focused on evidence inventory. One of the cookers they arrested evidently heard Aldrich tell Sorenson to deliver twenty-five ten-gallon keg loads to two different addresses, then to bust up the rest and get pictures the way we always did it. But, here's the problem. The cooker didn't say anything until he was in jail, then, he started telling his arresting officer he was going to blow the whistle on the game he knew the arresting agents were playing."

"That's not good," Sampson said. "What else?"

"Well, that was last week. Since then, there's been several office agents talking to Agent Aldrich about evidence-handling, but they've kept him out of touch with other agents. We can't get any details, so don't really know what's happening. I asked Sorenson about it. He said Aldrich knew he was in trouble, but was claiming many federal revenue agents sold evidence. Sorenson is afraid Aldrich will turn in those names to get a lighter sentence. The rest of his team is claiming they knew nothing about it and that, Aldrich always handled all of the evidence from their raids. Sorenson says that is the truth, and he never questioned what Aldrich was doing with the evidence."

"Well, Ambrotz, you and I discussed this type of thing before I left for Minnesota. What did I tell you to do if something like this happened?" Sampson asked.

"Immediately dispose of all evidence, sell it quietly, cheap and fast if we have time, and if not, by draining kegs into the ground if necessary. Get rid of every shred of evidence, keep your mouth shut, and act dumb," Ambrotz recited.

"Have you done that?" Sampson questioned.

"It's gone, Bob," Ambrotz said proudly. "I have all my pictures of our team axing kegs and stills, and standing ankle deep in moon. I showed them to Sorenson when he told me about Aldrich. Every picture is dated with a location written on it, and a list of the agents using axes. Sorenson was envious. He said they never took pictures and always let Aldrich manage evidence handling because that was the protocol they'd been taught by their team leader."

"Ok, you've handled it properly. Now just lie low. Make a big deal out of any raids, bust up the evidence on site, take more pictures, and don't keep a single drop of moon you find. You'll be questioned, too, all the agents will. If any of these suspicions of moon sales hit the Chicago papers there will be a witch hunt. Stick to your story, use your pictures, and tell any who question you, that is how I taught you to do it when I trained you as an agent. Remember, I always said "Destroy every drop and take picture to prove it." In those boxes of files I left with you and our team, I have pictures going back three years. I think you're safe; just stick to the story. Keep me posted daily. You can usually reach me, or leave a message at one of the two numbers I gave you between 6:00 a.m. and 8:00 a.m."

"Thanks Bob. I needed to hear that. This action scared the hell out of me at first. Then, as I followed your plan, it seems to be working out. I just needed to hear you say it again," Ambrotz finished gratefully.

"Keep me posted; that's important," Sampson said. "If they get tough with you I'll come down and fight for you, but timing is important. If something new happens let me know." he finished.

I think we're ok, Sampson thought. *Ambrotz followed the plan, has pictures, has the rest of the team's signatures, with dates on them, and all Ambrotz has ever done is occasionally drop some excess evidence off at a specific location. He has never seen or talked to anyone at that location and has no idea what happened to it after the drop off. Every one of his deliveries of evidence occurred after I left Chicago. I think we are ok, and if Ambrotz gets nailed, I think I'm ok. I won't let that happen to him . . . that's too close to me.*

Chapter 116

Ralph was just reeling up the hose from the gas truck, after filling two tanks of 100 gallons each, for Sanderson. His farm was about eight miles east of Cedarville. Ralph hadn't delivered there since December. "You must be getting ready for some serious, farming, Sandy. That's your biggest delivery of the year," Ralph grinned.

"Don' spread dat around, Ralph. I don' want dem feds snooping round here. My brother in Somerset says dem Revenue Agents take dose sales slip records from fuel suppliers and chase down cooking stills wid em. I don' need none a dat here," Sanderson grimaced. I bin cookin' for three years, you knowed dat, and never had no trouble, but dem agents is getting nosier and nosier. They makin' it tougher jest to git across dem bridges on da river!"

"I've heard that from more than one," Ralph agreed. "The guy that runs the ferry at Marine told a friend of mine that twice this month Revenue Agents have watched his crossings all through the night trying to catch bootleggers."

"They be tough to catch I bet. Dem boys wid da big engines meet me at a place down da road a piece. I bring dem cars to another place nobody knows of and fill em up wid moon, den bring em back to dem drivers waitin fer me. Gotta be careful wid da gas pedal on dem cars! I damn near went in da ditch last week, pressed down too hard, dem wheels spun me damn near inta da ditch!" Sanderson grinned. "Dey's fun to drive though, but I don want no Fed chasing me down da road. Dem bootleggers can do it."

"I need a couple jars of good moon myself. Can I buy it from you?"

"Sure, right now. Dis might be a little scratchy, cuz it's new, but it'll kick your ass!" Sanderson said. "I don't age nothin, jes cook it and sell it. You see dem jars in da snow by dem fence posts at da dances? Dems mostly mine. Dem dancers like da kick of old Sandy's White Lightning. It don' need no age. I get a dollar a jar, but if you keep quiet bout my gas usins . . . you can have dem both for a dollar, Ralph. Come over to da corn crib right dere an I'll dig em out."

After sweeping off a foot of loose corn, Ralph saw what he thought could be at least 100 more jars, before Sandy began sweeping the corn back in place over his inventory. Ralph took the two jars and put them into the tool box welded to the side of the tank-truck where it rested on the flat bed. He replaced the padlock, which kept people from stealing the tools he used to take tight caps off farmers gas tanks. Sandy was an old-time farmer, had been here forever, and now in his 70s was having the time of his life making illegal moon. It made him enough money to stay in groceries and gas and to keep those Saturday night dancers happy. Sandy told him, "My wife damn near left me when I started cookin' da moon, but after I started handin' her money she quieted down. Now, she don' say nuthun, just holds out her hand," he laughed. He appeared to Ralph to be about as happy a man as he knew in all of Stephens County.

What Ralph didn't see at Sandy's place, were the three barrels of fermenting mash sitting inside the barn. They were in one of the empty horse stalls, their loose covers carelessly set atop the barrels with open space into the barrels around the perimeter of the wooden covers. They were covered with flies, many of which were flying in and out of the barrel in erratic fashion. It was not uncommon for small still operations to be unclean, as this one was, and many were even worse. A hen stood on the loose-fitting barrel lid beside some fresh chicken shit.

Small batch moon operations were often a hodgepodge of undisciplined or experimental recipes. The stills were often homemade, using questionably dangerous combinations of metals that could chemically react to fermentation and cooking leaving toxic trace elements like copper, lead, and zinc in the product, with dangerous, sometimes fatal, consequences. It was a hidden industry, so secret there were no controls, or production requirements, to protect what users purchased from unidentified sources. It was not uncommon for people to die of alcohol poisoning after a big night on moonshine, and because of source secrecy, no way to blame anyone for the fatal outcome. It was estimated much small-still production was single-cook moonshine; the producers wanted to bottle and sell as quickly as possible to harvest cash. Second-cooking, as larger suppliers of moonshine practiced, removed much of those contaminants sometimes found in the single-cook product.

Adding to those dangers was the fact that the vast majority of people didn't know what moonshine should taste like in the first place, could not tell good from bad, and a high percentage of drinkers felt the worse it tasted the better and stronger it was. Most were ignorant of the fact that bad moonshine could kill them and labored under the false notion that moonshine was so strong it killed anything that could be harmful to the drinker. Prohibition was the perfect time for moonshine producers to get away with murder. Fortunately, it was generally the small producers that made most of the bad stuff. Ralph Johnson was a perfect example of the drinker-phenomena just described.

Most big producers were more careful, hired knowledgeable talent to produce their product, and strove for cleanliness and quality production. They wanted nothing to do with problems of bad moon.

Part V

Justice From
The Other Side
Of the Law

Chapter 117

By May, Andre and his crew had nearly doubled the production of moon at the Robinson place. There was over fifteen tons of fifty-pound sugar sacks stored on pallets in the basement of the new chicken coop keeping it reasonably free of moisture and crawly infestation over the winter. Hundreds of ten-gallon kegs were stored along the lower floor wall of the old coop, behind the stills, and the upper floor level was covered with so many mash barrels the workers could barely walk among them. They still kept them in lines, identified barrels with grease-pencil codes to not lose track of their estimated calendar date's of scheduled cooking. Andre, Ralph and their crew became increasingly detail-oriented as was demanded by the fermentation cycle. Mash, cooked before it was totally fermented, produced less alcohol than fully fermented, a waste that could not be tolerated. It now took one full-time man just to stir barrels of mash, and another to keep them properly filled and mixed with recipe ingredients in different states of fermentation. The big production, that Manny and Hutton demanded, was becoming a bigger job.

"You've done a good job of acquiring ingredients and containers, Andre," Hutton said. "Now the goal is to cook moon, fill those kegs, and get them off the premises as fast as we can. Sampson's men are active again down around Somerset and we know they'll be coming north. The faster we can process what we've got, the less we risk in a raid. I think Sampson and his boys will start digging harder to find stills. I've got Trade Lake producing even faster than here. They now have double-cook stills just like the three we've added here." Each of these new stills had two copper cows. The first-cook flowed into the second-cook cow, so the still could produce twice-cooked moon in just a little more time than it took to single-cook, before the change. "Trade Lake built up inventory of ingredients all winter, just as you did here, and they're shipping moon to a warehouse in Superior as fast as they can."

"We're going as fast as we can here too, Jim," Andre said. "I've got two shifts cooking. We've doubled last year's output, but it would be a mistake to try to do more than we're currently putting out. Our inventory of sugar, yeast and corn will be used up by the end of May. With those agents working the County, it's harder to bring sugar in than to get moon out. Got any more good ideas of how we can safely bring more ingredients in?" Andre asked.

"As I told you last month, I've rented two barns within five miles of here. They are off the main road. We are going to bring sugar in and store it there.

We've started hauling it north from the Twin Cities already and are crossing the St. Croix at Grantsburg, then coming down the back roads. So far, it's working, and the drivers say they've had no problems. We've already got ten tons in one barn. They've been hauling that north route in broad daylight. Our other Twin City source has been hauling mostly at night," Hutton smiled. "And so far no one has bothered the trucks you've been bringing in from the old saw mill. It's all a risk, but, it's one we're going to continue taking, Andre."

Andre and Ralph had been putting in long hours. Andre was taking the midnight to noon shift, Ralph the noon to midnight. It was working, but each of them had things to accomplish at home, too. Andre also had to keep Cartier Egg moving to have a legitimate enterprise to hide behind. Carolyn and Clair were making the whole chicken enterprise work at home, and Raft and Molly had taken over the chickens at the Robinson place. Carolyn and Clair took care of the twice weekly retrieval of Robinson-eggs, which were then combined with Cartier's for delivery. Everything was working, but the egg business was now getting more difficult. The new stores they'd added to their route began asking for weekday delivery to be ready for weekend demand. Carolyn had already stayed home from school twice to deliver eggs, but Clair couldn't tolerate that. She began driving egg deliveries herself and had told Andre, "This is how it's going to be, Andre. I can deliver eggs as well as anyone else in this family, and the kids are staying in school." Life with moonshine and eggs was becoming more complicated.

"I know you and the crew are working hard, Andre; we all are," Hutton said. "But, if we can continue to produce this way for May and June, we will shut down again here in July. If you get too tired, let me know and I will take a couple of shifts for you."

Andre was always impressed with Hutton's help and support. No matter the situation he seemed always to be there to help and seemed to know situations demanding attention before they occurred, or at least before Andre noticed. *Admirable qualities*, thought Andre. Andre also reflected on the thought, *there was still a lot no one seemed to know about Hutton, including himself. Everyone who knew him seemed to talk about Hutton, except Hutton.*

Chapter 118

Andre was driving his stake-bed truck back from St. Paul. He had a full load of 40 lb sacks of chicken feed piled from the flat-bed to the top of the stake-fence. Half of it was for the Robinson coop, the other half for home. There were also two five-gallon tin cans of a disinfectant he'd been sold by the St. Paul feed store mixed in with the load. Andre's Uncle told him he used the stuff to disinfect his chicken coop floor. He was told to mix a quart of the disinfectant with ten gallons of water, then, occasionally spray it with a pump sprayer over the coop's wood shavings and straw covering the plank floor. He said it kept the chickens healthier by eliminating growth of molds and crawlies on the floor. He was also told not to breathe in the spray and to keep the chickens out in the scratch yard for an hour or two after spraying. "Open all the coop's doors and windows and wear a scarf over your nose, Andre. Don't breathe that damn stuff, whatever you do!" his uncle had demanded. Andre thought, *our chickens seem to eat all the crawlies, but I am interested to see what, this disinfectant, will do on the floor.*

He was still on Highway 8 approaching Cedarville, when he noticed four cars and a truck stopped in his lane on the road ahead. As he pulled up behind a Model A Ford Coup, he watched one man in a suit talking to the driver ahead of him and another, looking into the trunk of the car ahead of the Model A. Then it hit him. They were Revenue Agents searching cars! *How lucky can I be?* Andre thought. *This is exactly what Jim suggested . . . get stopped with a full load of nothing but what you need for the chickens.*

The man closed the trunk of the sedan ahead and walked back and greeted Andre with, " Federal Revenue Agents inspecting cars and trucks to see what they are carrying," Eggert said. "What have you on the truck?"

"Chicken Feed," Andre answered with a smile. "Have a look."

"That's all?" Eggert asked.

"That's it. You aren't going to make me unload are you?"

"Just some of it," Eggert said, then added, "Pull over to the side of the road when that Model A leaves. It's dry, so you can unload onto the grass there beside the truck. Then, he walked up and waved the car back onto the road.

Andre thought, *no questions . . . just do it*, as he pulled over to the side.

"That's good," Eggert said as he walked to the back to where Andre parked the truck.

Andre set the emergency brake and opened the door. As he got to the tail fence of the truck, Eggert said, "I want you to unload the outside bags on the back row, so I can see what's inside of them."

Andre shook his head with a smile. "What are you looking for?" as he lifted the stake-fence from the slots on the bed of the truck.

"Booze, and moonshine" said Eggert.

"Well, I'm afraid there's none of that," Andre replied.

"That's what they all say," Eggert responded. "Let's get on with it," as he pointed to the back row.

Andre began unloading the three stacks of bags that occupied the width of the truck, as Eggert looked on. He didn't offer to help handle the bags. They were piled eight-high. As he got down to the third bag from the bottom, in the center row, he saw the top of a five-gallon can of insecticide appear. Eggert saw it too.

Eggert's ears almost lit up, thought Andre, *as he realized how suspicious the can must look hidden within the bags of Feed.* "That's disinfectant I mix for the chicken coop floors," Andre explained.

"Why is it hidden?" asked Eggert. "Set the can on the ground right there," he pointed. "Then open the top."

"Well, I didn't load it, the feed guys did. Be careful," Andre said, as he set the can down reaching for the screw cap. "They tell us never to breathe this stuff, especially before mixing a quart of disinfectant, with ten-gallons of water."

"They say that about moonshine, too," said Eggert with a frown. He was truly suspicious of the can, *probably because he can't see the label,* thought Andre. "I see it's not one can as you said," he added. "Bring the one behind it out, too."

Agents always smelled gas tanks, and containers of every sort, seeking the aroma of moon. Eggert did not believe the last two sentences of Andre's explanation about, "never breathe it," in fact it made him more suspicious.

As Eggert leaned towards the open top of the can, Andre again said, "Don't breathe that stuff! It really is disinfectant. Read the label on the cans. I have no moonshine!"

Andre sounded sincere to Eggert, so he did read the label. While he read it, Andre said emphatically, "Look, I'm in the chicken business, not moonshine. I can show you the invoice I paid this morning for everything on this truck. Just don't breathe that stuff!"

Eggert remembered his training in Stearns and thought, that's a great way to hide more cans on this truck. He bent further over and took a short sniff at the open can. His face puckered and he wiped his eyes. "Ok, Mr. Cartier. That's not moon. I need you to unload another row or two. Any more cans on this truck?"

"No, Just those two, and both are the same stuff," Andre finished, pointing at the invoice entry of "two cans of Abraham Insecticide," on the paper in his hand he held out before the agent.

Andre had half the truck unloaded on the side of the road when he saw Sheriff Maun pull up behind him on the side of the road. He had a big grin on his face as he said, "What the hell are you doing Andre, I thought that stuff was for the chickens?"

Eggert didn't smile at Maun's arrival, or even notice his presence in any special way. "Ok, Mr. Cartier. That's enough. You can load it up again."

"You don't have to worry about this guy," Maun motioned to Eggert, with a smile. "His mother-in-law is the Director of the local WCTU."

"I'll decide what to worry about, Sheriff," said Eggert, again without a smile. He'd never met Maun, only heard about him from Sampson, nothing good of course. He was even less impressed with the local Sheriff when he began helping Andre reload his truck. "Sorry to have made work for you, Mr. Cartier, but we have laws to enforce," said Eggert. "I got the name from the door of your truck; it is Cartier, isn't it?" he asked.

"That's right, Cartier Egg and Poultry. You'll see another pickup with the same name on the door, running around the County with a load of eggs. I hope you don't make my wife or daughter unload that truck, too," Andre added with a straight face, as Jason handed him another bag of Chicken Feed.

Eggert said, "We'll decide what to unload, Mr. Cartier. Be careful what you carry," he finished, as he walked to another car behind the Sheriff's.

"These agents are friendly, aren't they, Andre," Sheriff Maun grinned. Andre grinned back, shaking his head in agreement, but thinking, *you have no idea how happy I actually am about this inspection, Jason.*

Chapter 119

Manny and Jim Hutton were having breakfast at a restaurant in St. Paul. Besides their weekly telephone contact they tried to meet at least once every two weeks. Different things came up when they were eyeball-to-eyeball, often important things.

"You accomplished doubling production, Jim, and Chicago assures me they'll take all we can give them, so keep pouring it on," Manny said. "They like what you're sending and are getting better money for it since it became Minnesota 13. Your bonus this year, will recognize that idea you had two years ago, of moving over to Wisconsin. That was clever thinking. I'm just waiting for some of the Stearns producers to discover Chicago is receiving more Minnesota 13 than they are shipping," he smiled.

"It's working well, Manny. I've considered labeling some of what we are shipping to Superior the same way, but decided against it. Superior is a cheaper market. They don't go much for high-priced booze up there, so I think we're better off shipping it labeled only as "aged 3 years," than to call it 13. Chicago loves high-priced booze. I'll bet you could raise those kegs another $5 and still get it," Hutton smiled.

"We'll experiment," Manny nodded.

"The biggest problem we have, Manny, is bringing in supplies. We need so damn much sugar it's hard to hide the incoming loads. Now that the feds are back from the Dakotas it's going to be even harder. It's easier to ship moon because the loads are smaller than sugar loads."

"By the way," Manny nodded, "I've been meaning to tell you about my Chicago contact. He knows about that shipment his organization was expecting from their Chicago farm that got raided in Stephens County, last fall. I asked him how he knew and he said, "Because, God Dammit, my trucks never came back! The feds impounded them!" Manny grinned. "Then, two weeks later, my contact gets an offer via the grapevine, that somebody up north has 1300 gallons of moon ready for a quick, quiet, sale, and they seemed to know just who to talk to in Chicago. He bought it immediately, to fill the hole caused by the fed-raid of their farm in the Barrens, but when they received it they found the kegs marked with the same black grease-pencil-codes they used at their Barren's farm's stills, that were raided two weeks earlier."

"That's incredible," Hutton expressed. "He was buying back his own stolen moonshine!"

"That's right," added Manny, "He knew it, too. That kind of stuff doesn't sit well with the organization. It won't be tolerated. Since then, he has been doing a quiet, behind-the-scenes hunt. They haven't figured it out yet, because the tracks of the sale and delivery to Chicago were well-covered. But, I know those guys. They'll figure it out, and when they do, someone is going to have their hands full of more trouble than they can handle."

"I heard they destroyed all the moonshine, at that place, during the raid, even saw the pictures in the *Gazette*. I'll see what else I can find out. Maybe there's more to this than we thought," Hutton finished. "Thanks for the breakfast . . . gotta run, Manny."

Chapter 120

Ralph was laughing. "I can't help it, Andre; it's so damn funny!"

"This was, Friday night?" Andre asked.

"Yeh, it was right after the Village Council meeting. I guess they usually go over to Ted's Saloon after their meetings. They call it the Power House. Any one Ted knows can buy a drink in there. I've done it myself and Ted says he's never had a problem with the law."

"So, what happened?"

"Ted said they had a full house, like they do every Friday night. About 9:00 p.m. the door slammed open and that guy, Sampson, and his trout fishermen, all three of them, walked in saying, 'THIS IS A RAID BY FEDERAL REVENUE AGENTS. EVERYONE KEEP YOUR SEAT, THE EXITS ARE BLOCKED.' Ted said he thought it was a joke at first. Then, when someone tried to quietly exit the back door and that Sampson-guy, fired a shot into the ceiling and told them, 'sit down or get shot. Your choice.' Ted says they sat."

"My God," Andre said. That's serious stuff. Was Jason there?"

"No, and it's a good thing," Ralph grinned, "He would have had to help arrest every one he works for! They arrested the whole Village Council, except for the two women who went straight home from the meeting. It's even worse than that, Andre. They arrested the Mayor with a drink in his hand, and Anderson from the bank, was in there too!"

Andre couldn't help smiling, though his thoughts *dreaded the seriousness of this event. Just picturing the Mayor, the Village Council, and many of the local business men of the town in that position* forced a smile. *Do as I say, not as I do*, he thought, until all of a sudden *he saw himself as a candidate for a similar incident if those agents looked beyond his façade of eggs.*

"Ted said Jason showed up about a half-hour after the raid. When he did, the feds turned those arrested over to him, to jail for the night. Sampson told Jason they would meet with him and the Mayor Monday morning to discuss charges. I haven't talked to anyone since, so I don't know what happened the next morning. Ted said the County Attorney had just left the bar about five minutes before the feds arrived. Five minutes earlier and they could have had the County Attorney, too," Ralph laughed.

"Maybe they're going to raid saloons for a while, instead of stills. Let's hope so," Andre finished, wondering *what kind of a mess was Jason in now?*

"I won't be here this afternoon, Ralph. I've got to deliver eggs to the stores

Clair and Carolyn didn't get to Saturday. I'll be here at midnight, though," he finished. "This egg business is growing fast. I'm not sure we can handle getting into the fresh chicken meat side of the business for all the stores we now have. I'm going to need some more help."

Chapter 121

Not you again, Carolyn thought, as she saw the black Ford behind her. But, she saw it was a different man in the car waving her to the side of the road as he pulled in front of her Cartier pickup.

"Good morning, Miss," said Brown.

"I know, you're a Revenue Agent looking for booze," Carolyn said sarcastically before the agent had a chance to continue. "How many times are you guys going to stop me?" she added.

I've never stopped you," Brown said.

"No, it was a Mr. Samplund, I think," Carolyn responded.

"You must mean Sampson," Brown said. "He's the head Revenue Agent over here. You don't want to deal with him, young lady. He's tough!" saying it just as Sampson had instructed when he told Brown, "If you ever see that young Cartier girl driving that egg truck around, stop her and inspect her truck. I want her intimidated and scared. I think she lied to me last time I talked to her," was how Sampson had put it. "When did he stop you?" Brown asked.

"Two weeks ago," Carolyn answered. "He thought I might be smuggling booze. You too?" she asked.

"Your truck looks empty today," he said, glancing at the pickup's box in back. "Anything there I need to see?"

"Nope, I'm even out of eggs."

"Ok. You're free to go, but let me warn you. Don't mess with Sampson. He's dangerous. Tell him the truth if he questions you," Brown finished.

Chapter 122

It was 9:00 a.m. Monday morning when Sampson arrived at Sheriff Maun's office, the exact time Sampson said he would be there. Sampson had suggested to Maun, that after he had jailed all those arrested, the Sheriff should release them on bond, or a handshake, later that night. That would give each Councilman and politician a taste of what it felt like to be inside a jail cell. Sampson wanted to scare them into helping him. He let Jason be the hero, releasing them after their hour in jail, but wanted the council and the Mayor to meet him in Maun's office this morning at 9:00 a.m. sharp. Dictating the meeting time and place placed Sampson in charge.

The Council members and the Mayor all arrived between 9:00 and 9:05. It was crowded in the Sheriff's office, with seven people. The two women members of the council were not there because they hadn't been present during the saloon raid. Sampson immediately took charge of the meeting, by standing and staring down the conversation.

"My name is Federal Revenue Agent Robert Sampson. I am in charge of the Revenue Agents currently investigating Stephens County for revenue violations. Each of you was arrested Friday night at Ted's Saloon for violating Prohibition laws, by buying and consuming illegal alcohol on those premises. I know most of you have spent time since your arrest, thinking I cannot prove you bought, or drank, booze while there, but I have more than enough probable cause to hit each of you with a stiff fine and possible probation. Because of your positions as Mayor and Council members it is likely that you do not want such a thing to occur, or to appear in your local *Gazette*. Consequently, I am here to persuade you to cooperate with me and my assignment in Stephens County. I am willing to drop all charges and label the arrests as *insufficient evidence,* provided that I get a commitment from each of you. That commitment is, that you will encourage your local law enforcement to help me and my agents with our work to stop illegal manufacture and sales of illegal alcohol within this County."

Sampson and Sheriff Maun could almost feel the simultaneous sigh of relief from those gathered in the office. They had anticipated a bigger problem for the last forty-eight hours. None smiled, but each looked at others with visible relief, their eyes signaling, *ok, let's get on with it.*

Sampson continued, "I want the Council to encourage Sheriff Maun and officer Nyguard to provide me information and assist us with arrests whenever necessary for the next sixty days. With your assurance of that, we will proceed with dropping all charges, not just of yourselves, but any others arrested at Ted's Saloon Friday night. In addition, I will personally provide the Cedarville *Gazette* with a news release, which reads; "Federal Revenue agents raided Teds Saloon in Cedarville, Friday night, arresting a number of patrons under suspicion of buying and consuming illegal alcohol on premises. Upon further investigation, the agents agreed to drop charges due to *insufficient evidence*, but with the warning that the raid be heeded by all and the warning that more raids were yet to come. Because of dropped charges, names of those insufficiently charged will not be made public. All citizens are again reminded, there will be more raids and charges of subsequent raids will not be dropped." Upon finishing the reading, Sampson eyeballed those present, especially Sheriff Maun and the Mayor. He wanted them both to know what he expected in return for this gesture thankfully received by all in the room. "Do we have an understanding?" Sampson demanded.

"May we speak alone for a moment, while you step outside, Agent Sampson?" the Mayor asked.

"No," Sampson responded. "This offer is not open to discussion. Take it or leave it, and do it now." He demanded.

The Mayor's face reddened as he looked at the Council members present, then, said, "Does anyone disagree with accepting this proposal?"

Jason Maun was the only one that didn't shake his head to the negative. Instead, he nodded, affirmatively. "Just so you all know," he said, as he eyeballed each of them, "If asked to do more than I believe is my legal obligation, I will resign before complying. I also put you all on notice now, that I will no longer serve the bank's papers during foreclosures. In the mean time, I will agree to whatever you all decide."

Council members had already been warned of the Sheriff's attitude on foreclosures, so there was no resistance among them to Jason's statement. *The bank's Anderson will have apoplexy* they thought, *but, let him. We need to get off this, Sampson's hook, now.*

The meeting ended with no further conversation between Sampson and those present. When the office was empty, other than Sampson and Maun, Sampson said, "Sheriff, I don't want much. You already gave me that Chicago operation, but I am sure you could help me ferret out some additional tips. Why don't you see what you can do? I will have no further problems getting the Council to pressure your cooperation if I have to, but as one law officer to another, would prefer to not have to do that."

"It's been a busy morning, a busy weekend, Agent Sampson. Let me give that some thought and I'll get back to you," Jason said, as he invited Sampson out his office door.

Chapter 123

Maun knew he was between a rock and a hard place. With the event that had just occurred, been arranged by the feds actually, he knew he had but two choices. He could resign, or he could cooperate, to whatever degree demanded by the Council and the Mayor. He knew none of them would sacrifice either their political positions, or their status, on behalf of Jason Maun's philosophy about chasing moonshine. It was, put up or shut up, time.

He hadn't slept all night. Each time he'd dozed, he awoke with a start, *wondering how to face people he knew who might have something to do with the moonshine business, especially after turning them in as a tip to revenue agents.* None he was aware of had done any more than buy a jar or two of moonshine on occasion. Most had bought illegal drinks at places like Ted's; there were at least a dozen or more saloons like Ted's within the County. He knew people he suspected were running booze within the County for grocery money. He knew of old Sandy Sanderson's rotgut production on his farm, but suspected half the County knew of him. He also knew from which automobile trunks one could likely buy a jar at Saturday night dances at the town halls. Throughout the night, the less sleep he got, the longer the list became.

Jason rationalized all the next day. *Why do I feel like I'm guilty of treason if I turn in any of these people who are breaking the law? I'm a law officer for God's sake. I'm not breaking the law, they are. What do I owe these people? Nothing!* Going in that direction of thought, the pain eased. But, then he'd think *of some of those to whom he delivered groceries who might somehow have become involved in moon. He'd be grateful if one of them got a job to put food on the table. Jason knew some had little choice but to take whatever work was available.* These thoughts made him remember *serving papers of foreclosure.* The papers had nothing to do with moonshine, but they still helped warp his rationale on helping the feds.

By Tuesday night, he was saying to himself, *make a decision or resign, Sheriff Maun.* So, he did what many in similar circumstances might have done. He made half a decision.

His decision was helped along by the weekly issue of the Cedarville *Gazette* on Thursday. The headline read, CHARGES DROPPED ON SALOON RAID. The story belittled the raid as token law enforcement and a waste of time. The editorial claimed arresting all those people for having a drink, instead of putting stills out of business, was like putting out a major fire with a squirt gun. Maun was glad to see that article, because it took pressure off him, which helped him make his decision.

I will help them chase down bootleggers who transit Stephens County, he thought. *I don't know them, and they are bringing their crimes through the County I'm supposed to enforce the law within. Them, I will help arrest. I will continue to police the dances and will take a better look around the County for stills. I will try to answer Agent Sampson's questions in a more cooperative manner. If I see something suspicious I'll tell him. I will try to invent enough information to, at least, keep him thinking I'm cooperating. I feel as it must feel to prostitute. I don't like it, but, I can't afford to give up my job, nor do I owe my job to anyone. Ok, that's it. That's what I'm going to do. That's my plan*, he thought.

Jason smiled, then, wondered *why? What have I got to smile about?* The image that answered his mind's *smile*-question *was the image of Councilman Teggart, being arrested in Ted's Saloon.*

We'll see how this works, Jason thought to himself, with another *smile*.

Chapter 124

Months before, while posing as a trout fisherman, Agent Eggert had made notes about the teenager he had talked with who said he made his money driving jars of moon about the County. He had tracked that young man down again last week and had a threatening, but productive conversation with him. The long and the short of it was, "tell me who you are buying from and delivering to and you stay out of jail." And, of course, "no one will ever know you told us." It took Agent Eggert less than an hour to learn this teen was one of old Sandy Sanderson's runners. The teen had bought from Sandy for over a year, and Sandy didn't know, or care, where he was selling it, as long as no one knew it came from him. He had made the teen agree, that if ever caught he would say he bought it from someone in Somerset, someone he didn't know. *So much for that agreement* the teen thought, as he heard agent Eggert's words of, "and stay out of jail."

The next day, Eggert pulled into Sandy's farm yard just before daylight. There were lights on in the barn. The house was dark. He approached the barn, but couldn't get near enough to look in a window, because an old hay rake was parked just beneath it. As he opened the barn door and stepped in, an overweight barn dog that looked too old to get up, let out a muffled bark that seemed almost more of a groan.

Sandy was just twenty feet across the floor from the door, pouring moonshine from a galvanized bucket into quart Mason jars on a plank table. As the jar became full, he looked up at Eggert, nodded, and then began filling the next jar. "You wants to buy dis moon?" Sandy asked, with a smile.

"I'm afraid not," Eggert said. "I am a Federal Revenue Agent and you are under arrest for violation of Prohibition laws."

"I knowed who you was," Sandy said. "Been expectin ya for two years," he laughed. "Can you jes let me sell dis batch before you take me away? My wife needs dis money to feed her kin."

"I'm afraid not," Eggert said. "I have to ask you to shut things down, and come with me immediately, Mr. Sanderson."

"Ok, jes giv me five minutes," Sandy asked. He filled four more open mason jars to empty the bucket, screwed the tops onto the red rubber gasket atop the jars, and placed them on a shelf holding about twenty more.

Eggert was almost embarrassed. The man he was arresting was in his late seventies, bent over in neck and shoulders and apparently unable to fully straighten vertically. He limped as he walked and he didn't seem the least bit disturbed that he'd just been arrested, nor aware that it mattered. This was certainly not someone who worked with the likes of Scarface Capone. A small still sat behind Sanderson near the barn wall. There were three barrels of what Eggert thought were full of fermenting mash, the first two with loose wooden covers, the third uncovered with a stirring stick protruding from the top. Chickens roamed the barn. Eggert's own feet seemed to stick to chicken shit and straw on the floor. The smells made him feel like vomiting.

"Can I tell my wife before we go?" old Sandy asked Eggert.

"Certainly, I'll wait in the yard by the car. After you are booked at the County jail, I'll come back to destroy the moon," Eggert frowned. He had been an agent less than a year, had little arrest experience and this was the first one he'd done alone. Before becoming an agent assigned to Sampson, Eggert had sold crop seed for Northrup King. He was a good salesman, but found seed sales to be even more boring, than watching them grow. He'd lasted for almost two years before seeing an advertisement soliciting young men to train as Revenue Enforcement Agents to help America adhere to the lofty goals of Prohibition. He'd walked out of a grain elevator in Morris, Minnesota with an application in his hand and drove straight to St. Paul, Minnesota to the Federal Revenue Office. He spent the afternoon filling out the application to train as a Revenue Agent. Finishing about mid-afternoon, he drove directly to the office of Northrup King and resigned. My life is going to change to one of excitement, adventure, and accomplishment, he thought.

Today, it felt nothing like what he had envisioned then, as he watched old Sandy explaining to his wife, who looked older and even more frail than her husband, that he would be back this afternoon after he straightened this all out. As she stared at him from their front porch, Eggert wanted to hide. Sandy hugged her, then walked to the black Ford, whose door was held open by Eggert, inviting him in for his ride to the County jail.

Later in the afternoon, when Agent Eggert returned to the Sanderson farm, all of the moonshine was gone from the premises. So was Sandy's small, tired-looking still. There was only a shelf full of empty Mason jars. When Eggert asked Sandy's wife at their front door, what had happened to everything, she replied, "I have no idea. I'm not well, so I've been lying on my bed worrying about my husband all day. What have you done with him? I need him!"

"He's been arrested for violating Prohibition laws, Mrs. Sanderson. He must go before the Federal Judge tomorrow, so he will be in jail in Cedarville tonight. They may release him tomorrow, depending upon his sentence."

"I've never been alone here," she said. "Who will take care of me?"

"I don't know Mrs. Sanderson. I will tell the Sheriff to see if he can help."

She was crying now, tears running down her wrinkled cheek. "How much do they pay you to do this, young man?" she asked, as she slowly closed the door, not awaiting his answer.

Agent Eggert thought *of the calm waters* of the seed sales business, as he drove back towards Cedarville. He was unaware that the same teenager from whom he had forced the tip about Sanderson, had responded to Sandy's wife's phone call immediately after he left the farm. She asked the teen to come and get everything immediately and to take it to her sister's farm just a mile away. Her sister would be expecting it and would show him where to hide the still. He was to sell the moon as fast as he could, take twice his normal percentage, and return the rest of the cash to her. She didn't have to tell him to keep quiet about it. Her Sandy was not going to jail.

As he drove, Eggert thought mostly about *how he was going to explain to Sampson about leaving the moonshine evidence and still unguarded, while he delivered Sanderson to jail.* The Federal Revenue Agent involved in this raid now had no evidence with which to convict the man he had caught bottling moonshine. He also thought of *tears on those wrinkled cheeks.*

Chapter 125

"Your Agent, Eggert, found the Sanderson still," Sheriff Maun said to Sampson. "The judge suspended the sentence because there was no evidence to convict. He said even if there'd been evidence he would have sentenced him to just time served. He wasn't about to send a seventy-year-old man to prison for making a few quarts of moon. It's actually a good thing they let Sandy go home to take care of his wife. What would have happened to her if he was sent to prison?"

"It is not my job, to know, or to care, Sheriff. "My job is to shut them down. That's what I do," Sampson stared, coldly.

Shaking his head slowly, Maun said, "I really don't know of any other stills operating anywhere in the County. I have always suspected there were stills in the next County east, that's Bodine County, because so many bootleggers come through Stephens County headed west for the Twin Cities. Were I in your shoes, Agent Sampson, I would continue bridge watches at Stillwater, Osceola and Taylors Falls. To my way of thinking, that's your best bet for finding runners."

"We've done pretty well on the bridges, so I agree with you there," Sampson said. "But I am convinced there must be more stills somewhere in the Barrens. It's such a great place to hide. We are going to work Somerset again this week. Because the judges don't give stiff sentences to those we arrest they seem to get back into business, quickly."

"I think there are a lot of small runners, who just drive small deliveries throughout the County when asked by small cookers. I don't know where the cookers are," Jason added. "I sometimes think you'd do better watching for incoming loads of sugar and the other stuff they need. It takes a whole lot of sugar to make moonshine, but I never see loads of it coming into the County. I have noticed one thing, though, that I saw last summer. Every now and then there are loaded trucks parked in the parking lot of the old saw mill on the northwest side of town about two-miles out. I checked it out once last summer, but the truck was full of rolls of tar paper. I saw your man making Cartier unload his egg truck full of chicken feed beside the highway last week. Your agent said you sometimes find things, inside whatever is visible on the outside. I never did check inside that load at the sawmill, but it looked just like tar paper rolls to me. Another time there were two trucks there. They both had hay bale loads. I've never seen any sugar there, but I've noticed up to three trucks parked there a couple of times this spring."

"We'll check it out later this week," Sampson added.

Chapter 126

Ralph was driving Bill's gas truck towards Cedarville from the Barrens when he saw two black cars sitting at the crossroad ahead. As he drew nearer, a man stepped from one of the cars and flagged him to the side of the road.

Looks like it's time to talk to some fishermen, thought Ralph, *I recognize one of those guys from the gas station,* as he pulled to the side.

"Good afternoon. I'm Federal Revenue Agent, Brown. You've filled my car up several times at the gas station in town," he smiled. "We'd like you to step out of the truck while we look it over. My partner will do that while I ask you some questions."

Ralph nodded his agreement, as the other agent began to climb up the ladder, on the back of the tank truck. "Fine with me," he said as he stepped out of the truck.

"Where have you been making deliveries?"

Ralph turned back, reached inside the cab of the truck and grabbed a clipboard full of invoices off the seat. Paging through it he answered, "I was at the Johnson place, the Anderson farm, and John Everson's. I'm headed back to Bill's now.

"What do those three use all the fuel for?" agent Brown asked.

"Well, you can see by the invoices it's not a lot of fuel. They are small farmers; each has only one or two tractors. I think Everson has a generator for power, and I'm not sure about the other two. I just deliver what Bill tells me to bring them," he finished, raising his eyebrows and holding out his hand, palm up. Ralph watched the other agent open the caps on the three separate sections of the tank, designed to enable them to haul regular gas, high octane ethyl, and fuel oil all in the same load. After the agent raised the caps, he lowered his nose into the opening sniffing for a gasoline smell. Finding it in all three tanks he closed them and climbed down, giving a thumbs up to Agent Brown.

"Do any of those farmers operate stills for moonshine?" Brown asked.

"No, not to my knowledge," Ralph answered, then thought out loud, "Well, hell, how would I know anyway?"

The other agent walked over to Ralph and said, "Where's the key to the lockbox on the side of the truck?"

"It's on my key ring in the ignition," Ralph answered with a smile. Then, his mind froze, instantly-constipated by his recollection of *placing two jars of Sandy's white lightning in that same lockbox two days before,* and then, *forget-*

ting to take them out!

"I'll get the keys, you can show me which one is for the padlock," the agent said.

Ralph was in full panic, but trying not to show it. *Think, Ralph, what would Andre do? What would Hutton do? What are you going to do?*

The agent held the key ring up in front of Ralph waiting for his indication of which key. Ralph looked at them and said, "Oh, hell, I grabbed the wrong keys this morning. The lock box key isn't on this ring, just on the other one at Bill's. Sorry about that."

The agent looked at Brown, who shrugged his shoulders.

Ralph laughed, then said, "That lock box isn't big enough to hold my lunch. You don't think you'll find a barrel of moonshine in there do you?"

"Well," agent Brown said, "We'll follow you back to Bill's station and you can get the key there."

"Ok," Ralph nodded, *knowing he had at least bought more time to try and figure some way out of his dilemma.* "I don't know who drove the truck last, so I'm not sure where that key is."

Ralph's mind was in turmoil as he drove, ahead of the black Fords toward Bill's station. Instead of using the extra time, efficiently, and towards a solution, he berated himself with punishing thoughts. *How dumb can I be? First I sink a load in the river; I ask Hutton too many questions, now I'll get arrested for two jars of moon! This will implicate Bill and his gas business; make the feds suspicious of Andre because I work with him. I've let everyone down with another stupid mistake!* He was so busy downing himself; he nearly went through a stop sign. *That's the way, Ralph, go through a stop sign, have an accident. That will impress everybody.* He couldn't stop condemning himself, because he no longer had any forgiveness left for his mistakes, for what he had watched himself become. *What do I tell the wife and kids about this?*

Brown and Eggert were right behind him as he parked the tank truck behind Bill's station. Ralph had thought of absolutely nothing to help prevent, even deflect, what was about to occur. Almost before he was out of the truck, Brown and Eggert were walking beside him to the front of the station. Bill was standing by the cash register smiling. "Gentlemen," he greeted. "What kind of a visit is this? You look like you are delivering my own employee to me."

As he opened his mouth to speak, agent Brown cut Ralph off with, "Ralph needs your other key ring, the one with the key to the padlock for the tank truck lock-box."

Bill saw, from the expression on Ralph's face, that he was scared. He turned to the key board on the wall above the register, pointed to an empty hook and said, "It's not here. Jack must have taken it home with him again," he grimaced. "God dammit, Ralph, I keep telling you guys to leave the keys on the board!"

"It seems to me you people are a little too reluctant to open that lock, Bill," agent Brown said, almost accusingly.

Bill was mad, first at the missing keys, now at the tone of the agent's statement.

"Reluctant my ass! Come on," Bill shouted, waving them to follow. He walked through the shop of the station where they worked on cars. Without even slowing down, he grabbed two hammers from the open drawer of a tool box and quickly walked around the side of the building to the truck. All three were right behind him. Ralph seemed to be shrinking as he brought up the rear. Bill lifted the long shank padlock, setting its base atop the face of the biggest hammer, in his left hand. Then with a quick, but smashing blow of his right hand, with the other hammer, lock's base shattered into three pieces. Bill slid the lock's shank from the holes of the hasp holding the box-lid shut, turned to the agents and said, "Now, God dammit, don't be reluctant about buying me a new lock!" He turned abruptly and walked at an angry pace back towards the shop.

Brown and Eggert were almost embarrassed by Bill's actions, but he did it all so fast, they were stuck with the results. Ralph was about to piss his pants.

Agent Brown lifted the hasp, then the lid of the box. Both he and Eggert looked down into the box. Ralph lost about four drops down his pants leg. "Well, that was hardly worth a broken lock," agent Brown said as he dropped the lid. Eggert nodded. Ralph, white as a sheet, stared at the closed lid of the box. "Tell Bill we'll buy him a new lock," Brown said. You seem a little distressed, Ralph. Are you sure you don't deliver gas to anyone cooking moon?" he stared.

"I - - don't," he almost stuttered. "I am nervous," he stuttered, wiping his hand across his brow, "I can't afford to lose this part- time delivery job and Bill is really pissed about those keys! You guys stirred up something that could get me fired!"

"Well, I'm sorry we caused that, but you acted like you didn't want to open that box for us. We understand when people are nervous, Ralph. That's our job. Once more, are you certain you have no ideas about the people we are looking for?"

Ralph shook his head, "I keep telling you no. Now, I've got to go talk to Bill, before I'm out of work!" he finished, turning his back on the agents and walking away.

The agents got into their cars and left. Ralph tried to walk casually into the bathroom's outside door. Then, as his shaking hand fumbled with his buttoned fly, he pissed on his hands, the seat cover, the floor and the wall, thinking *what the hell happened to those two jars of moon?*

Washing his hands under the cold water, splashing into a dirty sink, Ralph thought *Bill must have found it yesterday. He is going to fire me! Balls, I have made another mess!* After wiping down the front of his work pants with an oil check rag he found in the bathroom, he walked into the station.

Bill looked at Ralph, with a grim expression, and then smiled. "How'd I do, Ralph?"

"What do you mean?" Ralph questioned, "How'd you do?"

"My act, for those agents?" Bill laughed, "I thought you were going to shit your pants! From the look on your face, when you came in with those two, I didn't think you were even going to make it back out to the truck," he laughed again. I found the jars yesterday. They're home in my booze cupboard. When I heard that key story from the agent I knew what you were doing. The hardest part for me was to keep from laughing. Was I mad enough?" he questioned, with an ear-to-ear grin. "By the way, Ralph, when we're done laughing about this I'm going to kick your ass for being so stupid with my truck."

"I'm sorry, Bill. I blew it!" Ralph apologized. "I just plain forgot about the jars after I left the Sanderson place."

"You owe not being arrested to old man Sanderson, Ralph. When I heard he was arrested yesterday, I went over to the jail. Maun let me talk to him. He's been a gas customer for ten years. I wanted to see if I could help him. He asked me to go out and see his wife, so she wouldn't be so scared about his arrest. Sandy said he sold you two jars and saw you put them in the lock box. I got them out last night. If it weren't for him, I'd be going over to see you in the jail, about now. You have to realize by now, you have to be more careful, Ralph. You didn't give those two any info on our customers, right?" He didn't give Ralph time to answer. "They're digging hard right now. Just keep telling them you just deliver gas where I send you. That's it." Bill knew this had to have been one of the worst days in Ralph's life. "I know you wouldn't say anything, Ralph," he said, reaching out to shake his hand. "We came through this one ok, but these guys aren't through with us. You better tell Andre about this, too."

"Do you think I have to tell them the whole story?" Ralph asked, embarrassed.

"No, just tell them about being stopped, and brought back to the station, without mentioning the jars. I just think they should know about *Uncle Ben being in town.*"

Chapter 127

Lundquist had asked Sampson to loan him Agents Brown and Eggert for the next two weeks. Stearns County Agents were setting up an elaborate network of road traps, trying to catch bootleggers all over the County at once. Because they were so underfunded and consequently shorthanded, feds frequently borrowed agents from other regions when involved with energetic arrest efforts. Once, five years earlier, Lundquist had arranged a thirty-agent raid in Somerset.

Because of the loan of his agents, Sampson was down to just him and Eastman. Because of the tip from Sheriff Maun about the overnight trucks parking in the old saw mill lot, one of them had been driving by that lot each morning before 4:00 a.m. The darkness, and the time of night they stopped, kept anyone from seeing them there. As quickly as they inspected any trucks in the lot they disappeared. In ten days, they'd found six different trucks left there overnight, but all with legitimate loads.

"Until this morning," Eastman explained to Sampson. "The one thing we never knew, was how long any of those trucks were left there. Then, it dawned on me, that truck loads could be left for just an hour or two, then picked up by someone else. The other thing was half the trucks you and I saw there were empty. I thought they may have been emptied and returned to the lot just before we got there. So, last night I pitched my tent in the woods by the lot. Two trucks were dropped off there at 1:00 a.m. I watched them until about 2:00, then, I was just going to go inspect the loads when a car pulled in. Two guys got out of the car, hopped into the trucks, and drove off north, with the car following them. That direction takes them right up into the Barrens, Bob, but by the time I ran to my car and then tried to follow them, without my lights on, I lost them. I realize now I probably should have approached them before they left the lot, but I didn't even know what they were hauling and I've never made an arrest alone."

"I'm glad you didn't," Sampson said. "Knowing this now, we'll have another chance to follow them. I want you to pitch that tent again for the next three nights. See if you can figure out if it is different drivers that bring trucks than take them away, or if you recognize any of them, and also whether or not they always go in the same direction. Once we pin that down, we'll double-team them one night and follow them to their delivery. This time, when they leave a truck, inspect it immediately to see what they're hauling. My bet is these midnight truckers are hauling sugar."

Now, a week later, Sampson said, "I knew it would be sugar. Good work,

Eastman. Chief Lundquist is chasing down those license plate numbers for me. Thursday night we'll both be there. There's almost no moon now, so even if it's not cloudy, we should be able to follow them. There will be no raid. Once we find the stills, we'll set up a more elaborate arrest. I want to find out who's involved. I suspect this will be big like that Chicago outfit. I'm still suspicious of that Cartier chicken business over at that Robinson place. Don't know why, just am," he said to Eastman.

After his last two statements, he thought, *my agents won't be wondering about any attention I give the Cartier girl on the road or of my nosing around the Cartier place, which I intend to do again, soon.* Sampson smelled blood. He was frustrated by the few stills they'd found in Stephens County, by the fact that they hadn't gained as much evidence, he could hide and sell on the side, as he had planned on and that, he hadn't found a suitable young woman in the region to ease his frustrations. *Eastman finding those loads of sugar at the saw mill was the needle I needed to find in the Stephens haystack* he thought.

Chapter 128

It was Saturday. Sampson hung around Cedarville's Main Street for an hour in the morning, wondering if he'd see a Cartier Egg truck delivering. About 10:00 a.m. he saw the pickup pull up outside the grocery store. Andre Cartier and a woman Sampson guessed to be his wife got out of the truck and entered the store. Sampson noticed the pickup box was full of egg boxes, making it appear they must just be starting egg deliveries for the day. *With both of them here, she is probably home alone. There's no school on Saturday. She said she had a brother; he could be there. This is as good a day as any for me to check out the Cartier farm for stills.*

Eight miles west of Cedarville, as he approached the first building beside the long driveway, he realized it was a chicken coop that looked identical to the one at the Robinson place. Cartier had told him that day at the Robinsons, that he managed two different egg operations. He drove past the coop and circled around between the barn and the house. Seeing no signs of activity, he pulled back down by the chicken coop and parked. He left his car, then, stood beside it, listening. He heard a tractor engine running in the field behind the barn, apparently doing some kind of field work. He opened the coop door and gazed down its length before stepping in. At the far end of the coop, stood Carolyn Cartier with her hand beneath a hen, who was nervously warming an egg in her nest.

As she set the egg into the basket on her arm, Carolyn saw the dark-suited agent, Robert Sampson, walk into her chicken coop. She wasn't sure why, but her first thoughts were, *Henri is dragging out in the field, Mom and Dad are in town, why is this guy here now?* She began walking towards the door where Sampson stood. She was wearing a scarf over her hair tied beneath her chin, and had on a dust shirt, unbuttoned over the white blouse beneath. Her slacks were the canvas pants she always wore for chores.

She looks good no matter how she's dressed, he thought.

"Good morning, Miss Cartier," he said, with an unemotional face. "We are inspecting farms for moonshine today and I drew the Cartier place. Since you invited me for a tour the last time we talked, I hope you can accommodate me this morning."

"Well, my father should do that, not me," she answered.

"Federal Agents decide who responds to their orders, Miss Cartier. We don't do revenue inspections at the convenience of those inspected. I want you to show me what I need to see," he directed in a stern voice.

"That's my brother dragging that field. Should I call him in?" she asked.

"No, you'll do, Miss Cartier; I have little time today." Then, Sampson added, "I need you to show me around, now," more sternly. Without giving her time to speak again, he walked towards the end of the coop where she'd been gathering eggs, saying, "How many chickens do you have here? Is this place the same size as at the Robinson place? How many of you does it take to keep up with this egg business?" he peppered, giving her no time to resist or respond between questions.

Wanting to keep him from inspecting the coop too strenuously, Carolyn decided her best move was to cooperate, as Sampson knew she would. She wanted to shorten the coop tour as much as possible, and move him on to other areas of the farm. She followed him as he walked, saying, "About 350 chickens, a little more than at the Robinson coop, and it takes about three of us, depending on how hard we work. Why are you here? Do you still think we are in the moonshine business? One of your agents stopped me again last week."

Sampson didn't respond, or even turn to look at her as he walked. He stopped at the end of the coop, turned, and said, "Yes, I do, Miss Cartier. I think your father is somehow in the moonshine business." *It worked in Chicago*, he thought. *God, she is good looking.*

"That's ridiculous," Carolyn said. "We are in the chicken business."

"What's beyond this door?" he asked, pointing to the wide door centered in the wall, which kept chickens from the supply room.

"Chicken feed, floor disinfectant, wood shavings, straw bales and tools," she answered. "Just open the door." *This has to be quick she thought. Invent a way to get him out of the chicken coop!*

"I believe you," he said, turning away from the door. He wanted to have some place he didn't inspect, so he'd have an excuse to come back again. Not entering the coop supply room would provide him that opportunity. He turned from the door and began walking back to the end he had entered first. "How long has your father been involved with moonshine?" he asked as they walked, without looking at her.

Why is he suspicious? she thought. *I need to convince him he's wrong, even more important, make him less suspicious of Dad at the Robinson place.* "I've told you repeatedly, he isn't!" she responded, as she followed him back to the other end. "Am I supposed to show you the barn and machine shed, too?" she asked.

"Of course," he answered. "I'm here to inspect the Cartier property, to find where your father hides his stills and moonshine. During my years in Chicago, when inspecting farms we often found moonshine, kegs and crocks, in barn haymows. I'm not sure you realize how serious it is, that your father is under suspicion of Revenue violations,

Miss Cartier. I once kept a young lady's father out of prison down there, after I finally discovered his hiding place."

"I thought Revenue Agents sent people to prison, not kept them out?" Carolyn said, as she opened the coop door inviting Sampson to follow her out. *We'll be better off anywhere than in the coop,* she thought.

"I was just doing her a favor because she was nice to me." Sampson smiled, for the first time. "We actually became good friends. I still hear from her and visit her, occasionally. Is there no running water in the chicken coop?" he asked, looking along the driveway side of the building.

"No. My dad says that was the biggest mistake. We have to haul water from the well every day. It makes extra work for us, but the chickens don't mind. Let me show you the barn, so you'll stop worrying about moonshine," she smiled, walking ahead, thinking, *he will follow.* He did.

She opened the barn door, then, looked down at his feet, seeing polished shoes. "No boots?" He shook his head. "Do you want me to find you some?" He nodded. "Just wait here," she finished, stepping into the barn. She came back out, handing him a pair of big pull-on soft-rubber boots, which would fit right over his shoes. He stepped into them, without thanking her.

As they walked through the barn, Carolyn said, "The stanchions are empty, because the milk cows are out in the pasture. The floor will be a mess, until my brother does afternoon chores. There's a half-dozen beef cows outside there, too," pointing to the barns west wall. "They stay out most of the summer, but winter, in that area there. You can see the horse stalls on that end, and that closed room down there is for supplies," she finished.

"Let's look in there," he pointed. Carolyn opened the door and scraped her boot soles on a piece of metal screwed to the floor, before stepping into the room. Sampson just stepped in.

"You'll find everything but moonshine in here," she smiled. "This is where we keep everything any of the animals need."

Sampson just did a cursory look at things, and then stepped back to the door. "How do you access the hay loft?"

"Right up that ladder there, in the center of the barn," she pointed.

"Let's go," he said.

Carolyn was so relieved to have him out of the chicken coop she relaxed a little. She almost stopped feeling threatened by his presence. She felt she had sort of saved the day by getting him out of there. She stopped at the base of the ladder inviting him, with a wave of her hand, to go first.

"Ladies first," he responded, waving her past him.

She scraped her boots again, then, started up the ladder. When she grasped her third rung, Sampson quickly started up, immediately behind her, which positioned his face near her waist line as he held himself out from the ladder by extending his arms.

Sensing his closeness, Carolyn said, "Be careful my boots don't mess up your clothes," as she climbed faster trying to create more space between them. Sampson countered by climbing as fast as she did, maintaining his position behind her. The ladder seemed longer than usual to Carolyn. Though lacking experience, her teenage mind and body were sounding alarm bells and throughout the twelve rungs, some portion of Sampson was touching some portion of Carolyn. She quickly stepped off the ladder, as her feet leveled with the hay mow floor, relieved to recapture some space beyond his reach. As he stepped away from the ladder she said, "There's moonshine beneath all that hay," she pointed, with a lopsided smile, just as she had the first time he'd stopped her in her pickup.

"I know you think you are being funny, Miss Cartier, but be aware that I am going to catch your father," he stared, watching to see if he got the same reaction he had that first day he'd asked her "if her father was in the moonshine business." Many law officers seem to have a sixth sense that tells them when someone is lying or scared. It sometimes saved lives, sometimes caught wrong-doers, and if used properly, often intimidated those being questioned. Sampson's sixth, had just worked again. He saw that same split-second reaction in Carolyn's expression, when he told her "he would catch her father."

It did scare her and she did show it. *How does this man know anything about my father?* She tried to make her expression look like anger, *but knew she hadn't fooled him.* "Why are you so sure my father is involved with moonshine? I know he isn't, but it scares me the way you talk about him. Why don't you come back when he's here, so he can convince you?"

"You invited me for a tour, remember, beside your pickup? Don't worry. When I catch him, I'll give you an opportunity to keep him out of jail. You've been nice to me."

"Who's been nice to you?" shouted Henri, his head and shoulders sticking out above the ladder hole. "What the hell are you doing up here, Carolyn, and who in hell is this? I've been looking all over for you."

"This is Federal Revenue Agent, Sampson, Henri, and he's looking for moonshine." Carolyn smiled.

"Well, you should have come and gotten me!" he said loudly, as he walked over to where they stood. "He doesn't belong up here without Dad or me," he said sharply to Carolyn, though looking at Sampson.

"Shut up, sonny! I am a Federal Revenue Agent, and I belong wherever I choose to be whenever I want. You don't tell me, I tell you," he glared. "Want to argue about it?" he sneered as he pulled his gun from the holster inside his jacket. It was a practiced move for Sampson and he knew exactly what response to expect. It got quiet. "Now, no more crap from either of you. He pointed at a fifty-five gallon drum sitting on the floor near the ladder. It had a wooden top on it, upon which sat a concrete cinder block like those in basement walls. "What's in there?" Sampson asked, pointing with his gun.

"Rock salt for the cattle," said Henri.

"You stand by the ladder, son," he pointed to Henri, with his pistol.

"You take the top off," he pointed to Carolyn, as he stepped over to the drum. Carolyn grasped the cinder block which weighted the wooden cover in place. She grasped the blocks partitions firmly, with thumbs and fingers, then squeezed and lifted it from the wooden top. As she turned in front of Sampson to set the heavy block on the floor, Sampson slowly swept his gun-hand in front of her allowing the back of his hand to slide briefly across the blouse covering her breast.

The touch of his hand so surprised Carolyn, that her split-second, autonomic reflex caused her to squeeze the cinder block harder! Without gloves, the sharp, protruding, roughness of the cinder block penetrated the skin of her fingers. The resulting pain told her brain to let go of the block. It fell directly onto the arch of Sampson's right foot! Dropping about two feet, its impact resulted in an instantaneous, v-shaped dent, about an inch deep, into the bones and flesh of the arch of Sampson's foot! Those bones, surrounded by nerves, flesh and veins, cracked, broke, parted, bruised and bled, as Sampson collapsed in a howl of pain onto the hay mow's floor.

He dropped his gun to the floor, as he fell and grasped his ankle, within the collar of the boots. Grimacing in pain, with teeth clamped, he snarled, "You little bitch, you dropped that on purpose! You've broken my foot!"

Obviously shaken, Carolyn said loudly, "If you'd kept your hands off me I wouldn't have dropped it!"

Henri jumped from the ladder, intending to first help Carolyn. When he saw she was ok, he looked at Sampson saying, "I think you're going to need some help, Mr. Sampson."

"Yes, for Christ's sake, help me," Sampson demanded as he rocked in pain. "I don't want that little bitch near me!"

"That little bitch, Mr. Sampson, is my sister, and if I hear her called bitch again, you can crawl out of here on your own," Henri said, trying his best to sound like his father the last time he heard him lose his temper. "What the hell are you doing here anyway?"

Sampson was exhibiting shock, sweating and moaning in pain. "I've got to get to my car to get to a doctor. Is there another way down besides that ladder?"

All of a sudden, Henri felt in charge of someone he thought, *was an intimidating bastard.* There was a wooden pallet on the floor beside the barrel Carolyn had moved the block from. Sampson grabbed his gun from the floor, fumbling it back inside the holster beneath his jacket. Henri said, "I'll help you onto that pallet. You can just sit on it. We will lower you to the ground with the hay lift."

Still moaning in pain, Sampson allowed Henri's hands under his arm pits from behind him. Henri helped him slide backwards onto the pallet. The pallet had four six-foot cables that ran from each of its four corners up to an eye ring centered above the pallet. Henri hooked the ring to the block and tackle chain hanging from the roof's metal beam above. Advising Sampson to sit still in the center of the pallet, he began pulling chain through the tackle-block wheels which slowly lifted the pallet and Sampson a few inches off the floor. Then, he began sliding the block's wheels slowly along the steel I-beam that ran the full length of the barn roof to the big hay mow door at its end. Opening the big door and seeing an expression of fear of height added to the pain on Sampson's face, he again told Sampson to sit still. Then, he slowly slid the pallet and Sampson six more feet outside the door. The pallet and agent Sampson now dangled beneath the rail some ten feet above the ground from the protruding rail they normally used to lift hay from wagons into the hay mow.

Carolyn continued pulling chain through the wheels, now in the opposite direction, Sampson was carefully lowered to the ground. Henri climbed down the barn ladder, exited the barn and ran to Sampson's black Ford. Finding Sampson had left the key in the ignition, Henri started the car and pulled it up beside Sampson as the pallet touched the ground. Sampson looked up at Carolyn in the hay mow door. "I'm not done here, Miss Cartier," Sampson threatened, in a tone he knew only she could hear. "I know your father is working moonshine. I'll be back."

Reluctantly, Henri helped Sampson into the passenger seat of the Ford. There was no way Sampson could depress a clutch or drive with that broken foot. He needed a doctor, quickly. As Henri got into the driver's seat, he said to Carolyn, "I'll drive him to a doctor in Cedarville, but if he calls you a bitch again, 'Sonny,' will leave him in a ditch!" loudly enough that Sampson must hear him, then added, "Call Sheriff Maun. Tell him we are coming in to the clinic in Cedarville, so he can help me get him out of the car. I'll ask him to bring me back home."

As they drove down the Cartier driveway towards the road, Sampson reached around behind his seat with his right hand. "I am in a great deal of pain!" he grimaced. As his hand came back to the front, it held a pint-sized, Mason jar, full of clear liquid. He unscrewed the lid, and drank two large swallows, took a deep breath, then another drink. He screwed the lid back on and set the jar on the floor between his feet. "Son of a bitch, that hurts!" He grasped his ankle again clamping his eyes shut.

Henri questioned Sampson during the eight miles to Cedarville, but received only answers Sampson wanted him to hear. He learned little beyond the fact, that Sampson was in charge, suspected Henri's father was involved with moonshine, and that, at least today, his sister had aggravated the agent enough to put her high up on his shit-list.

Sheriff Maun met them in Cedarville and helped get Sampson into the clinic. Because of another call for the Sheriff, Jason barely had time to talk to Henri about what happened before he had to leave. He had arranged for the town constable to give Henri a ride home.

Chapter 129

Eggert was explaining to Sampson, who was sitting with his leg elevated in a cast, "I stayed in that damn tent for four nights, before I found that truck load of sugar. I just finished checking under the tarp that covered it, discovered the sugar, got the truck's plate numbers, and was walking back to my tent in the brush when that car came in to the lot. They didn't see me. One man left the car, hopped into the truck and took off north. The other man followed him in his car. I was alone, so I didn't try to follow. But the next night I got there about 10:00 o'clock, and the same truck was sitting there, and full of sugar again."

Sampson, sitting in a reclining chair, was enjoying what he was hearing, in spite of being laid up with a crippled foot. *This was progress*, he thought.

"This time I followed, with lights off and at a distance, so they wouldn't see me. They went about six miles north on highway 87, then, turned west into a long driveway to another farm. Not wanting them to know they'd been followed, I left then, without going any closer. The next morning I drove back out to that farm. It looks empty, almost abandoned, no signs of life at all that I could see from the road. Not wanting to tip off what we knew, I didn't drive in. That farm is about five miles west of that Robinson place we inspected before, the one with the chicken place. I'm betting if we raided that abandoned farm we'd find stills. There was no sign of smoke, or anything else to indicate that, but why else would they be bringing all that sugar in there?"

"You're probably right," said Sampson.

"I went back to the mill and remained in my tent the rest of the night. About 7:00 a.m. a different car dropped off a different driver. He drove the empty truck south when he left the lot. The car followed him. I didn't recognize anybody. But, then, the next day, I saw that same truck, same plates, come through Cedarville full of cattle and headed for the Twin Cities. That was yesterday, Bob. It looks like they're hauling cattle, in, and sugar, home."

"That's what happens everywhere they're cooking moon," Sampson responded. "Truckers can't afford to deadhead empty one-way. I've seen this scenario before. If we arrest the truckers, they'll claim they just haul sugar and park their trucks in that lot. Then someone else picks the truck up and drives to where someone is using the sugar, unloads, and returns the truck to the lot. The trucker has no idea where the sugar goes, so they can't tell us. Most of the time, we can't scare the trucker into telling us who hires them to haul, and often they really don't know. They are paid cash in advance, delivered to them in an envelope, with instructions to pick up a load and leave their truck in the lot after dark. When they come back in the morning, the truck is empty, and a new envelope with cash and instructions is usually on the seat. There is nothing illegal about hauling sugar, unless we can prove their involvement with producing moonshine, and they make more money hauling sugar than cattle. It's impossible to stop. But, I want to know who's hauling for who, and who's organizing it?"

Sampson was scratching between the plaster cast and his ankle with a ruler, as he thought, *I'm not done with you, Miss Cartier.*

"What do we do next?" Eggert asked.

"Brown and Eastman come back from Stearns on Monday. We'll raid that location they're hauling sugar to on Tuesday or Wednesday. In the meantime, get comfortable in that tent. We want to know anything else that happens with those trucks. Keep track of what kind of trucks they are, I.D them if you can, get the plate numbers, and try to remember the people's faces."

Chapter 130

Sheriff Maun was talking to Andre at Bill's station, as Bill gassed up each of their vehicles. "Yeh, I helped Henri get him out of the car," said Maun. "He was so loaded with moonshine we almost had to carry him in. Doc says his foot was broken, so he was in a lot of pain."

Andre said, "I don't understand why he is so after Cartier Egg. He's stopped Carolyn on the road one day, and another of his other agents stopped her another day, then, that Sampson stopped her again. His agent made me unload my truck, that day you stopped and helped me reload. Next, he's going through my barn. What's drawing his attention to us?"

"I'm getting suspicious that it's, Carolyn, Andre," Jason said with a serious look. "I'm only guessing, and can prove nothing, but I am suspicious. Sampson told Henri as they drove in from your place with his injured foot that he was talking to Carolyn, because he learns more by asking kids about their parent's activities, but that doesn't fly with me. He's on my watch list now." he finished.

"Carolyn says she's not worried about him and really feels bad about dropping that block on his foot. She said he somehow made her drop it by the way he moved, or something. She insists he hasn't bothered her again since then, but is just as sure he doesn't like her, especially since his foot injury." She said he called her a bitch as she helped Henri lower him down from the loft. Henri verified that. It had better not happen when I'm around." Andre glowered. "That's not really law enforcement behavior is it Jase?"

"He's pushing me for information again, and now he's got the Mayor and the Council pushing me too. He's laid up with that foot, so he can't drive, but he's still sending his agents out. He's watching that old saw mill parking lot, because some truckers leave their vehicles there overnight. He thinks they might be sugar loads coming into the Barrens. That is a possibility, but I've never paid any attention to it," Jason went on. "He said they're going to work the bridges all this week, too. His agent, Brown, is driving him around and he's in a foul mood."

Andre's internal alarm bells went off when he heard Jason's comment about the old saw mill parking lot.

Chapter 131

As soon as Hutton heard from Andre about the feds watching the old saw mill parking lot, which was shortly after Andre found out about it from Maun, Hutton called The Cities to cancel two truckloads of sugar scheduled to be in the sawmill lot that night.

Over the next twenty-four hours, he had Andre round up all of Andre's trucking friends. By 8:00 p.m. five trucks, including Cartier Egg's stake-bed, had hauled tons of sugar from Hutton's abandoned farm warehouse, forty miles, to a barn at the Trade Lake compound. Running out of room indoors, they had a row of sugar-stacked pallets hidden beneath tarps along the hidden side of one of the buildings. The old farm where Hutton had been stockpiling sugar was now empty of all ingredients. Left sitting in the middle of the old barn floor, where just hours before had been tons of sugar bags, sat an old, dilapidated, small-volume, still, strongly resembling the one missing from the Sanderson farm when Sampson's agent returned there to inventory.

Driving one of the trucks that afternoon, was the teen-age runner of Sandy Sanderson, who Ralph had known for years. While the crew was loading the truck he was driving, he heard Ralph say, "We should leave an old beat-up still in here for the feds to find." The teen volunteered that he knew where one was available. Ralph discussed it with Andre, who discussed it with Hutton. Within five minutes, the decision was made to set up another diversion. When sugar hauling was completed, they sent the teen-ager and a pickup to Sandy's sister-in-law's farm to retrieve the small still. By 10:00 p.m., unloaded from underneath the canvas in the pickup, the Sanderson still was resting, cold on the floor of the former sugar-barn.

When Andre heard Ralph and the teen talking about the still, knowing Sampson was pushing Sheriff Maun for more information about stills, Andre thought Jason could use this info. Consequently, Ralph advised Jason Maun, that while looking for a possible gas customer for Bill, he had accidentally found an abandoned still on what looked like an abandoned farm. "Andre asked me to tell you about that still at the old Fitzharold place," Ralph finished. Sheriff Maun passed the information on to Agent Sampson that afternoon as a helpful tip.

Two days later, four Federal Revenue agents, in three black Fords, roared in the driveway of the farm five miles west of the Robinson place, the same farm the Bank's Anderson had told Sampson once belonged to Fitzharold. They found nothing but an old, decrepit, forlorn-looking still in the middle of the barn's floor.

Agent Eggert recognized the still, but didn't bring it up to Sampson or the other agents.

Sampson was pissed! Based on Eastman's reports he expected this barn to be full of sugar, with stills cooking. He had seen diversions orchestrated in Chicago and over in Stearns County. This one smelled of diversion, too. He needed to find out where Sheriff Maun had gotten this tip. Someone was messing around with him and his agents in Stephens County.

Chapter 132

Sampson was talking to Chief Lundquist. "Yeh, I am frustrated, chief. Whoever is messing with us over there has experience. I think some of these tips are just diversions to keep us busy. Other than that Chicago raid, most of the stills we've found are small. We've gotten tips from the Sheriff, from a couple of stool pigeons, and two from the local game warden. The warden's were both abandoned sites with torn up stills like they'd been raided before.

"We've seen a lot of diversions over in Stearns. Those farmers up there are clever as hell at hiding their cooking. What about those sugar loads you were talking about?" Lundquist asked.

"This damn foot has slowed me down a little, but we staked out that parking lot with one of my agents round the clock. He finally found two trucks that were definitely hauling sugar, but because he was alone that night he couldn't follow them. The next night he did follow and found a farm where they were leaving the sugar. We watched them haul two loads a night for the next two nights to the same farm. That's when we set up the morning raid two days later. I was sure we'd catch them cooking and with a lot of sugar on site. Then we raided and all we found was a derelict still and nothing else. We'd been set up . . . I'm sure of it," Sampson finished. "I don't have to like it, though. I've got a few names here I'd like to run by some of your Stearns agents to see if they recognize any of them. Can you arrange that for me?"

"Sure, give me the list. Maybe you'll get lucky."

"Cartier, Maun, Johnson and Hutton are the ones I'm curious about," Sampson said.

"Hutton rings a bell right away. There was a James Hutton in Stearns County that we chased for two years. He was always a step or two ahead of us. We thought we had him one day, I was certain, but when we triggered the raid, the stills were still cooking in the building, but there wasn't a soul around. We shut it down, wrecked everything, but never pinned it on anyone. The farmer claimed he just rented the space to someone from The Cities. That was last year. Then this Hutton just disappeared. I haven't heard of the other names, though," Lundquist finished. "Let me run them by some of my agents. I'll get back to you."

"I got that name, 'Hutton,' from Anderson at the bank in Cedarville. He said Hutton was a real estate agent," Sampson added.

Hutton, Sampson thought as he drove towards Cedarville. *Sheriff Maun also said Hutton was in real estate around the County, but none of us have ever seen him. That could be who's messing with us. Somebody over there really knows what's going on with moonshine in the Barrens. I'm going to find out who.*

Chapter 133

The big Cadillac sedan rolled north above Janesville, Wisconsin. The car had left Chicago that morning. There were three men within, all dressed in dark suits. All were somber, serious looking, and their attitude signaled a sense of purpose. They had all been summoned to a meeting the day before by, Vinnie Restor, who was currently the traffic manager of one of the Chicago syndicate's liquor distribution networks.

"Somebody up around Minneapolis got hold of one of our shipments of moonshine a little over a month ago. The feds raided one of our production setups in Wisconsin. They destroyed the stills, said they destroyed the product, and turned our site manager over to the feds in Chicago. He didn't sell us out; in fact he's working for us again down here now. Then, about three weeks later, some unknown made me an offer for about the same amount of moon the feds claimed to have destroyed after that raid. I bought it for a premium price because we needed it so badly. When it got here, the markings on the kegs, confirmed that we'd just purchased, our own booze!"

The three muscled-suits, who had been summoned to the meeting, began to understand the mission they were about to undertake. Vinnie was looking for someone, seriously. They were going to find him.

Vinnie went on, "We followed the sale and transport of the moon back through three different middlemen, but have not been able to ID the real source, yet. I smell a dirty fed. We've had them down here since Prohibition started, so it's not hard for me to believe they are up there as well. I want the three of you to leave today. Go to Minneapolis. I've arranged for some guidance from my contact up there. He thinks he might know something about this. We'll go over the rest in a minute."

"How do we handle it if we find him?" one of the four asked.

Don't take him out, but I want him to know he's made a mistake. We'll discuss that, if you find him, or them. We need more details before we can make that decision."

Chapter 134

Sitting in the Cedarville bank's office, Sampson asked, Anderson, "How many places has he bought in the County in the last year or two?"

"Well, he hasn't bought any. He's a real estate agent, but working with us, he arranged the sale of the old Robinson place to a wealthy land owner in the Twin Cities. He said he had sold a couple of places east of our County as well. I think he works mostly in the Cities." Anderson finished. "He's a good man. Everybody likes him."

"So, he doesn't own the Robinson place?" Sampson asked.

"No, it's another owner from Minneapolis. That's the man who is fixing the place up and who started the chicken business out there that Cartier manages. Andre Cartier manages both that one and the one at his own farm as well and is doing well with the business he's expanded. They are both growing nicely, and he intends to begin shipping eggs to Twin Citie's stores next year."

"Well, who owns that place we raided two weeks ago? It's about five miles west of the Robinson place."

"That used to be the Fitzharold place, but we didn't hold the mortgage. It went into foreclosure two years ago, and has been vacant and unfarmed since. I don't know who owns it now."

"I want to talk to this Hutton. How do I find him?" Sampson asked.

"I have his card right here in this file. I can give you the office listing for the Twin Cities."

"So, you don't think this guy could be hooked up with the moonshine business?" Sampson asked.

"I don't think so, but he knows about real estate."

Chapter 135

On the phone, Sampson told Hutton he was looking for real estate in Minnesota or Wisconsin and was told by banker, Anderson, that Hutton would be the man to talk to. He did not tell him he was a federal agent. "I'm interested in something just north of the Twin Cities and either east like Stephens County, or west in the area of Stearns County. My wife doesn't want to be more than an hour or two away from The Cities. Do you know those counties?" Sampson asked.

"Well I don't know Stearns, but I've looked around Stephens a lot in the last year. I probably know that region as well as anyone. My client wants me to find him two or three more places over there in Stephens County, especially on lakes. He thinks that will be the vacationland the wealthy Twin Cities people are going to want when the Depression ends," Hutton said. Sampson had called him the day after he spoke with Anderson at the bank. "I'll be back over there looking at more property next week, but I'll be in southern Minnesota for the next three days. If you want to meet in Cedarville I can arrange it."

Sampson made an appointment for the following Wednesday. They would meet at Cedarville's Coffee Time restaurant for lunch. Sampson would have one of his agents take their picture somehow. He wanted to get a copy of Hutton's picture to Lundquist to see if they were speaking about the same James Hutton.

Hutton's alarms went off as soon as he got Sampson's call. He called Anderson at the bank right after Sampson hung up. "So, who is this guy, Sampson?" he asked Anderson.

"According to Sheriff Maun, he is the lead Federal Revenue Agent enforcing Prohibition for this region of western Wisconsin," Anderson said.

"Thanks, I appreciate that information. I thought there was something funny about the way he was expressing interest in land over here. I don't want to waste my time as a real estate agent. This guy probably wants me to help him find stills in Stephens County. No thanks. That's his job, not mine. Thanks again for the information."

Chapter 136

Hearing of Hutton's existence, of his involvement in real estate in Stephens County and that he was the one who arranged the sale of the old Robinson place, which Sampson and his agents had already raided, seemed like too much coincidence to Sampson. When he added Lundquist's comment of, "Chased him for two years, he was always a step ahead of us," it made the hair on the back of Sampson's neck stand. Still, he said he knew nothing of Stearns County real estate, only about Stephens County, *but that's what he would say*, Sampson thought, *just too much coincidence. There is more I need to know before I meet with him Wednesday.*

Sampson's foot was healing. Fortunately for him, though the doctor at first thought it to be a real mess, he only broke one small bone. The walking cast was to come off this week. He had seen nothing of any Cartiers since his foot injury. Sheriff Maun had told him Carolyn felt badly about the accident, but also that she still insisted Sampson had caused it. "He didn't have to make me lift that concrete block!" she'd told Maun. "Why did you make her lift it?" Maun had asked Sampson. "In my investigations, Sheriff, I do things my way," he answered, feeling *no explanation necessary, especially to a local officer, nor did he want to discuss his hand brushing her breast.*

Lundquist had borrowed Brown and Eggert again for another raid in Stearns County. With just he and Eastman there was little he could accomplish in Stephens. Consequently, he put Eastman back on bridge watch for the week, alternating between the bridges at Taylors Falls and Osceola. Eastman had called him at 11:00 a.m. that morning with some good news. "It was that same guy that's been coming through the last three weeks with a carload of kids hanging out the windows. I decided this guy was having too many birthday parties or something, so I pulled him over at Taylors Falls. All six of those kids were under ten-years old, Bob! There were two in the front seat and four sitting on a layer of carpet in the back seat. When I rolled that carpet back, just an hour ago, I found ten, five-gallon crocks, of moonshine! We let him slip through our bridge stops at least four times before because of all those kids! I've got them all sitting in that car right here on Main Street. How do I make this arrest, boss? Just him, or do I arrest the kids, too?" Eastman asked. "Just him, Agent Eastman, and then give each of the kids a ride home and inform their parents they were being used to hide this guy's bootlegging. That should make him popular." Sampson finished. "Get pictures when you bust those crocks of moon, Eastman, and bust every one of them. Get pictures of the kids in the car, too."

Telling Eastman to continue the bridge watch, Sampson began setting up his evening's work. Coincidence and the name "Hutton," were scratching at his mind. He was still suspicious of the Robinson place. Though he had invented suspicion of Cartier Egg to maneuver closer to Carolyn Cartier, he was beginning to really suspect Andre Cartier because of, coincidence. When they raided the Robinson place, it was Cartier who was present and cordially provided a tour of the property. For all Sampson knew, Cartier could be on Hutton's payroll for more than just eggs. That second building Cartier had shown the agents didn't really make sense as a chicken coop, because of those two different floor levels and they only used one end for chickens. Too many unanswered questions itched in his mind, and Sampson was positive there was still another big moon operation somewhere in the County.

Sampson was going to do some night exploration of the Robinson place, without anyone discovering he was there. His foot was getting strong again and didn't hurt much anymore if he was careful. He had acquired some dark clothing, a head net for his hat to keep those damned mosquitoes from draining his blood, and two Eveready flashlights. He would also carry his Leica camera, though he would likely not use it in the dark, and his pistol. He wanted to find out what went on over there at the Robinson place at night.

He parked his car out of sight, in a wooded area a half-mile from the Robinson place and on the side opposite of the driveway, at midnight. With his pant legs taped tightly around his ankles to keep out mosquitoes and ticks he began walking through the forested part of the Robinson property.

Chapter 137

Ralph had three men cooking, stirring and mixing mash. It was the first week of July, and they had produced double-cook moon approximately sixteen hours a day, for the last four weeks. That schedule provided them seven or eight hours a day to clean up the stills and the floors of the building before starting the next sixteen-hour cook. The ten-gallon kegs were quickly moved to either the coop at Robinson's or Cartiers, where they would be recorded, dated and labeled, to begin their expedited aging process, before leaving for Chicago.

Over the last year and a half, the process had become routine, accept for this year's doubling of production with the help of the new and larger, double-cook stills they were all having problems keeping pace with. It was heavy, sometimes messy, work. The fact that the transportation of the product had to be accomplished in secret made it that much more work. That they had been able to produce such volume of quality moon and ship it without discovery had its impact on everyone's behavior, though. Things were becoming *routine*, a major danger to secrecy.

To the three different crews of workers, who were becoming exhausted from long hours seven days a week, it had all become . . . just a job. They were making good money, better than any other work options available to them, but the unending routine of the schedule was sapping the energy and extra caution stealth required. The present danger, growing by the hour, was that someone would somehow make a mistake allowing transparency to evolve. Intensely aware of this possibility, more so than any others, was Andre Cartier who thought endlessly about that possibility. *We've been lucky for so long*, he thought, *how much longer?*

What he and the others didn't know was that fate was creeping through the woods during the same seconds as his last thoughts.

Chapter 138

Sampson walked slowly through the underbrush to avoid injury. He kept his flashlights off letting his eyes adjust to the blackness. Clouds and trees prevented the glow of the moonlight from reaching the forest floor. A couple hundred feet into the wooded area he began to see specks of light ahead, specks which grew, as he progressed. Soon they became a row of lighted windows in what Sampson knew was the older of the two chicken coops. Knowing there was action ahead, he slowed his walk, conscious of the danger of alerting anyone to his presence. As the lighted windows grew he began to hear sounds from the building. There was a low, nearly imperceptible, hum that grew louder as he approached. As he reached the end of the building he recognized the sound as likely that of burners boiling and making steam, which were exactly the sounds he was hoping to find. In addition he could hear the louder noise of a single-cylinder gas engine on the other end of the building, which he guessed to be a water pump for cooling. His revenue agent activities in Chicago had made him keenly aware of the unique combination and patterns of sound connected to the cooking of moonshine. Once again, Sampson smelled blood.

All of the activity seemed to be inside. He sat for ten minutes, carefully watching and listening. No one entered or exited the building. Knowing no one was moving about Sampson crept to the first available window. Standing, his line of vision went directly through the center of the window. Staying far enough back so the window's light would not reflect and reveal his presence through the dirty windows, Sampson saw four busy men, moving about three active stills. Sampson thought, *Hutton, Cartier, Johnson, and who else will I soon be bringing to their knees?* He was also lustily thinking, *I hope it's Cartier. That little bitch and I have a date.*

Chapter 139

"I'm sorry to call you so late at night, Jim, but I felt you had to have this information," Manny said.

"No problem, Manny, I know it must be important," Hutton responded.

"I told you I was checking with my Chicago contacts about that raid on that Chicago-based farm. Once they discovered they had just bought their own moonshine back from someone who stole it, they began an intense hunt to discover how it had occurred. They tell me they are now onto something. They think it is a dirty fed, up here, in Minnesota. They have traced it to a building in the Twin Cities. We are careful to never mess around in each other's territories, so they have asked my help now. We were told 1300 gallons of moon came from that raid in Stephens County in that article you showed me in that copy of the Cedarville Gazette, with pictures of the moon being destroyed after the raid. There's something phony about that picture in the paper, Jim. There was no 1300 gallons destroyed in the pictures you showed me. I need you to help me find out more information about that raid. Do some quiet snooping around. If we have a dirty fed, we need to know about it. That kind of information can be worth its weight in gold. The feds are never as good at hiding things as we are. I'm betting you can uncover this mystery," Manny finished.

"I know how to handle that, Manny," Jim smiled. "I have to place an ad in the *Gazette* tomorrow, just to keep my real estate image intact in the County. I'll find out where those pictures came from and see what else I can learn."

"Get back to me right away with any information, Jim. Though they've asked me for help, I know these Chicago guys are still on a hunt of their own. I'd like to shut that down, before they stir things up unnecessarily, but need more information to do it. I don't like them up here digging into this, because that can cause us problems," Manny said as he hung up. *Hutton will do it*, he concluded to himself.

Chapter 140

Sampson had a huge smile on his face. Standing in the dark, just outside of the light's reflection, he was salivating like one of Pavlov's dogs, as he stared through the window at Andre Cartier's face! *This could not end any better* he thought. *I will end this operation and have another big inventory of evidence to sell. I'll be a hero to Lundquist and gain a shit-load of money. My retirement is coming soon! I'll let Carolyn Cartier keep her father out of prison.* He felt that same quiver of excitement that always thrilled through him when he slapped a woman into submission, or an adversary to his knees. In his mind, *he had just hit the jackpot*

Sampson watched through the night. There was no getting tired. He could not have had more energy. Often, people tend to follow a single-purposed shot of energy, but tonight, Sampson's emotions were motivated by much more. He was about to obtain, both legal and illegal gain, add heroic stature to his revenue agent image, and best of all, sexual fulfillment from that lying little bitch that broke his foot. *This could not go any better.*

He circled the building through the night, carefully staying out of sight, but getting a precise view of what different people were doing. He identified those he already knew – Andre Cartier, Ralph from Bill's gas station, Raft, who he'd been told worked in the coop, - and committed the rest to memory as best he could. He intended to do nothing tonight but gain info, ID people, and figure out how big this operation really was. This was too big an opportunity to activate a raid impulsively, no matter how badly the smell of blood urged him to do so. He needed a day or two of calm, cold, thinking, to determine how to best maneuver this new wealth of information into his desired conclusion. At the top of that list was, Miss Carolyn Cartier.

He held his camera up to a window on three different occasions, not sure what he'd get because he had never used the camera at night without a flash. The inside the building was well-lighted though, so he was quite sure it would be worth trying. He was back in his car at 4:00 a.m. with torn pants, a bleeding hole beside his left eye from a hanging branch he'd walked into, but even that could not erase the smile from his face.

Chapter 141

Manny was sitting behind his desk, talking to the driver who had driven the Cadillac from Chicago. "Vinnie said you would be arriving today. I will not have the information you need until tomorrow, or the next day. I will have one of my people direct you to our guest apartment here in Minneapolis. The three of you can stay there tonight and tomorrow night if you are here that long. My man has also set you up for a free ride in visiting the Washington Avenue speakeasies and anything else you need. Enjoy yourselves, stay quiet, and I will get hold of you as soon as I can."

As gracious as Manny's words were, the Cadillac driver knew he was receiving directions not to be questioned. "Thanks, I'll wait to hear from you," was his brief response, as he turned for the door. "Vinnie told me to contact you for the word and to take no action without first informing you. That's how it will be."

"That's how we want it," were Manny's dismissing words, as the driver left the room. "Tell the two who are with you the same."

Manny and Vinnie had rubbed elbows in syndicate happenings for years. They had never really been partners in anything, just occasionally done each other small favors. They often shared information, one or the other always knowing what they could and could not ask for, since syndicates were usually competitors over territory. A simple, "You know you can't ask me that, but I suggest you talk to so-and-so, who works for what's-his-name," would usually do the trick.

Consequently, when Vinnie needed some info about the Barrens of Wisconsin, the first thing he did was call Manny.

Chapter 142

"I need three copies of the *Gazette,* that had those front page pictures of that Chicago-bunch of stills," Hutton said, to Cedarville *Gazette* owner, Jay Roberts. "I've got some real estate clients looking for land in Stephens County. That story and pictures make them comfortable. They love the fact that Stephens County enforces the law," he smiled.

"We've had a lot of requests for copies of that issue," Roberts answered.

"Did you take those pictures?" Hutton asked.

"No, one of the agents, Sampson, I think was his name. He came by the day after the raid and gave me three photos. He even had a roughed out story he'd scribbled on a paper. I picked the best of the three pictures and up popped the front page," Roberts smiled.

"I don't want to be a bother, but would you show me the other two pictures?" Hutton asked, with his best salesman's smile.

"Yes, they are right here," sliding open a file drawer, as he answered.

Hutton talked, as he noticed there were no more than five kegs shown in any of the three pictures. "Good pictures make a great front page. Thanks," Hutton smiled, as he headed for the door. According to Manny's information, lots of ten-gallon-kegs were missing from the photos. What happened to them? Both Chicago and Manny smelled a dirty fed. Jim Hutton's nose was beginning to itch. I may be closer to that fed than anyone, Hutton thought as he reached for the phone in his Forest Lake apartment and dialed Manny. "Manny, here's what I've found so far."

Chapter 143

Sampson planned carefully. He wanted prioritized results. First and foremost, he wanted Carolyn to, desperately want to keep her father from jail. Consequently, he had to keep Andre Cartier out of the visible picture, at least, for now. He decided that when he made an arrest it would be Ralph because he was sure he could both coerce Ralph into admitting guilt, and that he would likely try to protect Andre Cartier from being discovered. Ralph had already been stopped and questioned by Brown. Sampson thought it likely Carolyn did regret, damaging his foot, which was possibly another ounce of persuasion he could use. He knew Carolyn was smarter than the girl he mastered in Chicago, but hoped her regret might make her feel even more obligated. He wanted her to feel she was the only one, capable, of *quietly,* keeping her father from prison. He was sure this conquest would not be easy, but just as sure, it would be worth the effort. Desire was trumping logic, and because *the desire was his*, Sampson was unaware of it.

He decided he would wait as long as a week before triggering a raid. That gave him a week to work on Carolyn. Two of his men would be over in Stearns for the rest of the week and Eastman was on bridge watch. He was free to pursue his quests, with no one else aware of what he was doing. Sampson was beside himself, deep into fantasy of his coming conquest. *Today is Friday* he planned. *The Cartier girl does egg deliveries tomorrow. She will again be stopped in the Cartier Egg and Poultry truck by Agent Robert Sampson.*

Chapter 144

About 10:00a.m. Saturday morning, just outside of Cedarville, Carolyn again saw the Ford in her rear view mirror. Irritated, she automatically pulled the pickup to the side of the road. She was tired of this treatment, and was about to let it be known.

"Good morning Miss Cartier," Sampson said as he placed his hand on the sill of her door's window.

"Not 'you little bitch' today?" Carolyn responded sarcastically. "How's your foot, Agent Sampson?"

Sampson immediately took charge. "Ok, you want it to be that way, little bitch? Listen to this. I warn you not to say one word to anyone about this conversation. If you do, you will forever, regret it. I now have absolute, irrefutable proof your father makes moonshine."

Carolyn was hearing the words she dreaded most, "absolute, irrefutable proof." A wave of cold fear swept over her and the look she saw in Sampson's eyes told her it was true. She saw her own eyes mirrored in Sampson's and knew by his reflected visual reaction, she had just confirmed his declaration.

Seeing her expression crumble told Sampson, *strike now!* "He cooks moonshine in the old chicken coop at the Robinson place. Ralph Johnson is working with him, so is Mr. Raft and others. Though they do not yet know it, I have seen it, watched and taken pictures of them, and I have all the proof I need to send them all to Leavenworth Prison," Sampson said, with words inspiring fear to her very core.

He knows too much. This is real. We are all going to jail! Carolyn's emotions burst from control. Tears streamed down her face as she shook her head. Still trying to deny his accusations, with tears dripping from her face, she cried "Why won't you leave us alone?"

Behind his stern expression, Sampson grinned with satisfaction, but seeing her current state of desperation kept his expression to one in which she could perhaps see a glimmer of hope. "I always knew you were lying, so it took me a while to find the truth, Miss Cartier. But, as your tears confirm, I have proof now. Why did you do such a stupid thing?" he asked, in a manner aimed at making her feel, she was the only one involved. "Why the unending lies, the breaking of my foot, and now, again today, when I have proof . . . just more lies?" Sampson pulled a photograph from his inside coat pocket. He held in front of her a picture of her father taken through a chicken coop window. It was a dark, grainy picture, but she could immediately tell who it was.

"I didn't do it," she cried. "I just got involved." Carolyn was in shock and didn't know what to do, what to say, or how to act at the moment. Desperation reminded her of a question she didn't want to ask, the question that had kept surfacing in her mind the last few weeks, *but she now knew she had to.* Wiping tears from her face with her sleeve she said, "When you inspected our farm, you told me you once kept a young lady's father from going to jail. How did you do that?"

How perfect can this thing go? Sampson thought. "She was a very caring young lady," Sampson said sincerely. "She never lied to me and through her cooperation, she saved their whole family the embarrassment and pain of prison time and how it would have affected the rest of all their lives. She is still grateful, today, and still a friend."

"How?" Carolyn asked again.

"We had a long, private conversation and worked it out; however, I haven't made that offer in your case. It is very dangerous for me to even consider such a thing with you. Why should I? You are the little bitch that made me limp, probably, for the rest of my life!" he said harshly. "How could I even trust you would keep your promise, should I arrange such a thing?"

Carolyn sensed hope, exactly as Sampson thought she might, thinking, *if the other girl kept her family from prison, why couldn't she?* She had to find a way out of this. "You could trust me. I swear you could."

"I sense you are sincere, but you are the same girl that's been lying to me for months," he added. "How do I know you are not lying now?"

She knew it would take some kind of decisive and demonstrative action on her part to take advantage of any opportunity Sampson was dangling, no matter the price. She had to make this pending disaster disappear. She reached for his hand on the door, then, resting hers on the back of his, She said, "I'm not lying."

Sampson's pulse quickened, but he resisted making anything extra of her move. He simply said, "Ok, Miss Cartier, I will try to believe you. When will you be finished delivering eggs today?"

"In about an hour. I've one stop left in Balsam Lake," she answered, again wiping remaining tears from her face.

"It's 3:00 now. Meet me in the parking lot of the old saw mill at 4:30. You'll find me parked behind the old building that's falling down. Don't be late, and don't breathe a single word to anyone about this. If you do, your father and others will be in Leavenworth very soon. This must be kept absolutely between us. I cannot stop the law from working. If you let this leak out, I will be helpless, and no longer able to help you." He hesitated for a few seconds shaking his head, then, smiled his friendliest smile directly into her eyes, saying, "I can only help you, if you help me make it happen. I don't make the laws you broke, and

I didn't tell you, to break them. That was your decision, Miss Cartier, just like your lies. I can only help you, now, if you work with me on this. 4:30, then," he finished as he walked back to his car.

Sampson entered his car, as Carolyn drove off, thinking *there is nothing she could say that could hurt me. She is telling the truth now. This couldn't have gone better. It's going to work, again.*

A little over an hour later, Sampson was sitting in his car as the *Cartier Egg & Poultry* pickup rounded the corner of the disintegrating building at the old mill. Carolyn pulled up beside his car. He waved, suggesting, she come into his car.

She had spent the last hour delivering the last of the eggs, simultaneously, trying to rationalize the unfolding situation. She was not experienced enough to know the details of what she was facing, but knew enough to be certain it would be nothing she would ever have considered on her own. She had spoken to no one, but Jorge, at the store and to him nothing that did not involve eggs. Her plan, as best she could have one, was to listen to Sampson and somehow buy time for consideration of what she must do to keep the disaster she helped cause from happening. The only thing she was certain of, at this moment, was she would never see her father or family in jail if there was any way she could prevent it. Sampson said there was, and that he could help her accomplish it. What she thought of and feared most, *was the cost.*

As she sat down in the passenger seat of Sampson's car, she left the door open. She listened for several minutes as Sampson talked. Midway through their discussion, Sampson gently held her hand. For a minute or more, he placed his other hand on top of hers, as he talked. When he finished she nodded in agreement. He purposely released her hand saying, "I'm glad you are finally being honest and, I'm glad I won't have to turn all of you in to higher authorities," as he showed her more pictures, obviously taken through the Robinson building's windows. The pictures were dark and fuzzy, but she immediately recognized the people in them. In the center of one photo was her father pointing out something on a still to Ralph. Sampson let her hold it for a few seconds, to erase any resistance she might have saved. Then, after another severe warning about not disclosing their agreement to anyone and that there could be no possibility of changing her mind on this, he told her to go home. His last words to her were, "Just go home and don't worry about this now. I will invent a way to keep your parents from jail and you and I will just ease our way into getting to know each other as my friend and I did in Chicago."

Carolyn cried the pickup home, stopping twice along the road to wipe her eyes and to try to regain enough composure, to show up at home for dinner.

Chapter 145

Clair was readying the dinner table, wondering why Carolyn was nearly an hour later than usual, after her Saturday deliveries. As she was about to bring it up with Andre and Henri, she saw the pickup coming up the driveway. She walked out to meet her. Carolyn looked sick as she stepped from the truck. "What's wrong, honey? You look ill," Clare asked.

"I don't know, Mom, I feel sick," Carolyn answered, grasping her stomach. "I can't eat supper. I'm just going to lie down for a while."

"Did you eat anything while you were in town?" her mother asked.

"No, nothing, I don't know what it is. I just want to lie down for a while, Mom."

"Ok, hon, go ahead. I'll explain it to the others."

Carolyn lay on her bed for an hour reliving the words of Sampson. She had never known anyone so powerfully evil, threatening, or as in command as she now saw him. He was an officer of the law, which to her had always represented something good. But, he had the power to send her father, possible her whole family and others away to prison, yet based on his private talk with her belonged there himself! No one, not even her girlfriends, had ever spoken to her of things Sampson so nonchalantly spoke of, hinting of pending intimacy between them, yet telling her not to worry about it, that she would grow to like what he discussed, and would likely become his close friend as the Chicago girl had. Best of all, he'd added, her parents would not be in prison and she alone would have saved them from it. He explained he would never take such a risk for most, and had he not had the first experience with the Chicago girl, would not even be considering it with Carolyn. He had ended with, "Were I not so attracted to you, I wouldn't even consider helping you with your parent's problem."

She sensed the slanted words he used were to scare her into compliance, but she also knew the situation was real. She told him she had to have tonight and Sunday to finish convincing herself, but would answer him Monday and that it would likely be a "yes." Those words seemed to work with Sampson and supported her plan of buying more time to think of some alternative way out.

After one last dire threat, of what would occur if she spoke a single word of this to anyone, he had reached out his hand for hers. Resisting every thought or impulse in her mind, she allowed it. He held it for what seemed an eternity to her, but was actually only as long as it took him to say, "You will not regret this. You will like it."

After getting dinner started Clair left Andre and Henri at the dinner table and returned to Carolyn's room carrying a bowl of fresh tomato soup and some crackers, which she set on the table at her bedside after seeing Carolyn slept. She sat quietly by her bed for several minutes, gently stroking her hair. Motherly instincts and love of her daughter told Clair this was all bigger than an upset stomach. As Carolyn awoke, Clair said, "Remember when you asked me about the weird behavior of that boy, Dan? When things are too big for us alone, that's the time to ask for help, honey. I can help you with whatever this is, too."

Carolyn melted into her mother's arms with sobs that shook the bed and it was several minutes before she could stop crying enough to coax out some words. Clair was frightened now by the immensity of her daughter's emotions. She listened to every word she cried, sobbed, and choked on, as she hesitatingly told the rest of her Sampson story in bits and pieces, as though afraid to face the whole situation at once. Over the next hour, too embarrassed by the sexual nature of her pending problem to include her father, Carolyn told Clair the entire story of all three encounters with Revenue Agent, Robert Sampson. She was exhausted before she could begin speaking of the last encounter, today. To admit to her mother, her agreement with Sampson, made her seem worthless to herself. When finished, she cried exhausted tears again as Clair reassured her of how much she was loved, that she was safe, that Sampson's plan would never be enacted and her parents and others would not go to prison. It took over an hour before Carolyn lay exhausted and again asleep in her mother's arms. Then, Clair gently released her, covered her with a blanket and slipped from the room, exhausted herself.

She went right to Andre, hoping he could convince her, that the outcome would turn out as she had assured Carolyn it would.

Chapter 146

Anticipating what could become an almost single-handed raid, Sampson was amazed at how recent developments had unfolded in a manner coinciding with his plans. He credited himself, as usual, for all that had occurred. His suspicions had been correct. His decision to night-probe the Robinson place was spot-on and his set up of the Cartier girl over recent months had been finessed. His bank accounts in Chicago would soon fatten when new evidence was again sold to his new account in the Janesville region. He had especially liked being paid in silver and gold instead of paper currency, whose value was approaching questionable status.

So impressed was he with what he saw as Carolyn Cartier's imminent capitulation, that he concluded delaying the raid up to a week would not be a problem. It would provide him the opportunity of further exploring who else might be connected in support of the Robinson stills. He could already envision the *Gazette's* headline of his single-handed arrest of the Robinson group while his men were off in Stearns County. Perhaps he could make an even bigger story of it. He would use his truckers from the Somerset region to transport the Robinson moon to his Minneapolis warehouse, before Brown and Eggert returned from Stearns County, and keep Eastman busy with the bridge-watch.

Sampson had everything planned except his final inducement of the Cartier girl's surrender. He was not dumb. He knew he had to use extraordinary caution, but felt he had done so. His prior success enjoyed in Chicago encouraged his belief he was about to succeed again. He knew Carolyn was near-petrified with fear, and with her hand in his at the mill, had sensed her near submission. He also knew, the longer he waited now, the less likely it was to happen. He had to keep things moving. The remaining questions were, when, where, and how. The biggest challenge right now, was to figure out how to trigger the raid, without arresting Andre Cartier. That would insure a longer relationship with his daughter. If Cartier's involvement was discovered later, Sampson could explain it as, simply not having deduced the entire operation's help-roster, as well as, having been seduced by Cartier's daughter to delude him about her father's involvement in the moon operation. Sampson's logic was now clouded by lust, to the degree that his normal cautions and strategies were fading beyond his visions of the young Cartier girl. Actions, that a month before he would never have considered, now seemed his only path. He was also convinced, by his most recent encounter with the young woman in Chicago, that Carolyn Cartier would, too, be grateful.

Chapter 147

Knowing the emotions about to be triggered in Andre, Clair waited until Henri had retired, then, asked Andre to go for a walk with her.
She made him first promise he would take no action until Clair agreed with it, before she would tell him about Carolyn. Sensing the importance of the issue he knew nothing of, Andre agreed. Clair explained how Carolyn had come home sick, then, repeated verbatim everything Carolyn had told her. Andre experienced rage he'd never known as he listened to Clair's words. Then, sadness, that his daughter had been forced into such ugly compromise by his decision to become involved with moonshine, then guilt, as he watched Clair's tears periodically interrupt her explanation of their daughter's encounters with Sampson. Clair broke down and wept after her last words. They held each other beneath the stars, as a gender-mix of tears fell to the ground.

It was minutes before they spoke. Andre said, "Now, we must think very carefully, Clair. I want to beat this man to a bloody pulp, but I don't want to go to jail, or cause the sky to fall on us all. This is bigger than just the Cartier family. I want Jim Hutton's help with this. I'm going to call him now. Clair knew he was right and quickly nodded her agreement. They both knew they were in over their heads.

Andre called Hutton at 10:00p.m., explaining carefully, as one had to do on a party-line, they needed an immediate meeting with him because, *Uncle Ben was arriving in the morning.* It was going to be a long Saturday night.

Hutton arrived at the Cartier's home at 11:30 p.m. At 1:00 a.m. he drove from Cartier's into Minneapolis to talk with Manny. Hutton, Andre and Clair agreed to meet the next morning at the Cartier farm to plan their response to Sampson's moves on Carolyn. There plan must also address, Sampson's optional strategy, for arresting them all. As a federal revenue agent, he now had irrefutable proof that could send Andre, his employees, and maybe even members of his family, to Leavenworth. None of the Cartier family had ever faced a crises of this magnitude.

"I'll be back out there tomorrow by 10:00 a.m. Andre," Hutton said on the party-line to the Cartier home. "I'm sorry to make you miss church, but this can't wait. I am confident I can get what we need by tonight. I promise you, we will be completely ready for Uncle Ben's visit." Any neighbor, listening on the party-line, would think they were arranging an impromptu family reunion.

The Sunday morning meeting lasted until 2:00 p.m. and included Carolyn and Henri. With Manny's Chicago contacts, on and off the phone more than once, he and Hutton had worked out a strategy during the night. During the next morning's meeting, Hutton laid out what he and Manny had decided should be done in the best interests of all involved. Andre and Clair were so relieved by their proposal they immediately bought into the plan. He and Clair then explained it to Carolyn and Henri. Andre had to take Henri aside, to carefully explain man-to-man the intrigue and details of what Carolyn had faced, alone, and what they now all faced, together. It took a few explanations, by both Hutton and Andre, before Carolyn's fears became manageable. But, by 3:00 p.m., after a couple more private conversations between Carolyn and her mother, she and Henri were both ready, almost anxious for Saturday's planned results.

By 3:30 p.m. Andre was on his way to the Robinson place. Wanting to pick up Ralph and two of his workers along the way, Andre verbally kicked his neighbor off the party line so he could phone Ralph and the others to tell them, "Uncle Ben's in town and he's coming over to see us!" Raft was drafted into the work force as they drove past the Robinson farm house he now lived in.

The purpose and plan of each who had been in the Sunday morning meeting, was based on the agreement made between Sampson and Carolyn, at the old mill. With her hand in his, Carolyn had promised Sampson she would give him her "yes," sometime Monday. To maintain secrecy, they had agreed her "yes" would be a white scarf tied around the base of the mailbox post at her driveway. Then, she had reluctantly worked out details for their next meeting with Sampson. The scarf would be tied to the post by Monday night so he could simply drive by and see it. "If it's not there," Sampson had said, "I will have no choice but to let the law take over. I cannot help you after that, Carolyn," was how he had again penetrated her defenses. While cautioning her, he used his handkerchief to wipe the tears from her cheeks, as though he genuinely cared for her well being. There was no way she could invent a reason to be anywhere but home at their farm for their next meeting, which would again give Sampson and her the opportunity to talk. Following the scarf's signal, Sampson would officially come to the Cartier farm the following Saturday morning to complete the inspection he aborted when he injured his foot months before. Saturday morning, Carolyn had said, her mother would be in town at a scheduled event with Carolyn's grandmother. Carolyn would arrange that her father and Henri would be delivering eggs for her that morning, because she would feign not feeling well enough to do the deliveries herself. Sampson felt the white-scarf was likely safer than any other communication they could arrange. Having aborted his first inspection, gave him a legitimate reason for being there and an unsuspicious opportunity for again talking to Carolyn. The only downside to this plan was, it prevented him, from raiding the Robinson place, for one week.

Once again, desire for Carolyn, was trumping logic. His holding of Carolyn's delightfully warm hand, during the close encounter with her at the mill, convinced Sampson it was worth the one week delay. She was the priority, not the raid. His desire for Carolyn, and Carolyn's love-generated need to protect her family, were the emotional mix on which imminent actions would unfold.

Manny met the Chicago Cadillac team Monday morning. At that time, he already knew there would be a white scarf around the Cartier mailbox by afternoon. He explained again, it would be four more days before he would have what they had been sent to Minneapolis to find. Their free party on Washington Avenue would go on for those days; they could remain in his guest apartment and he would advise Chicago as to their whereabouts and why the delay. The Chicago men knowingly, again followed Manny's directions.

By Monday afternoon, Hutton, Andre, Ralph, Raft, some additional help and their usual truckers, hauled the last load of ingredients, containers, and stills from the Robinson place, to the empty barn on the abandoned Fitzharold' farm, where the feds had found old Sandy's still, two weeks before. That was a shorter distance than hauling to Trade Lake, which they'd done during their first emergency shutdown. Hutton felt it unlikely the feds would look at the Fitzharold place again so soon. All kegs were hauled and stored in both the Robinson and Cartier chicken coop-basements removing the last evidence from the cooking scene before they began to dismantle the stills. The hoses used to run fresh water to the stills were removed. The main water pipe from the pump was rerouted to appear the water source for the chickens in the other end of the building. Most of Tuesday was spent removing the last clues of moonshine activities from the property. They even went so far as to fill the building with hay bales, so there was barely room to walk between the edge of the bales and the walls. The stacked hay bales smothered the silage-like moonshine aroma and stirred up a great amount of dust, which re-settled throughout the building making it appear to have been there a long time. It looked like the place had always been a dusty old chicken coop and hay bale storage area.

Clair spent all day Sunday and Monday close to Carolyn. During the Sunday morning meeting, Carolyn had been told by Andre, Clair, and Hutton she was to continue with the exact agreement she had made while holding hands with Sampson. She was reassured again and again, that though she was to keep her "yes" agreement, there was absolutely no chance that what Sampson planned would actually occur. Finally, Carolyn believed. She would do it.

At 3:00 p.m. Monday, Carolyn tied a white scarf around the mailbox post at the base of her driveway. At 4:00 p.m., Henri, who had been posted inconspicuously in the hay mow of the barn, saw a black Ford sedan drive down the road past their driveway. Just moments later, it returned heading in the other direction, but slowed slightly as it passed the mailbox. Though it was too far away for Henri to specifically identify the driver, he could tell its sole occupant was staring at the mailbox and had almost certainly been Sampson. Since the morning meeting, the day before, Carolyn had not even seen her Dad on Monday or Tuesday because he was so busy at the Robinson place.

Anticipating activities of the coming Saturday, the rest of the week, Clair and Henri, and Andre when home, were especially close and supportive of Carolyn. She had never felt so loved, and the assurances left her more emotionally prepared to handle the upcoming rendezvous with Sampson. Henri left her mostly with her mother, but sneaked into her room twice during the week and sat by her bed on the floor. "We are going to get that bastard, Carolyn," saying the word just as he'd heard Andre use it on an old bull that once chased them from their fields. All week in school, neither of them said a word to anyone about Sampson, or the meeting at their farm. On Thursday afternoon, half-way through her geography class, Carolyn found herself thinking, *I wish Sheriff Maun knew about all this. I trust him.* Her instructions were, "Not one word to anyone who was not in the Sunday meeting, Carolyn." *I wish Jason Maun had been there, though,* she thought.

Chapter 148

Sampson was euphoric as he drove past the Cartier driveway. The scarf immediately triggered arousal. Even, knowing it doubled the possibility of his being seen, he could not resist turning around to drive past the scarf-wrapped mail box a second time. His plan was working down to the smallest detail, exactly as he had envisioned it. *No wonder the O'Hara's and the Lundquist's of law enforcement can't keep up with me,* he thought. *I should be sitting in their chairs.*

He knew he must still exercise caution. Planning out the balance of the week he tried to eliminate potential problems. He called Lundquist and told him bridge-watch was paying off, so the Chief could keep Eggert and Brown for another week to work Stearns County as Lundquist had asked. "I'm sniffing out something big over here and would just as soon continue on my own. I've got Eastman on bridge-watch and he caught another regular bootlegger yesterday." Lundquist agreed, feeling he could use the help. Sampson met with Eastman, listened again to his arrest of the man with a car full of kids, then assigned him to continue with bridge-watch another week thinking, *that will keep Eastman out of my way. I will stay completely away from the Robinson place, so no one discovers that I know about it. I'll tip off Sheriff Maun that Eastman is on bridge-watch, and that I am setting up another Somerset raid. If he is tipping off shiners, the Robinson people will hear I'm not working their area, so they'll just keep producing for the week, which leaves me free to consummate my arraignment with the Cartier girl.*

Sampson's street sense kicked in, more than once, asking, *"Is this going too well?" Be careful,* he thought but then rationalized, *there is no danger in simply completing the Cartier property inspection, which was aborted when I was injured. That is totally within my legal realm. It's a legitimate visit, which will give me another opportunity to evaluate her willingness, before I make my next move.* That satisfied his rationale.

Chapter 149

It was 10:00 a.m. Saturday morning, as Sampson drove his black Ford sedan up the Cartier driveway. He was wearing a fresh hair cut and shave, what he considered his best black power suit, shined shoes, filled shoulder-holster, and his shiny Federal Revenue Officer's badge. *He looked*, he thought, as he felt, *smart, powerful, dangerous, and sexually attractive, like the only man on earth, that could keep Andre Cartier out of jail.*

His emotions were hinting at that same feeling he so often got after striking a blow, especially the one that brought a woman to submission, or an adversary to his knees. He wanted to feel it again.

The cautions of a trained agent, were still with him, but suppressed by his growing desire. He drove a circle around the Cartier farm yard. The two trucks labeled, "Cartier Egg & Poultry" were both absent, accounting for the absence of Carolyn's father and brother, as Carolyn had said would be the case. The Cartier's sedan was not parked in the yard, which confirmed her mother's absence as well. All appeared to be, as Carolyn had suggested it would, when he held her hand at the old mill. There was no hint of activity anywhere he could see.

Carolyn had said he would likely find her in the new chicken coop gathering the morning's eggs. He parked his Ford by the upper end of the coop. Remembering the approach, he had practiced repeatedly in his mind, Sampson stepped from the Ford.

Just as he shut the car, Carolyn stepped from the chicken coop door. "I thought I heard someone," she said, nervously.

"Is anyone else on the farm?" he smiled.

"No," she answered softly.

She looks scared, he thought. They are always scared at first. She was wearing corduroy slacks and a white blouse. *If she had been gathering eggs*, he thought, *she must have just removed the loose dust coat she'd worn the last time I saw her in the coop.* There was not a smudge of dirt on her blouse, which had immediately captured his attention.

"Where are they?" he asked, again with his friendliest smile.

"My Dad and Henri are delivering eggs, my mother is in Cedarville with her mother at the WCTU meeting I told you about," she answered, speaking more, *at* him, than, *to* him, yet looking into his eyes. She was obviously uneasy, while describing their *aloneness* to Sampson, which was contrary to what she would normally ever have done in this circumstance.

"Let's go back inside," Sampson said, pointing at the door.

"In the chicken coop?" she asked, in a surprised manner.

"Yes, in the supply room on the far end," he said, with a hint of purpose. "I didn't look in there the last time I was here. She opened the coop door and stepped into the swarm of knee-high chickens. Sampson entered behind her, closing the door behind him. He touched her back, nudging her in the direction of the door at the far end. Carolyn did not react to, or resist his touch, so he kept his fingertips moving in a circular pattern on her back as they walked through the chickens.

She was petrified, but trying hard to not show it. *Do exactly as he tells you,* she remembered them saying. It seemed then, it would be easy, but now, was terrifying. But, she was doing it.

"How long before any of them come back?" he asked, as they walked.

"An hour, maybe a little more," she answered, *with dread.*

"That will give us time to get acquainted," he smiled, more to himself, than to her.

Carolyn reached for the door knob as they reached the supply room door, twisted it and swung it open. She stepped inside, holding it open for him, his hand still caressing her back.

Sampson closed the door behind him, with his other hand, then, gently pushing her ahead of him, walked to the double-door in the end wall of the coop. He turned the locking mechanism, on the handle, to the locked position.

Carolyn watched their aloneness increasing. *Exactly as he says,* her thoughts reminded her.

He looked at her appreciatively, from her eyebrows to her toes, then, smiled warmly. "This doesn't have to be difficult, Carolyn. I want it to be easy for you, just as it was with my other friend. Nothing has to happen today, other than the two of us just getting to know each other a little better."

She was immediately relieved at, "Nothing has to happen today," and exhaled more fully, which she hadn't done since they entered the coop together. The room was cool, but she felt very warm. The slight zephyrs of breeze through the screened, but open, windows prevented the room from overheating. It was tension that had her sweating

"Good, I'm glad to hear that," she said with a slightly forced, smile. "So why are we here?"

"I want to confirm your commitment to me. You've told no one of our agreement?"

"God, no!" she exclaimed. "They would shoot you, then they'd all go to prison anyway," she stammered. "I've done everything you asked, so what now?" she demanded, as coached by Hutton and her parents earlier.

"We'll just get to know each other a little better today. Then, I'll arrange a way we can meet and be undisturbed for a couple of hours, as my other friend always asks of me." he smiled again.

Carolyn's expression appeared, again, as a hint of a smile, but was actually more relief of her fears.

"So how do we get to know each other?" she asked.

"It's quite warm in here," Sampson smiled. "Start, by taking your blouse off," he said, gently touching the top button, on the front of her blouse.

Chapter 150

No one, but the school nurse or her mother, had ever *asked her* to do such a thing. This man *told her* to. *Exactly as he says,* her brain repeated, as she reached for the top button. Sampson's smile appeared warm, almost friendly, but Carolyn could see right through it to his calculating, cold heart, *if there was one*, she thought. She unhitched the second button. *"Nothing of Sampson's proposal will ever occur,"* she remembered her mother saying. As she reached for the third button, her mind screamed for help! She had unbuttoned each of the first two, slowly, trying to buy time, which tormented Sampson. Carolyn heard not a sound beyond the clucking of chickens, but the *seeming sound* of the aroused expression on Sampson's face was deafening! *Where are they? Help me,* her fingers screamed, as they stumbled to slip the button through the hole of her blouse.

"You've nothing to fear," Sampson persuaded. "We are just looking at each other," he smiled. "I told you nothing would happen today. As you have not lied to me, I will not lie to you. Don't be afraid," he finished.

Unhitching the last of her four-button blouse, and not wanting him to see more, she let it simply hang, draped in unbuttoned repose across her breasts.

"Now, take it off," Sampson said.

Exactly as he . . . were her thoughts, as her mind again screamed *help me!* She moved her arms down behind her, allowing the blouse to fall from her wrists behind her back.

Sampson was aroused beyond distraction, as he watched the blouse sleeves slip from Carolyn's wrists to the coop floor. "Now, take . . ." but his demand was broken midsentence, as the outside double-doors burst inward with an explosive, BANG, a screech of metal hinges, and flying wood splinters, as each of the ruptured doors slammed against the inside walls of the coop!

Two large, dark-suited men, with guns in hand, lunged into the supply room with the slamming doors. Sampson knew instinctively, if he reached for his pistol, he was dead. Though stunned, his training caused him to drop into a crouch, as he tried his first ploy of shouting, "I am Federal Agent Robert Sampson, put those damn guns away!" he watched for the suit's reaction.

"Thanks, Sampson. We needed to know it was you," said the larger of the two men. "We work for the boys you stole moonshine from," he grinned, "and then was dumb enough to sell it back to," he continued as he reached inside Sampson's suit coat stripping his pistol from its holster. "Your fedral job's over, Sampson. Our boss told your boss, about all a your dumb moves yesterday, includin rapin that Chicago girl and now trying the same thing with this young lady here . . . and stealin booze from the government too," he laughed, "Both in

Minnesota and Illinois." His partner was patting down Sampson as the other spoke with his pistol pointing at Sampson. "You're a popular guy, Sampson," he grinned, "You're wanted by both da feds and da syndicate in two states!"

"You can't do this to me, for Christ's sake, I'm in the middle of a raid! These people make moonshine and I have evidence to prove it!" Sampson yelled.

"We ain't cops, Bob. We don't give a shit what you're doing, except to dis nice young lady and dat don look like no raid to me. Dat, we give a shit about. We don't like dat. Now, shut up and listen. I'm only sayin dis once't," he directed, with deadly assertion.

Sampson shut up.

"Der's only one way you stay alive, Sampson. Forget about dis place. Dis here place you're trying to raid never existed. Dese here people, including dis young lady, don exist. If you talk bout dem to anybody you're dead. Got it? Nothin to nobody bout dis here place. If you do, you're dead." The talking man's partner grasped Sampson's wrists and cuffed them behind his back. "You gets one chance, one, to repay the Chicago boys for the stolen booze you sold them. You're comin wid us now, to arrange dat payback. If, you are still alive after dat, you can worry about it den. If not, it won't matter. You won't care when yer dead. Da boss says you'll be on da fed's most wanted list by tomorrow. You got nowhere to go and only one way to live, Sampson. Payback!" With that, each of the men grabbed Sampson with a hand under each armpit and half-carried, half-dragged him through the open double-door. The biggest man stopped them at the door, turned, and looked at the shocked expression on Carolyn's face, as she wrestled a tangled blouse sleeve onto her arm. "Apologize ta her ya asshole," he said slapping the flat of his gun to Sampson's ear, "Say yer sorry."

Sampson could not look at her, but mumbled, "Sorry," reacting to the rap on the ear.

"Louder!" the man said, grinding the side of his gun against Sampson's ear hard enough to draw blood from the scrape.

"SORRY!" Sampson shouted in pain, still not looking at her.

The men lifted him through the door by his arms, as Carolyn buttoned the top button of her blouse. She watched the two men half-carry, half-drag, Sampson to the black Cadillac sedan parked further down the driveway toward the mailbox with the white scarf wrapped around its post. One man opened the car's rear door, the other threw Sampson into the back seat. Slamming the back door, the big man waved at those standing outside the chicken coop, then entered the Cadillac.

Carolyn watched as the Cadillac drove on down past the mailbox at the end of the driveway and turned onto the main road. She'd heard it would be going to Chicago. As she watched the car disappear down the road, she saw the white scarf's ends, flutter gently, in the breeze.

Some Verifying Information

Historical fiction always leaves unanswered questions, as well as, the urge to verify some of the history we accrued growing up which still lingers in our minds. For those readers familiar with the regions of this story, here are a few more facts;

- Arrest records of Wisconsin's Polk County (called Stephens County in the book) between 1920 and 1926, tend to reflect Northern Moon's story of continued growth towards 1933's Repeal. Prohibition based **arrests** from jail records of those years are below;

1920 – **19**   1921 – **59**   1922 – **52**

1923 – **55**   1924 – **41**   1925 – **91**   1926 – **116**

Moonshine sales continued to grow right up to repeal, in 1933.

- Arrests shown are from Polk's County Sheriff records, which indicate little cooperation between local law enforcement and Federal Revenue agents.
- Syndicates often paid for moonshine in cash, using silver dollars and gold, rather than paper money.
- Research verifies the purchase of farms and land, through banks in western Wisconsin, with pails of silver and gold, no questions asked.
- Ferries mentioned in Northern Moon all existed.
- The wooded and rolling hills, of western Wisconsin provided ideal landscape to conceal stills, ingredients, and finished moonshine from the law.
- Research has confirmed some syndicate people did pay to build chicken

coops on farms to hide stills, and also paid some fines their producers of moonshine were sometimes assessed by the law.

➢ Research indicates Priest's garb as a favorite disguise of some bootleggers when driving loads of moonshine.

➢ There is no town of Cedarville in this region of Wisconsin.

➢ Moonshine recipes depicted herein are not accurate for use.

Author's Notes

I have long wanted to write about the times of Prohibition. I've always been big on writing, small on research, so because of business demands; I successfully procrastinated for years before tackling *Northern Moon*.

Ward Moberg, who loves research, as I love writing, wrote and published his historical newspaper called, The Dalles Visitor for several years which I used to place business ads within. Years later, while listening to him speak to a historical society group about *Prohibition;* Ward reignited my desire to write of the same. He has been extremely helpful to me and it is his research that enables me to say, "Many events in Northern Moon actually did occur." Only the names of some people, places, and activities have changed to make Northern Moon historical fiction. Thanks Ward!

A special thanks to Cathy Wimmer and Robert Haskin for technical assistance and layout.

A special thanks to Carolyn Wedin and Phil Peterson II for editing assistance.

Northern Moon is the first book of a trilogy, to be followed by, Northern Moon **Light,** and Northern Moon **Shadows**, each of which encompass some of the years between the Crash of '29 and the repeal of Prohibition in 1933.

There are many books about Prohibition. If you are looking for a quick glimpse of enlightenment on the topic, one of the best I've read is, Elaine Davis', *Minnesota 13,* copyrighted in 2007 and printed by Sentinel Printing Co. of St. Cloud, Minnesota. Another excellent book is, *Last Call, the Rise and Fall of Prohibition*, by Daniel Okrent.

Phil Peterson Sr.   callphil@ecenet.com

Phil would be happy to hear your brief appraisal, of this first book, of the Northern Moon trilogy.

Enjoy a preview of the first chapters of

NORTHERN MOON LIGHT

Second book in the Trilogy – Available 2012

Chapter 1

Sampson sat alone in the back of the Cadillac. The two men, who had dragged him from the Cartier chicken coop, sat in the front seat. Neither had said a word since they drove out of the Cartier driveway and onto the highway that would take them to the Twin Cities. Sampson was trying to make sense out of what had just occurred. He couldn't. What he had interpreted, as a resounding success with the Cartier girl, had turned into a disaster. He was now a prisoner of syndicate men from Chicago, who knew he was the dirty cop who had stolen moonshine from them, then sold it back to them. What shocked him the most is they had somehow set him up for capture during what he had planned to be the finishing of his seduction of the girl he'd watched for months. He knew he was in the biggest trouble of his life. Consequently, he was repeatedly reviewing what the two men in the car had said to him after they burst into the chicken coop stopping his undressing of the teenage girl. He remembered their words, explicitly.

"*Thanks, Sampson, we needed to know it was you. We work for the boys in Chicago that you stole moonshine from and then was dumb enough to sell it back too.*"

Sampson deduced from that statement they must work for one of the Chicago syndicates he had sold the evidence moonshine too.

Next, he remembered, "*Der's only one way you stay alive, Sampson. Dis here place, you're trying to raid, dis here chicken coop, never existed. Dese here people, including dis sweet young lady, don exist. If you talk bout dem, to anybody, you're dead. Got it? You never say nuttin to no one bout dis here place, da moonshine, or the daddy of dat little girl you was tryin to use. If you does, you're dead.*"

He interpreted that to mean, *he was to say nothing about the Cartier's, Andre, or the Robinson moonshine operation, ever.*

His mind continued to echo, "*You gets one chance, one, to repay the Chicago boys for the stolen booze you sold them. You're cumin wid us now, to arrange dat payback in Chicago. If, after dat you are still alive you can worry about it den. If not, it won't matter. You won't care when yer dead. Da boss says you'll will be on da Fed's most wanted list by tomorrow. Dey sent Lundquist a package of info on you. You got nowhere to go and only one way to live. Payback!*"

That told him *he might have an opportunity to give the money he pocketed from selling the stolen moon back to the syndicate, if he lived through the process.*

He remembered every word they had said. The last ones were, "*Apologize ta her you asshole! Say yer sorry."* His ear still bled from the wound inflicted by his captor's gun grinding into it.

Sampson knew there was no love for him in this Cadillac. He knew death was nearby, but not before Chicago. For the moment, he decided his best tact was silence. The two men in front had not uttered another word, to him or each other, since leaving Cartier's farm an hour ago. They were apparently following a well-rehearsed plan, as the Cadillac pulled into the parking lot of Sampson's Minneapolis apartment building.

The driver pulled up by the front door entrance. The door opened, as a third black-suited man stepped from it into the back seat of the Cadillac, roughly shoving Sampson over against the other side's door. The car immediately pulled out of the parking lot back onto the street.

The driver said, "Anybody need to pee before we head for Chicago?"

"No," said the front seat.

"No," also came from the new man in the back seat. "I used the john in Mr. Sampson's apartment," he grinned at Sampson. He held a paper bag in his hands toward Sampson in a gesture. "I found some interesting papers in there the boss will like. Mr. Sampson keeps books. A few addresses too."

These guys know too much. They've been onto me for a long time for this whole thing to happen this way. This is not going to have a happy ending. So certain was he on the degree of trouble he sensed, he was beginning to wonder why he was still alive. Then he remembered. Payback.

Chapter 2

Jim Hutton was reevaluating his life. This last episode at the Cartier's farm, watching the Cartier's, especially, Carolyn, agonize over their dealings with Sampson, and finally watching Sampson disappear down the road in that Chicago-Cadillac made him realize he had become involved in something much bigger than he originally planned it to be. Small-time moonshine and working his way into real estate had been fine. From then on it had been almost, inadvertently, that he had worked more and more with Manny Goldfin. He had to admit he liked Manny and liked working with him. It was Manny that had arranged taking care of Sampson and told Hutton how to go about it.

Over the last year, since he had moved from Stearns County into the Barrens of Wisconsin, his participation in illegal activities had grown dramatically. His moonshine activities were bigger, involved a lot more money, and what bothered him most, was their enterprise now involved several more people's lives than just his own. To Hutton, it was one thing to risk his own future with an illegal enterprise, but he was now doing it with other's lives as well. Jim Hutton had always liked to help other people. Logic, love, and leadership were natural and normal qualities of his life. Initially, moonshine in the Barrens had enabled him to help the people he was soliciting into moon activities. They were going broke, losing their farms, and he helped some of them avoid those dire circumstances. Their efforts at the Robinson place, Trade Lake and with the Cartier's had gone so well he had been able to enjoy outsmarting the feds and spent little time worrying about those working with him.

The Sampson episode, however, had alarmed him of the real circumstances he and his employees now found themselves enmeshed in. After working with Manny, and before moving to Wisconsin as a full-time partner, he knew Manny was involved on the other side of the law, but he never dreamed he was as big with the syndicate as it now appeared. Manny always seemed to know someone, who knew someone else, who could always come up with answers when they were needed. Whatever Hutton needed, to make things work, Manny, was able to come up with. This characteristic was easy for Hutton to work with and take advantage of. The two of them, working together, produced results. Hutton was making more money than he'd ever dreamed and helping others do the same. He really hadn't wanted to change anything before Sampson happened.

As Hutton thought his way through the last year, he realized he had just seen the head Federal Revenue Agent disappear down the road in a syndicate Cadillac! That disappearance, arranged by Manny and others, somehow involved *interstate* syndicate cooperation and Jim Hutton, himself, had been thoroughly involved in the entire episode! *"I've evolved from a small moonshine entrepreneur, into a participant in big moonshine law-breaking, which is now connected to kidnapping! What's next, Jim, murder?"* he asked himself.

When he heard of Carolyn's dilemma with Sampson and that they were all about to be arrested because of Sampson's discovery of the Robinson operation, he received help from Manny. Manny, in normal fashion, had taken charge. He made a few calls to Chicago first, then proceeded to tell Jim Hutton exactly what moves to make, and how, when, and where. Manny eliminated the threat of Carolyn being violated, of everyone's potential arrest, and his plan was so well thought out it was easily implemented. The plan succeeded and all threats were erased but one; Hutton and the Cartier's were now involved in more serious crime than simple moonshine. Hutton realized he, no one else, was responsible for it all and was keenly aware that should the disappearance of Federal Agent, Robert Sampson, ever be solved, they could all be even worse off than now.

Manny told him, "Don't worry about it. Just set it up exactly as I've told you. The Chicago boys will take care of Sampson. That solves your immediate problems. They will also deal with the Revenue Department over Sampson's disappearance. The feds don't want a lot of attention broadcast about a dirty-cop, Jim. Just do everything as we've discussed. It will work out."

It had been two weeks since Sampson left for Chicago. No one in Stephens County had heard his name since. None of his men were working Stephens county as before and no one had seen any of them. Not only was no one looking for Sampson, it was as if no one even knew he was gone! Hutton had a cup of coffee with Sheriff Maun, just yesterday, and throughout the conversation there was no mention of Sampson, the Revenue Department, or moonshine. No one besides Hutton, the Cartier's, Manny and the Chicago boys seemed to know anything had even happened to a revenue agent. Ralph, Raft and a couple others who helped the recent move at the Robinson place only knew the move was to, again, avoid detection. They knew nothing of Sampson's exit. *How far have I gotten myself and others into something we can't get out of* Hutton worried?

Chapter 3

Mike Nelson had just shut down the burners; his still was well-hidden in a machine shed on the back side of the gravel pit he operated. The pit was on 50 acres of land half-way between Somerset and Hudson, Wisconsin, to the south. He had operated the still for the last year, during his down times of processing gravel, sand, concrete aggregates and a variety of stone sales from his display yard. The Depression had slowed his aggregate business so much he couldn't have remained open without the income he'd added in the last year from his moonshine.

"Ok, today's cook brings us up to twenty, five-gallon crocs, Jack," he said to his younger brother. We'll make a run tonight and our cash is made for this month."

"I keep reading in the papers about Fed raids, Mike. How come they never bother us?" Jack asked.

"We are hidden here in the shed, and we usually don't cook unless we have the gravel crusher going. That puts out enough exhaust, dust and noise to make the still's steam and aroma almost invisible. Our dump trucks don't look like anything that would be hauling moonshine. I guess that's about it," Mike said, and then added, "And, we've been lucky."

The shed-door suddenly opened and two men in dark suits walked into the machine shed holding up wallet badges to Bill and Jack. "Federal Revenue agents," one said. "This is a raid, you are under arrest," then pointed and said, "Sit down on those chairs."

"What was that about luck?" Mike said to his brother.

"Looks like it's just run out," Bill added.

The agents questioned them quickly. They saw the twenty crocs, wrapped in burlap to cushion breakage, stacked against the back wall of the shed. "Is that all of it?" one agent asked, pointing at the crocs.

"That's it," said Mike. "I can cook some more if you want to wait," he added, sarcastically.

"Don't get cute with us," the agent warned pulling the lapel of his suit coat back to expose his shoulder holster. He turned to the other agent and added, "Ok, have these two load those crocs in the back of the truck. I'll do a quick inventory while you load. When you're done I'll take these two in for booking."

The other agent pointed at the crocs and said, "Let's go boys. Load em up! You'll find us much easier to get along with if you move when you're told to." Mike said to Jack, "Ok, let's get it over with, Jack." As he picked up the first croc and headed for the door. Jack followed suit, and in less than ten minutes, the crocs were loaded into the pickup driven by the agents. As they reentered the shed, the agent that did most of the talking said, "Ok, I'm done in here. The two of you come and sit down. I want to talk to my partner outside." He turned to his partner saying, "I'll book these two while you haul that stuff," and stepped outside with his partner, closing the door behind him. Mike and Jack heard them talking and the truck's engine starting. The agent stuck his head back in the door and said, "You two sit tight. I want to look around out here a minute. The door closed and they heard the truck pulling away from the building.

"What's going to happen to us?" Jack asked his brother.

"I don't think much. He's not going to find anything else out there no matter how much he looks around. We'll maybe get a fine and a hand slap. I don't think we're big enough for them to waste much time on."

A half hour later, when the agent didn't return from "looking around," Mike went outside to find him. Two minutes later he came back in, shouting, "Son of a bitch, Jack! We've just been robbed! They weren't agents . . . they stole our moonshine! They're both gone!"

Enjoy the second and third books of Phil's trilogy on Prohibition.

Northern Moon Shadows
Available in 2013.

Northern Moon Light
Available in 2014

Additional books by Phil Peterson Sr.

ALL THINGS ARE POSSIBLE, The Verlen Kruger Story, 100,000 Miles by Paddle, by authorized biographer, Phil Peterson Sr.

See website **verlenkruger.com**

Six Knots for Everyday Life – Simple, practical, the only six you need.

Songs of the Sea – Poetry written at sea, by Phil Peterson Sr.

Around The World and Then Some – A Fifty-Year Sailing Adventure

By authorized biographer, Phil Peterson Sr.

Go to **philpetersoncreates.com** for information on all of Phil's books.

To communicate directly with Phil - **callphil@ecenet.com**

Made in the USA
Lexington, KY
25 September 2017